NEUROPSYCHOLOGY OF VISUAL PERCEPTION

INSTITUTE
for RESEARCH
in BEHAVIORAL NEUROSCIENCE

Jason W. Brown, Series Editor

BROWN

Agnosia and Apraxia: Selected Papers
of Liepmann, Lange, and Pötzl

BROWN

Neuropsychology of Visual Perception

PERECMAN

The Frontal Lobes Revisited

PERECMAN

Integrating Theory and Practice
in Clinical Neuropsychology

NEUROPSYCHOLOGY
OF
VISUAL PERCEPTION

Edited by
Jason W. Brown, M. D.
New York University School of Medicine

LAWRENCE ERLBAUM ASSOCIATES, PUBLISHERS
1989   Hillsdale, New Jersey   Hove and London

Lawrence Erlbaum Associates, Inc., Publishers
365 Broadway
Hillsdale, New Jersey 07642

The IRBN Press
New York, New York

Library of Congress Cataloging-in-Publication Data
Neuropsychology of visual perception.
    Includes bibliographies and indexes.
    1. Perception, Disorders of. 2. Visual perception.
 3. Neuropsychology. 4. Neuropsychiatry. 5. Imagery
(Psychology) I. Brown, Jason W. [DNLM: 1. Vision Dis-
orders—physiopathology. 2. Vision Disorders—psychol-
ogy. 3. Visual Perception—physiology.   WL 105 N494]
RC382 · 2 · N49 1989   617 · 7   88-30932
ISBN 0-8058-0284-3

Printed in the United States of America
10 9 8 7 6 5 4 3 2 1

Contents

Contents

Preface

The central problem in neuropsychology, Paul Schilder once remarked, was the relation between the image and the object, a relation, he thought, that went to the very heart of the transition of private mental experience to externality. Schilder not only thought about the problem, he carried out some ingenious studies to explore the perceptual basis of imaginal states. For example, in a study of cases with delirium and hallucination, he induced vertigo in the hallucination through caloric stimulation; in another study, he described rotatory dreams in patients with vestibular disorders. The hallucination was shown to follow the same laws as the perception. Morris Bender and his collaborators also looked at imagery and object perception and documented close links between certain perceptual deficits and image phenomena.

What one can say from the work that has been done, not only the studies of Schilder and Bender but the observations of Lhermitte, De Morsier and Pötzl on hallucination in organic disease, the papers of Morel on acoustic "scotoma" during auditory hallucinations, Jacob's work on palinopsia reviewed in this volume, or Klüver's classic studies of eidetic imagery, is that the findings so far seem to support a close association—I would venture to say an inner bond—between objects and mental images. Morel went so far as to declare that hallucination and agnosia were different expressions of the same disturbance. More recently, studies with positron emission tomography seem to show a common metabolic substrate for percepts and hallucinations, while studies on the generation and rotation of mental images in normal subjects indicate that images are scanned like objects. The inference is that images and objects have mechanisms in common. The papers of Alan Paivio and Martha Farah in this collection extend such findings to problems of brain function and neuropsychology.

In contrast to the scattered literature on disorders of imagery with focal brain lesions, descriptions of perceptual defects abound. By and large these are accounts of the various forms of agnosia as reviewed here in the chapter by Frank Benson, or investigations of "elementary" deficits as described in Zihl's review. Some syndrome's that have been especially well-documented are described in papers on topographical defects by Jane Riddoch and Gwyn Humphreys, spatial impairments by E. Bisiach, hemineglect by Guido Gainotti and colleagues, and visuomotor ataxia by P. Rondot. The paper by Jon Kaas reviews experimental studies on the "new" anatomy of the visual system that are essential to understand the clinical material on a neurological basis.

Disorders of object perception have traditionally been interpreted as the result of damage to areas (components) in the cortex which normally mediate the function that is lost or impaired. Or, the disorder is attributed to interruption of the connections between the various cortical areas (components). There are points of contact between the clinical literature and current physiological studies from the standpoint of modular organization. Some of the implications of this approach are discussed by Pöppel. In pathological case studies from this perspective, the different forms of perceptual deficit or agnosia are usually considered in relation to the widely accepted idea of a staged in-processing of sensory information and the transmission of 'raw' percepts to parietal or temporal lobe mechanisms which subserve spatial, conceptual and experiential analysis, updating and storage. Abnormal imagery, for example hallucination or illusory phenomena, is interpreted as a later revival of perceptual information. On this account, an image is linked to a perception as a type of perceptual memory. The image results from the deposition and storage of a perception and its reworking in memory; it is a secondary occurrence and not an intrinsic part of the perceptual process.

More recent work has looked at imagery from the standpoint of propositional behavior, though this cannot begin to explain eidetic and after-images, phantom limbs or visual perseveration and the metamorphopsias. A theory of imagery, if it is to be more than a local model for one type of image, that is, if it is to be more than a theory of thought or imagination imagery, eidetic or after-imagery, needs to explain a great variety of normal and abnormal phenomena. This is because there are no sharp boundaries between the different image types. Moreover, the evidence for a link between image and object points to the need for an account of imagery in the context of a theory of perception. Even if imagery is considered to be independent of object perception, a theory of object perception will obligate the approach that is used to explain the nature of the image. This is because the way we explain the world around us determines the way we understand the world within our heads. Further, if an image is interpreted as a form of memory, as a trace of a past perception retrieved from a memory store, a theory of imagery will also entail an understanding of the relation between perception and memory. The point is that the image lies on the interface of our memory of the world and the world as we see it. It raises fundamental questions about the nature of the world and how it is represented; it touches, as Schilder knew, on the deepest problem for a theory of mind, whether objects elaborate a memory of the world or a memory of the world elaborates the objects of perception.

My own view on imagery and object perception is that it is not a matter of shared subsystems or overlapping turf that the two have in common but a difference in processing stage in a single system that distinguishes them. Images and objects are mental representations; they both develop out of memory but the object undergoes further processing. In this processing, the volumetric space of imagery is derived to the Euclidean space of the external world. An object and its external space are what result when an image and its private space are more fully drawn out and articulated. Some images—eidetic images and hallucinations—can resemble an object but they are not object-like in their appearance or in the space within which they appear. Still, to the extent that they approximate an object, such phenomena indicate that the presence or absence of sensory input is not a *crucial* difference between imagery and perception. The object is just a transformed image. Sensation is important in that it shapes and facilitates this transformation.

This is not a simple thing to understand. Images develop more or less autonomously while objects are a response of the organism to external stimulation. There is an obvious difference that drives the folk belief that images are mental constructs while objects are real entities. How can this difference be reconciled with the idea of a common system for image and object formation? In my view, it requires that we think of an object as a result of sensory constraint applied to the process of image formation. This is more like a shaping or sculpting of an image than a piecemeal construction. This shaping effect configures the image so it models an object 'out there' in the external world. As Henri Bergson put it, a memory is a "nascent perception . . . (in which) the virtual image evolves toward the virtual sensation" and not the other way around!

This hypothesis, which is the core of my paper in this volume, is an attempt at a basis in theory for the more focused papers on imagery and perception that make up the greater part of this book. These papers constitute a state of the art survey of work in this area and provide data that are essential for the development of models of normal image and object formation. Regardless of one's approach to the clinical disorders, however, there is a need to rethink the many basic assumptions that are implicit in whatever approach one chooses, and part of this rethinking involves a notion of how images are related to objects in a theoretical context. A sensitivity to this issue should serve as a guide for the way that individual cases are evaluated, so important in the study of subjective phenomena. It is certain that the outcome of clinical work on this problem will have implications not only for theory in neuropsychology but our thinking about the nature of objects, mental states and philosophy of mind.

Jason W. Brown

I
Organization of Visual Cortex

1

Changing Concepts of Visual Cortex Organization in Primates

Jon H. Kaas

Introduction

Our understanding of the organization of the visual system of primates has rapidly increased over the last 20 years (for earlier reviews, see Kaas, 1978, 1986; Maunsell & Newsome, 1987; Van Essen, 1979, 1985; Weller & Kaas, 1981, 1982). Although information has come largely from studies of both Old and New World monkeys, it is highly likely that features of organization revealed in these monkeys are basic to primates, and that many aspects of visual processing are similar in monkeys and humans. Because so much of the neural processing related to object vision and visual attention is at the cortical level, the principle theme of this review is the functional organization of visual cortex. The subcortical visual system of primates has been recently reviewed elsewhere (Kaas & Huerta, 1988).

Early views of the organization of visual cortex divided visual cortex into two or three serial processing stations. The importance of primary visual cortex (area 17 or striate cortex) in vision has long been appreciated, since lesions of this cortex produce such dramatic impairments that individuals are often described as cortically blind (see Campion, Latto, & Smith, 1983, for review). As a result, the role attributed to primary cortex was that of sensation (see Merzenich & Kaas, 1980, for review). In contrast, lesions in adjoining cortex changed visual capacities in less dramatic ways. Thus, this adjoining cortex was termed psychic cortex (Campbell, 1905; Elliot Smith, 1906), and was thought to be essential for perception. Brodmann (1909) and Elliot Smith (1906) both described two levels of psychic cortex, "areas 18 and 19" of Brodmann and "parastriate" and "peristriate" cortex of Smith (Figure 1). Cortical levels of visual processing were thought to start with striate cortex and sensation, and relay through two basic and higher levels related to perception in areas 18 and 19. This basic outlook was expanded to include subsequent processing in multi-

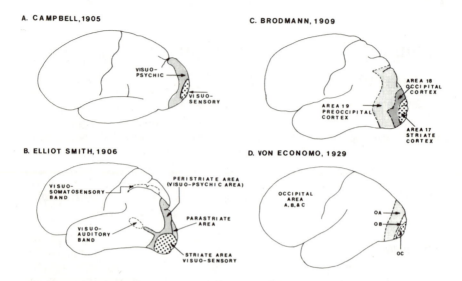

FIGURE 1 Early views on the organization of visual cortex in the human brain, A. Campbell (1905) divided visual cortex into a primary "visuo-sensory" field and a secondary visuo-psychic field. B. Elliot Smith (1906) included a primary visuo-sensory (striate) area, peristriate and parastriate visuo-psychic areas, and visuo-auditory and visuo-sensory (somatic) bands of "association" cortex. C. Brodmann introduced the widely used numbers, area 17 for primary (striate) cortex, and area 18 (occipital area) and area 19 (preoccipital area) for two band-like visuo-psychic fields. D. Von Economo (1929) parcelled visual cortex into visuo-sensory striate cortex or occipital area (OC), a parastriate "association" area (OB), and a peristriate area (OA) for "commemorative" functions.

modal association cortex, and has served as a framework for modern concepts of cortical organization.

Modern concepts of information processing in visual cortex stem from three basic and highly significant advances. First, we now recognize that visual cortex in primates is much larger than previously thought. Visual cortex contains many subdivisions and includes not only cortex in the occipital lobe but cortex in the temporal and parietal lobes as well. Dramatic experimental evidence that cortical areas important in vision extend beyond occipital cortex was first obtained when Klüver and Bucy (1939) discovered that bilateral temporal lobectomy in monkeys produced severe impairments in object recognition. Mishkin and others (see Mishkin, 1966; Mishkin, Ungerleider, & Macko, 1983; Ungerleider & Mishkin, 1982) subsequently used ablation studies to help localize the visual region to inferior temporal cortex and show that the visual functions of temporal cortex were dependent on the relay of visual input from striate cortex. Even earlier, eye movements produced by electrical stimulation of parts of posterior parietal cortex and frontal cortex (Ferrier, 1874) implicated these regions in visual performance, and parietal lobe damage in humans was known to sometimes produce a defect in the perception of the contralateral half of the body and visual space known as contralateral neglect (see Hyvärinen, 1982; Mountcastle, 1975 for reviews).

Although it became clear rather early from ablation and electrical stimulation studies that a vast amount of cortex is visual, recognition of the large number of functionally significant subdivisions and the complex patterns of interconnections that mediate processing streams was not possible until microelectrode mapping and modern pathway tracing methods were developed. Early surface recordings showed that regions of the temporal and parietal lobes, as well as occipital cortex, responded to visual stimuli (Doty, Kimura, & Mogenson, 1964; Woolsey et al., 1955), but determining how these regions of cortex are subdivided into multiple maps of visual space depended on a fine-grain analysis of connections and microelectrode mapping procedures. Accurate studies of cortical connections first became possible with the advent of the Nauta method for revealing axons and axon terminals degenerating following lesions of the cells of origin (referred to as "the Nauta revolution" by Ebbesson, 1984). An early and influential paper of Kuypers, Szwarcbart, Mishkin, and Rosvold (1965) demonstrated projections from striate cortex to the prestriate region and to cortex in the upper portion of the temporal lobe (also, see Jones & Powell, 1970). Extrastriate visual cortex in the occipital lobe was in turn found to project to inferior temporal cortex, posterior parietal cortex, and a part of frontal cortex related to eye movements (the frontal eye field). Finally, inferior temporal cortex and parts of posterior parietal cortex were found to have connections with the frontal eye field and prefrontal cortex. Thus, early anatomical studies confirmed the involvement of vast amounts of cortex in visual processing, and revealed the broad outlines of basic processing sequences.

The second major advance in thinking about cortical processing in the visual system came with the recognition that many cortical fields are not functionally homogeneous. The concept of "modular" or "columnar" organization within fields became popular with the proposal of Mountcastle (1957) that primary somatosensory cortex is subdivided into a mosaic of small (less than 1 mm diameter) processing modules extending from white matter to surface and devoted largely or exclusively to information from either cutaneous or subcutaneous receptors. Although there are reasons to modify specific statements on the organization of somatosensory cortex (see Sur, Wall, & Kaas, 1984), the notion that primary and nonprimary cortical fields in the visual system contain mosaics of functionally distinct groups of neurons has been well supported. The best evidence is for striate cortex. Initial support came from the trailmaking electrophysiological studies of Hubel and Wiesel (1968 and 1977, for example) demonstrating that primary cortex can be subdivided into patterns of specific orientation selective cells and patterns of ocular preference cells. More recently, anatomical as well as physiological evidence has been marshaled to support the conclusion that nonprimary visual areas of cortex are functionally heterogeneous (Albright, Desimone, & Gross, 1984; DeYoe & Van Essen, 1985; Krubitzer & Kaas, 1987; Shipp & Zeki, 1985; Weller, Wall, & Kaas, 1984).

The third major advance in understanding visual processing in primate cortex stemmed from the discovery in cats that three or more distinct parallel visual pathways originate in the retina (see Stone, 1983). These pathways have become known as the X, Y, and W pathways, and a similar terminology has been applied in monkeys, although the terms have been used for monkeys in other ways as well, and controversies remain over possible homologies (see Kaas, 1986 and Kaas & Huerta, 1988 for reviews). The X pathway appears to be the important source of visual information for object recognition and creating our experience of the visual world. The Y pathway contains information about where changes occur in visual space, and therefore the Y pathway seems to be involved in visual attention and the detection of visual motion. The functions of the W pathway are poorly understood, but the initially separate W pathway largely converges on parts of the X system in primary visual cortex and thereby the W system may modulate or potentiate aspects of the X system. The broad significance of the existence of the three pathways is that parallel processing of visual information starts in the retina, and there is now clear evidence that the X and Y streams continue as partly separate processing streams in extrastriate cortex as well.

The X, Y, and W streams from retina to cortex

The principle characteristics of the X, Y, and W pathways from retina to cortex have been reviewed elsewhere (Kaas, 1986; Kaas & Huerta, 1988; Rodieck, 1987; Rodieck & Brening, 1983; Stone, 1983). In brief, the X (or parvocellular or P) pathway originates from a dense array of medium-sized (relative to others at the same retinal location; cells become larger from central to peripheral retina) retinal ganglion cells that project almost exclusively to the medium-sized cells that constitute the parvocellular layers of the lateral geniculate nucleus. The parvocellular layers, in turn, relay to particular sublayers of area 17 (Figure 2). About 80% of retinal ganglion cells and geniculate neurons are components of the X system. Most of these cells are concerned with central and especially foveal vision. Axons of X cells conduct impulses at relatively medium rates. The X cells of the retina and geniculate are typically color selective, maintain a discharge to steady stimuli, and have small receptive fields (again relative to others at the same retinal location; receptive field sizes decrease from periphery to central vision). The above features are all consistent with the proposed importance of the X stream in object vision. The large number of neurons in the pathway and the disproportionate emphasis on central vision

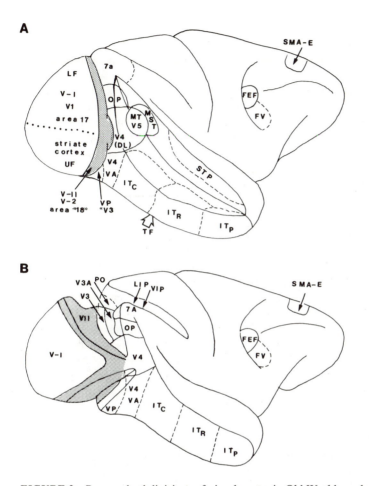

FIGURE 2 Proposed subdivisions of visual cortex in Old World monkeys. A. a lateral view of the brain with the superior temporal sulcus opened; B. a lateral view with the lunate, intraparietal, parieto-occipital and inferior occipital sulci opened. A dotted line separates dorsmedial V-I (area 17 or striate cortex) representing the lower visual field (LF) from ventrolateral V-I representing the upper visual field (UF). Other visual areas include the Ventral Posterior area (VP), the Occipital Parietal area (OP), the Middle Temporal area (MT), the Medial Superior Temporal area (MST), the caudal, rostral, and polar subdivisions of inferior temporal cortex (IT$_C$, IT$_R$, IT$_P$), the Superior Temporal Polysensory area (STP), the Frontal Eye Field (FEF), the Frontal Visual area (FV), and the eye movement segment of the Supplimentary Motor area (SMA-E). See text for other abbreviations and details.

reflect the amount of information that is coded in the retina for object vision (different classes of ganglion cells for four types of color coding and two types of luminance selectivity) and the fact that detailed object vision is only possible in the central visual field. Color is obviously important in monkey and human object vision, and relatively small receptive fields are necessary to preserve information about local details. Maintained discharges may be important for object vision during short fixations. Medium-sized axons with medium rates of conduction are fast enough and yet not too slow for a system that requires some moderate amount of cortical processing time. Object vision is cortically mediated, and the relay of X information is almost exclusively to striate cortex.

The Y system depends on only a small proportion of retinal ganglion cells (about 10%). However, this small proportion adequately covers the visual field because the receptive fields of Y-cells are relatively large and subclasses are limited to those sensitive to increases and those sensitive to decreases in luminance. Color is not coded, but cells are sensitive to low levels of contrast and short periods of stimulation. Neural responses are transient at stimulus onset and offset, and information is conducted rapidly over thick axons of the relatively large retinal Y cells to the large cells of the magnocellular layers of the lateral geniculate nucleus. A subsequent relay is to the upper half of layer IV of striate cortex. The Y cells of the retina also project, largely via collaterals of axons terminating in the geniculate nucleus, to the superficial layers of the superior colliculus. Thus, Y cells tell the central visual system where in visual space a local change in luminance has taken place, most often as a result of stimulus movement. The transient responses to stimulus change and the sensitivity to low levels of contrast provide a framework for the detection of even rapid stimulus movements, but the large receptive fields and lack of color coding mean that the system neglects details of form and color. The rapid conduction of information is consistent with the importance of being able to rapidly respond to stimulus changes. The relay to both the geniculate and colliculus immediately involves both cortical and subcortical centers in the parallel processing of the same information. The superior colliculus is known to be important, via brainstem projections, in visual fixation and orientation, and thus an important function of the Y input is to allow regions of change in visual space to be rapidly foveated for further examination and object identification. Deactivating this part of the system by ablating the superior colliculus produces defects in eye movements and visual attention. Y cell information is probably the main component of the relay from the colliculus to two nuclei of the inferior pulvinar complex, and this pulvinar information is the only nongeniculate source of visual information to extrastriate cortex. However, because damage to striate cortex produces "cortical blindness," that is a lack of conscious awareness of objects, the pulvinar relay of afferent Y cell information to extrastriate cortex apparently does not relate to object vision. The direct relay of Y cell information to the lateral geniculate nucleus and hence to striate cortex provides extrastriate cortex with information about rapid local changes commonly resulting from stimulus movement, and thus the Y system is well designed as the input subsystem for the cortical processing of information relative to visual detection of luminance changes and movement, attention, fixation, and tracking.

The W cell group apparently contains several classes of neurons with several probable functions, some of them relating to subcortically mediated visual reflexes (Stone, 1983). However, a major component of the W cell group relates to cortical visual mechanisms via projections to the lateral geniculate nucleus and the superior colliculus. The W ganglion cells are relatively few in number (about 10%) and small in size, but they typically have large receptive fields. They often are poorly activated by visual stimuli and conduct information slowly over their axons to central structures. They project to a scattering of small interlaminar and sublaminar neurons in monkeys and presumably other higher primates, and to two narrow koniocellular layers of rather small neurons in the lateral geniculate nucleus of nocturnal prosimians (Weller & Kaas, 1982). Inputs to the superior colliculus appear to provide a second source of W cell information to the same regions of the primate lateral geniculate nucleus. The slow conduction times, low discharge rates, and large receptive fields seem to rule out the W cell inputs as being important in the detection of sudden local changes in visual space or in coding details critical in object vision. Instead, the W cell inputs seem suited for functions spanning longer periods of time than detection of rapid changes in the visual environment and rapid object "identification." We suggest that the W cell inputs to cortex modulate and enhance neurons related to object vision and attention, especially the X system, by altering the responsiveness of cortical neurons over relatively long, (perhaps seconds) time periods. The greater development of the W cell system in nocturnal primates suggests that such an enhancement is especially important during conditions of dim lumination.

THE SUBDIVISIONS OF VISUAL CORTEX

Present concepts of the organization of visual cortex in primates stem from proposals made in the late '60s and early '70s for Old World macaque monkeys by Zeki (Zeki, 1971, 1978) and for New World owl monkeys by Allman and Kaas (Allman & Kaas, 1971a, 1976).

Old World Monkeys

In studies on macaque monkeys, Zeki (1969) used degeneration methods to demonstrate three separate projection zones of area 17, fields he termed V2, V3 (thought to be successive concentric rings around primary cortex), and a region on the posterior bank of the superior temporal sulcus (see Kuypers et al., 1965 for an earlier description and Cragg, 1969 for an concomitant description). Further studies by Zeki expanded the scheme so that V3 was subdivided into a V3 and a V3a, a V4 was added and then subdivided into a V4 and a V4a, and the focus in the superior temporal sulcus (STS) become known as the "motion area" (for the responsiveness of its neurons to moving stimuli) and subsequently as "V5." More commonly, the field in the superior temporal sulcus is known as MT or the middle temporal visual area after the description of the retinotopic organization and architectonics of the area in owl monkeys (Allman & Kaas, 1971a) and subsequently in macaque monkeys (Gattass & Gross, 1981).

More recently, reports from a number of laboratories have indicated the probable locations of additional visual areas, and have pointed out visual regions of uncertain organizations. Figure 2 summarizes some of the current concepts. Van Essen and coworkers (see Van Essen, 1985) argued that the region of cortex previously assigned to ventral V3 differs enough in connections and neural properties to be considered a separate visual area, ventral posterior or VP. Although experimental support for this conclusion is substantial, the conclusion does raise the problem of having visual areas devoted exclusively to the upper visual quadrant (VP) or the lower visual quadrant (V3). Given this problem, it is not surprising that some investigators prefer to consider VP as ventral V3 (see Desimone and Ungerleider, 1986). The ventral extent of V4 (or the V4 complex since the number of fields in the region remains uncertain) has been a point of question, with some investigators having V4 extend ventrally onto the ventral surface of the brain (Desimone & Ungerleider, 1986), while others argue for a separate visual area, ventral anterior or VA (see Maunsell & Newsome, 1987; Van Essen, 1985), similar to the VA field of owl monkeys (see below). Maunsell and Van Essen (1983c) introduced the term, "medial superior temporal area," or MST, for the projection zone of MT in the superior temporal sulcus. However, the connection pattern suggests that MST contains two separate areas (Desimone & Ungerleider, 1986). The ventral intraparietal area, VIP, was also identified by projections from MT (Maunsell & Van Essen, 1983c). An adjoining lateral interparietal region, LIP, was denoted by Anderson, Asanuma, and Cowan (1985) as a source of strong connections with the frontal eye field. Nearby, the partietal-occipital area, PO, was established by electrophysiological mapping methods (Covey, Gattass, & Gross, 1982; Gattass, Sousa, & Covey, 1985). Connection patterns have suggested that another field, the dorsal prelunate area (DPL) is dorsomedial to V4 (Van Essen, 1985). In the temporal lobe, behavioral, electrophysiological and anatomical evidence supports the contention that inferior temporal cortex contains several subdivisions (see Weller & Kaas, 1987 for review), and recent anatomical studies suggest that caudal IT also contains at least two visual areas (Felleman, Knierim, & Van Essen, 1986). In addition, a distinct architectonic field in the ventral temporal lobe, area TF, has connections with other visual areas (see Weller & Kaas, 1987).

Several other fields can be considered visuomotor or polysensory in nature.

A large region in the superior temporal sulcus, the superior temporal polysensory region (STP), was shown by Bruce, Desimone, and Gross (1981) to be responsive to visual, auditory, and somatosensory stimuli. A number of studies have discussed the visual and visuomotor functions of the region of posterior parietal cortex known as 7a (see Anderson, Asanuma, & Cowan, 1985 for review). In the frontal lobe, both the classical frontal eye field, FEF, (Huerta, Krubitzer, & Kaas, 1987, 1988) and cortex ventral to the frontal eye field have connections with other visual structures and are capable of evoking eye movements with electrical stimulation. The FEF is interconnected with a large rostral portion of the supplementary motor area (SMA), and electrical stimulation of this SMA eye field results in eye movements (Huerta et al., 1987).

In summary, present proposals indicate that a large number of cortical areas relate to visual function in macaque monkeys. Some of these proposed areas have considerable experimental support, while some are only suggested by patterns of connections. Thus, present proposals will undoubtedly be modified both by corrections and additions.

New World Monkeys

The development of concepts of how visual cortex is subdivided in primates occurred along somewhat different lines in New World monkeys, since the early emphasis was on microelectrode mapping methods rather than patterns of connections. In a series of experiments in owl monkeys (Figure 3; Allman & Kaas, 1971a, 1971b, 1974a, 1974b, 1975, 1976), the primary (V-I) and the secondary fields (V-II) were mapped and related to architecture, and systematic representations of the visual hemifield were discovered and related to cortical architecture in the temporal lobe (the Middle Temporal visual area, MT), the lateral occipital lobe (the Dorsolateral visual area, DL), the medial occipital lobe (the Dorsomedial visual area, DM), and occipital cortex of the medial wall of the cerebral hemisphere (the Medial area, M). Less complete electrophysiological evidence was gathered to suggest the locations of other visual areas including the Dorsointermediate area (DI), Posterior Parietal visual cortex (PP), and Ventral Posterior (VP) and Ventral Anterior (VA) visual areas (see Newsome & Allman, 1980). More recently, anatomical methods have been used to help define and locate other presumptive subdivisions such as the Superior Temporal area, ST, which may contain two fields and corresponds to MST of macaque monkeys (Weller et al., 1984), caudal (ITc), rostral (ITr), polar (ITp) and medial (IPm) subdivisions of temporal cortex (Weller & Kaas, 1985, 1987), and the temporal parietal region (TP; Weller & Kaas, 1987).

Microelectrode stimulation methods and connection patterns were used to define the frontal eye field, the frontal visual region, FV, and the eye movement portion of the supplementary motor field (Gould, Cusick, Pons, & Kaas, 1986;

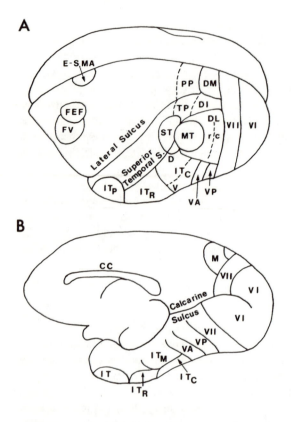

FIGURE 3   Proposed subdivisions of visual cortex in New World owl monkeys. A.
Dorsolateral view. B. Medial view. The dorsomedial area (DL) has rostral (r) and caudal
(c) subdivisions, while caudal inferior temporal cortex (IT$_c$) has dorsal (D) and ventral (V)
subdivisions. See Fig. 2 and text for abbreviations and details.

Weller & Kaas, 1987). Finally, connections between caudal but not rostral DL
and area 18 in squirrel monkeys (Cusick & Kaas, 1988a) suggest that the DL
region contains two visual areas.

Other Primates

Much less is known about visual system organization in prosimian primates
(see Weller & Kaas, 1982), apes and humans. Given the evidence for V-I (striate
cortex) in all mammals, V-II in a wide range of mammals including prosimians,
monkeys, apes, and humans, and MT in prosimians, monkeys, and possibly
humans, it seems likely that at least these three fields exist in all primates.

Furthermore, there is clear evidence that visual cortex of all primates consists of a number of fields, but the extent to which the organization is similar or different in the major primate lines is not yet certain.

THE FUNCTIONAL ORGANIZATION OF PRIMARY (STRIATE) CORTEX

Primary visual cortex (area 17 or striate cortex) is especially important in primates because it receives the input of all but a few of the relay cells of the lateral geniculate nucleus (see Kaas & Huerta, 1988). Thus, lesions of striate cortex profoundly deprive extrastriate visual areas of activating inputs, reduce monkeys and humans to having only a few crude visual abilities, and deprive humans of conscious visual experience (see Campion et al., 1983). There are several organizational features of striate cortex that relate to its important functional roles.

As is well known, striate cortex is retinotopically or visuotopically organized (Figure 4). Cortex of each hemisphere represents the contralateral visual hemifield and there is a major expansion of the representation of central as compared to peripheral vision. In addition, the map is somewhat anisotropic with the vertical dimension of the visual hemifield expanded slightly (about $1.5\times$) in comparison to the horizontal dimension (Tootell, Silverman, Switkes, & De-Valois, 1982). This expansion appears to be related to the fact that the inputs from the geniculate layers are initially segregated in some primates, including all Old World monkeys and all higher primates including humans, so that alternating bands of receptive cells are exclusively activated by the right or left eye (see Figure 6). This ocular dominance decreases in cells more removed from the direct geniculate inputs, but the ocular dominance bands, in a sense, mean that there are two maps in striate cortex, one for each eye. However, most cortical neurons are binocular (responsive to both eyes), and hence the anisotropy is not 2:1.

The obvious significance of the visuotopic map is that neurons in any particular location, to the extent that they are dependent on local connections, compute information for only a limited region of visual space, and influence adjacent cells that relate to highly similar regions of space. However, some lateral connections in striate cortex are reasonably long (see below).

A conspicuous feature of striate cortex is its laminar organization. Striate cortex is so markedly laminated in histological appearance compared to other fields that its boundaries and location are easily recognized in most animals, especially in primates. Cortical layers are generally numbered according to the six layer scheme of Brodmann (1909), although in striate cortex sublayers are

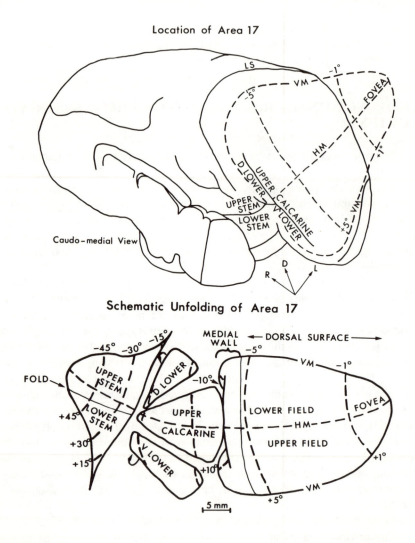

FIGURE 4 The location and retinotopic organization of primary (striate) cortex in macaque monkeys. A caudomedial view of the brain shows the representation of the central 5° of the contralateral visual hemifield on the dorsolateral surface of the brain. More paracentral and peripheral parts of the visual hemifield are represented in the folds of the calcarine fissure. The unfolded map of area 17 includes cortex from the calcarine fissure and the dorsolateral surface of the brain. Coordinates are for a polar map with concentric distances in degrees from the center of gaze (fovea). The representation of the upper visual quadrant is ventral to that of the lower visual quadrant, the zero vertical meridian (VM) forms the outer boundary of striate cortex, while the representation of the zero horizontal meridian (HM) bisects the field. LS, lunate sulcus. Modified from Weller and Kaas, (1983).

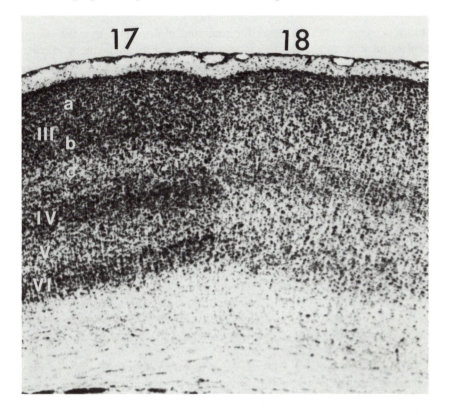

FIGURE 5 Cortical layers of primary visual cortex according to the scheme of Hassler (1966). Brodmann (1909) included layers IIIb and IIIc of Hassler in layer IV. Comparisons with layers in area 18 support the scheme of Hassler. Marmoset monkey. See text for details.

obvious and it is useful to denote them (Figure 5). Another complication is that it is not completely certain what layers in striate cortex of primates are homologous to layers in striate cortex of other species or serially homologous to layers in other regions of cortex in primates and other mammals. Brodmann (1909) regarded layer IV (4) in higher primates as broad, with three clear sublayers (A, B, & C). The sublayers of layer IV were thought to narrow and merge to become a single IV in adjoining cortex (area 18). Hassler (1966) and others have argued that the apparent merger does not really occur, and that only IV C of striate cortex is continuous with layer IV of adjoining cortex, and therefore layers "IV A" and "IV B" are really sublayers of layer III. Because comparative data (see Weller & Kaas, 1982) support Hassler's (1966) view, his less common laminar terminology is used here.

Layers are important in striate cortex because they reflect the grouping of neurons according to functional roles (e.g., Blasdel & Fitzpatrick, 1984; Dow,

1974). 1. Layer IV is specialized for receiving information from the lateral geniculate nucleus, modifying this input slightly, and then relaying it to more superficial and deeper layers. Cells in the upper (outer) half of layer IV (IVa) receive inputs from the magnocellular Y-like geniculate neurons and have response properties much like the magnocellular geniculate cells. Neurons in the lower (inner) half of layer IV (IVb) receive inputs from the X-like parvocellular geniculate layers, and reflect those properties. Thus, for higher primates, layer IV cells are X-like or Y-like, and generally geniculate like in that they are typically monocular, with circular (nonoriented) receptive fields. Neurons in other layers are typically more complex, binocularly activated, and selective for stimuli of a particular orientation. The cellular mechanisms for producing these more selective neural responses to visual stimuli are not well understood. However, the layers above and below layer IV can be described in terms of their overall cell properties and functional roles in providing information to other structures.

2. Sublayer IIIc is specialized for further processing of Y cell information from layer IVa, and relaying this processed information to extrastriate cortical areas (largely V-II and MT; see below). The neurons in IIIc are basically Y-like, but they are also sensitive to stimulus orientation and direction of movement.

3. Neurons in sublayer IIIb receive a direct input from the X-like parvocellular geniculate layers, and they typically have monocular, nonoriented, color-selective receptive fields, much like layer IVb cells.

4. Sublayer IIIa can be subdivided into systematic arrays of clusters of cells with high metabolic activity (the cytochrome oxidase patches; see below), and surrounding neurons with lower metabolic activity. Cells throughout sublayer IIIa appear to be dominated by X-like geniculate properties, and thereby seem to be basically concerned with processing information from the X channel. However, the neurons in the patches appear to be especially concerned with color coding, and typically have circular receptive fields and lack selectively for stimuli of particular orientations. The patches receive W cell geniculate inputs directly from the lateral geniculate nucleus, but they do not obviously reflect W cell properties. Thus, the significance of the W cell inputs is unclear, but it could be important in maintaining the high levels of activity. The interpatch neurons in layer IIIa are typically selective for stimulus orientation, and vary in being selective or nonselective for color. Layer IIIa neurons provide the relay to the second visual area, VII.

5. Layer II has cells that respond rather poorly to visual stimuli, and activation may depend on the W cell system.

6. Layer I is important in that it contains apical dendrites from cells in lower layers, and these dendrites receive the W cell inputs from the lateral geniculate nucleus to layer I. The significance of this W cell input is unknown, but it may relate to relatively slow changes in local activity levels in cortex.

7. The inner layers, V and VI, provide the outputs to subcortical centers. Layer VI provides feedback to the lateral geniculate nucleus. The neurons in the upper half of layer VI (VIa) have X-like features; and they receive some direct collateral input from parvocellular neurons, and they send back strong projections to the X-like parvocellular geniculate layers. The lower half of layer VI (VIb) is Y-like, with collateral inputs from magnocellular geniculate neurons and strong projections to magnocellular neurons. These feedbacks apparently modify receptive field center and surround properties of geniculate neurons (Marrocco & McClurkin, 1985). Other interconnections of layer VI neurons are with the claustrum, and these connections help mediate the property of "end-stopping," the reduced responsiveness of neurons to stimuli over some optimal length (see Sherk, 1986 for review).

8. Most of the layer V neurons appear to be dominated by the Y subsystem, especially in the inner half of the layer. The neurons are selective for stimulus orientation and often direction of movement, and are strongly binocular. Major projections are to the pulvinar complex, the superior colliculus, and the pons. The projections to the colliculus and pons are clearly related to the functions of these structures in producing eye and head movements and directing visual attention. The large pyramidal cells at the lower boundary of layer V project to both the superior colliculus and the cortical visual area, MT (Fries, Keizer, & Kuypers, 1985).

A final notable feature of primary visual cortex is its modular organization (Figure 6). As noted above, the geniculate inputs of many primates are unevenly distributed according to the eye of activation, so that alternating bands of layer IV cells are activated by the right or left eyes. Such "ocular dominance columns" (see Hubel & Wiesel, 1977) are not present in most mammals, and are absent even in many primates (Florence, Conley, & Casagrande, 1986). Furtheremore, the output cells of striate cortex are binocular. These observations suggest that the initial segregation of inputs by eye of origin in some primates does not have direct functional importance, but may result from selection for other factors (see Kaas, 1987).

A second type of module in primary visual cortex is the "orientation column." Many neurons in striate cortex of a wide range of mammals are best activated by bars or lines of a particular retinal location and *orientation*. In monkeys (e.g., Hubel & Wiesel, 1977), cats, tree shrews, and probably most other mammals, neurons selective for particular orientations are grouped into vertical columns (Figure 6), that, when viewed from the brain surface, are band-like in tree shrews (Humphrey, Skeen, & Norton, 1980), but are less regular in macaque monkeys (Blasdel & Salama, 1986). Bands of cells best activated by vertical stimuli are maximally spaced from bands related to horizontal stimuli, and intermediate orientations are systematically arranged in between. The arrays of bands probably represent gradients of activity rather than discrete steps.

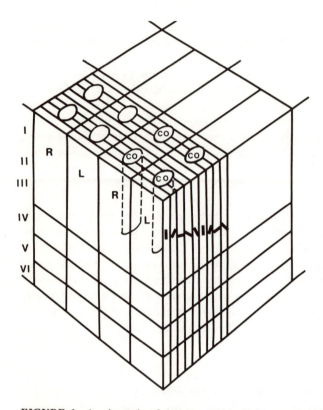

FIGURE 6 A schematic of the proposed modular organization of area 17 with ocular dominance bands (Right, R, and Left, L), bands of orientation selective cells (narrow slabs with bars), and cytochrome-oxidase patches (CO) with neurons related to color processing. Modified from Livingstone and Hubel, (1984a). See text for details.

A third type of module in area 17 is superimposed on the orientation and ocular dominance models in most primates (Horton, 1984), but is apparently absent in other mammals. Arrays of patches (Figures 6 & 7) of neurons with high metabolic activity are revealed by stains for the mitochondrial enzyme, cytochrome-oxidase. The neurons in these patches differ from those surrounding the patches in that they lack the property of orientation specificity. In addition, many of the neurons are color coded (Livingstone & Hubel, 1984a), and there is evidence that yellow-blue opponent cells are concentrated in some patches while red-green opponent cells are concentrated in other patches (Ts'o, Gilbert, & Wiesel, 1986). The patches are also distinguished by being broadly interconnected in the same hemisphere (Cusick & Kaas, 1988b; Livingstone & Hubel, 1984b; Rockland & Lund, 1983) and callosally in some primates (Cusick, Gould, & Kaas, 1984).

The existence of modules suggests that primary visual cortex contains several disrupted maps of visual space, and functions as several distinct visual areas.

THE SECOND VISUAL AREA, V-II

The existence of a second visual area adjoining the primary visual area was postulated by early investigators such as Brodmann (1909), Campbell (1905) and Elliot Smith (1906) on the basis of clinical and architectonic observations. Evidence of a second systematic representation of the visual hemifield was first obtained in electrophysiological mapping experiments in cats by Talbot (1941). Somewhat later, Woolsey and Fairman (1946) introduced the term V-II for this second representation. V-II has been termed a "second order transformation" of the visual hemifield, because in primates, at least, V-II is split along much of the representation of the zero horizontal meridian (Allman & Kaas, 1974b). As a result, the upper and lower visual quadrants are separated into lateral and medial portions in the band-like V-II, and the outer boundary of V-II is formed by the

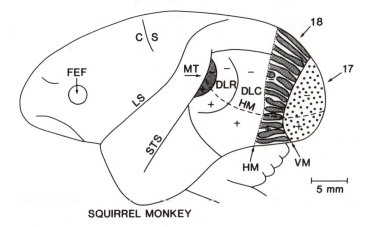

SQUIRREL MONKEY

FIGURE 7 The arrangement of cytochrome-oxidase dense bands in area 18 of a squirrel monkey (shading). It is common to further divide the bands into "thick" and "thin" bands containing neurons of different response properties and having different connections (see text). Adjoining visual areas are area 17, and caudal (DLC) and rostral (DLR) divisions of the dorsolateral visual area (DL). The Middle Temporal visual area (MT) extends into the superior temporal sulcus at the rostral border of DL. The zero horizontal meridian divides these five fields into dorsomedial and ventrolateral representations of the lower (–) and upper (+) visual quadrants, respectively, and forms the rostral border of area 18. The frontal eye field (FEF) is also indicated. CS, central sulcus; LS, lateral sulcus; STS, superior temporal sulcus, VM, zero vertical meridian. Based on Cusick and Kaas, 1988a.

zero horizontal meridian. V-II is coextensive with a distinct architectonic field which was termed area 18 by Brodmann (1909) in cats and New World monkeys. Unfortunately, Brodmann included much more than V-II in his "area 18" of macaque monkeys and higher primates, and therefore there is some confusion in the use of the term "area 18." However, given our present understanding, it seems reasonable to restrict the use of the term "area 18" to the architectonic field that is coexistensive with V-II, regardless of species. As far as we know, V-II exists not only in all primates, but in all mammals (Kaas, 1980).

Recently, it has become apparent that V-II of monkeys and perhaps most primates is characterized by an interesting type of modular organization. In brain sections reacted for the metabolic enzyme, cytochrome oxidase (CO), area 18 of monkeys is characterized by alternating dense or light bands of CO reactivity that extend across the width of area 18 (Figure 7; Cusick & Kaas, 1988a; Kaas, 1987; Livingstone & Hubel, 1984; Tootell, Hamilton, & Silverman, 1985; Wong-Riley & Carroll, 1984). Under close inspection, the CO dense bands can be divided into sets of alternating "thick" and "thin" bands. The connections of the thick bands, the thin bands, and the interbands differ (Krubitzer & Kaas, 1987; Livingstone & Hubel, 1984a; Shipp & Zeki, 1985). One set of bands receives inputs from the CO dense patches in area 17, have many neurons related to color-coding, and relay to the DL-V4 complex and ultimately the temporal lobe. The other set of bands receives inputs from the Y-like cells with orientation selectivity and broad band color responsiveness of area 17, have broad band color and orientation selective cells, and relay to the middle temporal visual area, MT. The interbands receive inputs from the X-cell dominated regions of area 17 that surround the layer III CO patches (the interpatch regions), have orientation selective cells, and relay to the DL-V4 complex and then to temporal cortex. Thus, there is evidence for three parallel systems in V-II, two related to form vision and further processing in temporal cortex, and one parallel system that relays to a motion detection system in MT and ultimately parietal cortex (see below). Intrinsic connections within V-II appear to be largely restricted to interconnecting bands or interbands of the same subsystem (Livingstone & Hubel, 1984a). More widespread feedback projections from the rostral targets of V-II may provide some integration of the three subsystems (Krubitzer & Kaas, 1987).

THE MIDDLE TEMPORAL VISUAL AREA, MT

MT is a subdivision of visual cortex in the upper temporal lobe of primates (Figures 2 & 3) that is defined by a systematic representation of the visual hemifield and a distinctive architectonic appearance (Allman & Kaas, 1971a). Like V-I, the map of the visual hemifield in MT is without splits or tears, and therefore it is termed a first order representation (Allman & Kaas, 1974b). MT has been mapped with microelectrodes in prosimian galagos (Allman, Kaas, & Lane, 1973), owl monkeys (Allman & Kaas, 1971a), macaque monkeys (Gattass & Gross, 1981; Van Essen, Maunsell, & Bixby, 1981), and has been demonstrated by topographic projection patterns from area 17 in squirrel monkeys (Spatz, Tigges, & Tigges, 1970) and marmosets (Spatz, 1977). Connection patterns with area 17 suggest that a homologue of MT may exist in at least some nonprimates (Sesma, Casagrande, & Kaas, 1984). In retinotopic organization, MT is basically a small mirror image of V-I. Thus, central or foveal vision is represented caudally or caudolaterally in MT, peripheral vision is rostral, while the upper and lower quadrants are lateral (or rostrolateral) and medial (or caudomedial), respectively. The retinotopic organization of MT is less precise than that of V-I, since the neurons of MT have receptive fields that are roughly 10× larger than those of V-I. As for other visual areas, the representation of the contralateral hemifield is distorted in MT so that proportionately more of the field is devoted to central vision. In appropriate histological preparations, MT is easily recognized by dense myelination and by dense staining for cytochrome oxidase (see Allman & Kaas, 1971a; Gattass & Gross, 1981; Tootell et al., 1985). This ease of histological identification has been useful in a number of single unit and lesion studies.

The receptive field properties of neurons in MT have been extensively studied (see Albright, 1984; Dubner & Zeki, 1971; Felleman & Kaas, 1984; Maunsell & Van Essen, 1983a, 1983b). Almost all neurons in MT demonstrate some preference for direction of stimulus movement and stimulus axis. Neurons across the thickness of cortex have similar preferences, and neurons with different direction of movement preferences are systematically arrayed across MT much in the manner of the orientation-selective bands of neurons in V-I. Thus, in some sense, MT contains multiple, disjointed, and slightly offset maps of the visual hemifield, i.e., different maps for different directions of movement.

MT receives the broad-band Y-like inputs from V-I directly or after a relay in V-II, and therefore neurons in MT are unselective for color, but responsive to low levels of contrast (see Kaas, 1986; Maunsell & Newsome, 1987). Neurons are only slightly inhibited by increasing the length of optimally oriented stimulus bars beyond the activating receptive field, but they are very selective for stimulus width, preferring widths much less than the width of the receptive field (Felleman & Kaas, 1984). Neurons have spatially and temporally homogeneous activating receptive fields (Felleman & Kaas, 1984), but they also have large antagonistic receptive field surrounds that extend beyond the classical receptive field (Allman, Meizin, & McGuinness, 1985). As a result of the interaction between the receptive field and the broad surround, neurons in MT are highly activated by small stimuli moving relative to a patterned background. A number of recent lesion studies have shown that information relayed through MT is critical for behavioral abilities involving visual tracking and judgments of motion. Newsome, Wurtz, Dursteler, and Mikami (1985) discovered that small partial lesions of MT produced defects in the ability of monkeys to smoothly track visual targets with pursuit eye movements. In related experiments, small lesions of MT in monkeys produced an eight-fold increase in the psychological threshold for the detection of shear motion (Siegel & Andersen, 1986). Finally, Newsome and Pare (1986) found that MT lesions produced an impairment in the ability of monkeys to detect correlated motion of dots imbedded in uncorrelated motion. Although, the lesion studies point out the importance of MT in tasks related to detecting and tracking moving stimuli, it should be noted that, in all these experiments, animals improved to normal levels over a few days of testing, showing that other visual structures or other parts of MT are capable of compensating for the lost tissue.

PROCESSING STREAMS IN VISUAL CORTEX

One of the more interesting proposals for considering the organization of the visual system in primates is that of "two cortical visual systems" as outlined by Mishkin, Ungerleider, and Macko (1983) and Ungerleider and Mishkin (1982). One cortical system involves a hierarchical sequence of interconnected processing stations that ultimately include inferior temporal cortex, and this system is concerned with the visual recognition of objects. The other system consists of stations and pathways that finally include posterior parietal cortex, and this system mediates functions related to localizing objects in space and visual attention. This proposal of two visual systems stems from the early evidence that projections from primary visual cortex diverge and subsequent visual stations project to temporal and parietal lobes (Kuypers, Szwarcbart, Mishkin, & Rosvold, 1965), and the observations that lesions of inferior temporal cortex disrupt discriminations based on differences between objects while lesions of posterior parietal cortex disrupt discrimination where the spatial arrangement of objects indicates the correct choice.

When the known interconnections of the subdivisions of visual cortex are considered, at first they seem too complex to support a "two visual systems" theory. Figure 8 shows some of the ipsilateral cortical connections of visual cortex of owl monkeys, and undoubtedly more connections exist. In addition, the summary does not include callosal connections (see Cusick et al., 1984) and connections with subcortical structures (see Kaas & Huerta, 1987). Each cortical visual area typically has interconnections with three to six ipsilateral visual areas, perhaps three contralateral visual areas, the claustrum, and two or three subdivisions of the pulvinar complex. Thus, the processing of information in any field is subject to the influences of many inputs, and each field influences, directly or indirectly, many other fields. Yet, there are reasons to believe that it is both productive and justifiable to conceptually simplify the connection pattern in order to reveal the basic framework of the processing sequence. Connections

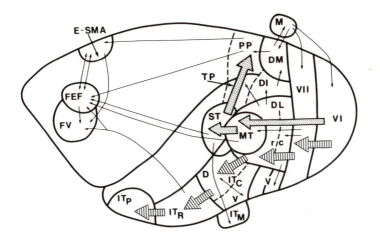

FIGURE 8   Some of the ipsilateral cortical connections of visual cortex of owl monkeys. Two major processing streams are distinguished (compare with Fig. 9). See Figures
2 and 3 and text for abbreviations and details. Modified and expanded from Kaas (1987).

between structures certainly differ in magnitude and differ in significance
according to laminar pattern in cortex (see Weller & Kaas, 1982). Although the
evidence for cortical fields is limited, some inputs appear to be responsible for
the major response properties of the neurons, while other connections modify
these basic properties. As an example from the thalamus, neurons in part of the
pulvinar complex with inputs from both visual cortex and the superior colliculus
have response characteristics resembling the cortical inputs and are almost totally
dependent on those inputs (Bender, 1983). If the major "feedforward" or activating connections are considered, then a simplified summary of a serial and
parallel processing system emerges (Figure 9). Similar but more complex processing hierarchies have been outlined by Maunsell and Van Essen (1983c) and
Maunsell and Newsome (1987). The scheme in Figure 9 can be made more
complex by adding other visual areas and more connections. Interpretations of
the levels of given fields in a hierarchy depend on evaluations (often guesses) of
the significance of inputs. For example, the scheme in Figure 9 places MT and
V-II at comparable second stages of processing since they both receive major
direct inputs from V-I. However, since MT also receives "feedforward" projections from other fields such as V-II, Maunsell and Newsome (1987) place MT
at the fifth level of cortical processing. Allowing for these differences in interpretation there is widespread agreement that the connection patterns and
proposed hierarchies are supportive of the "two streams of processing" theory.
    The two streams of processing not only involve cortical areas, but begin
much earlier, at the level of the retina. In brief, the X, Y, and W pathways are
largely segregated from retina to striate cortex, although the W pathway appears

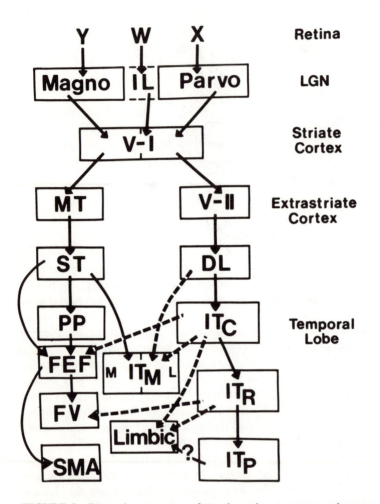

FIGURE 9 Processing sequences from the retina to cortex and over parallel "object vision" (right) and "motion detection" streams in extrastriate visual cortex of monkeys. The Y, W, and X channels from the retinal are segregated into magnocellular, interlaminar, and parvocellular regions of the lateral geniculate nucleus (LGN), respectively. Modified and expanded from Weller and Kaas (1987). See text for abbreviations and details.

to influence both X and Y pathways via layer I terminations and largely the X subsystem via W cell terminations in the cytochrome oxidase patches, while the X and Y subsystems remain more distinct.

The Y-like output of area 17 is directly to MT and indirectly to MT via one set of CO bands in V-II. A sparse alternative path that probably is based on Y-cell information is to DM (V-III). MT relays to ST (or MST). Most neurons in

ST-MST have response characteristics reflecting the inputs from MT, but some are remarkably different from MT neurons in that they continue to respond to a visually tracked moving stimulus after it has been briefly turned off (Wurtz & Newsome, 1985). Thus, neurons in this field could help maintain visual pursuit when the object to be followed is briefly obscured by other objects in its path. ST-MST relays to subdivisions of posterior parietal cortex where neurons are more complexly related to visual tracking, and appear to have roles in visual-spatial perception, visual attention, motion perception and visuomotor integration (see Andersen, 1988 for review). Some of these functions are mediated via connections with prefrontal cortex, especially the frontal eye field and adjoining frontal cortex, and the superior colliculus.

The X-cell pathway is relayed almost exclusively to V-II from the color dominated cytochrome patches in V-I to one set of bands in V-II, and from the orientation selective layer III interpatch regions of V-I to the interbands of V-II. Both of these X-dominated portions of V-II appear to relay largely to the DL-V4 complex, where further segregation may occur. At least some parts of V4 appear to be strongly related to the processing of color information and color constancy (Zeki, 1973). On the other hand, a large proportion of neurons in the region are selective for stimulus orientation, width, and length (Desimone, Schein, Moran, & Ungerleider, 1985), properties consistent with the view that these neurons are in a subsystem related to form discrimination. Of course, color is an important parameter in form discrimination in primates. Although DL appears to contain subdivisions (Figures 3 & 7; see Cusick & Kaas, 1988a) and the dense inputs from V-II are to caudal DL, parts of the DL complex are interconnected and all parts relay to the caudal divisions of inferior temporal cortex (Weller & Kaas, 1987). Neurons in caudal inferior temporal cortex have large bilateral receptive fields including the fovea and some of the neurons are selective for features of complex objects, especially important objects such as faces (Gross, Rocha-Miranda, & Bender, 1972; Desimone, Albright, Gross, & Bruce, 1984). The main "face selective" neurons are in a subdivision of IT cortex in the superior temporal sulcus; Desimone et al., 1984; Baylis, Rolls, & Leonard, 1985). Caudal IT cortex relays within at least two subsequent divisions of inferior temporal cortex, and outputs of these fields relate to the hippocampus and amygdala, structures important in assigning significance to stimuli and implimenting the storage of visual memories (Mishkin et al., 1983).

CONCLUSIONS

Early concepts of central processing in the visual system of primates including humans, was that of a simple hierarchy with three serial cortical processing stations followed by multimodal association cortex. The system is clearly more complex. Present evidence argues for three distinct parallel subsystems from the retina to primary visual cortex, and the existence of two major streams in cortex, one related to form vision and the other to visuomotor performance and attention. The number of cortical processing stations dominated by the visual modality is astonishingly large, with present evidence supporting the existence of a number in the range of 20 areas for higher primates. In addition, some fields, perhaps all, function as several fields by having several disjointed maps dispersed over repeating and functionally distinct processing modules.

REFERENCES

Albright, T. D. (1984). Direction and orientation selectivity of neurons in visual area MT of the macaque. *J. Neurophysiol., 52*, 1106–1130.

Albright, T. D., Desimone, R., & Gross, C. G. (1984). Columnar organization of directionally selective cells in visual area MT of the macaque. *J. Neurophysiol., 51*, 16–31.

Allman, J. M., & Kaas, J. H. (1971a). A representation of the visual field in the posterior third of the middle temporal gyrus of the owl monkey *(Aotus trivirgatus). Brain Res., 31*, 85–105.

Allman, J. M., & Kaas, J. H. (1971b). Representation of the visual field in striate and adjoining cortex of the owl monkey *(Aotus trivirgatus). Brain Res., 35*, 89–106.

Allman, J. M., & Kaas, J. H. (1974a). A crescent-shaped cortical visual area surrounding the middle temporal area (MT) in the owl monkey *(Aotus trivirgatus). Brain Res., 81*, 199–213.

Allman, J. M., & Kaas, J. H. (1974b). The organization of the second visual area (VII) in the owl monkey: A second order transformation of the visual field. *Brain Res., 76*, 247–265.

Allman, J. M., & Kaas, J. H. (1975). The dorsomedial cortical visual area: A third tier area in the occipital lobe of the owl monkey *(Aotus trivirgatus). Brain Res., 100*, 473–487.

Allman, J. M., & Kaas, J. H. (1976). Representation of the visual field on the medial wall of occipital-parietal cortex in the owl monkey. *Science, 191*, 572–575.

Allman, J. M., Kaas, J. H., & Lane, R. H. (1973). The middle temporal visual area (MT) in the bush baby *(Galago senegalensis). Brain Res., 57*, 197–202.

Allman, J. M., Meizin, F., & McGuinness, E. (1985). Stimulus specific responses from beyond the classical receptive field: Neurophysiological mechanisms for local-global comparisons in visual neurons. *Ann. Rev. Neurosci., 8*, 407–430.

Andersen, R. A. (1988). Visual and visual-motor functions of the posterior parietal cortex. In P. Rakic & W. Singer (Eds.), *Neurobiology of neocortex* (pp. 285-295). New York: Wiley.

Andersen, R. A., Asanuma, C., & Cowan, W. M. (1985). Callosal and prefrontal associational projecting cell populations in area 7A of the macaque monkey: A study using retrogradely transported fluoresent dyes. *J. Comp. Neurol., 232*, 443–455.

Baylis, G. C., Rolls, E. T., & Leonard, C. M. (1985). Selectivity between faces in the responses of a population of neurons in the cortex in the superior temporal sulcus of the monkey. *Brain Res., 342,* 91–102.

Bender, D. B. (1983). Visual activation of neurons in the primate pulvinar depends on cortex but not colliculus. *Brain Res., 297,* 258–261.

Blasdel, G. G., & Fitzpatrick, D. (1984). Physiological organization of layer 4 in macaque striate cortex. *J. Neurosci, 4,* 880–895.

Blasdel, G. G., & Salama, G. (1986). Voltage-sensitive dyes reveal a modular organization in monkey striate cortex. *Nature, 321,* 579–585.

Brodmann, K. (1909). *Vergleichende Lokalisationslehre der Grosshirnrinde.* Leipzig: Verlag Barth.

Bruce, C. J., Desimone, R., & Gross, C. G. (1981). Visual properties of neurons in a polysensory area in superior temporal sulcus of the macaque. *J. Neurophysiol., 46,* 369–384.

Campbell, A. W. (1905). *Histological studies on the localization of cerebral function.* Cambridge, England: Cambridge University Press.

Campion, J., Latto, R., & Smith, Y. M. (1983). Is blind sight an effect of scattered light, spaced cortex, and near-threshold vision? *The Behavioral and Brain Sciences, 6,* 423–486.

Covey, E., Gattass, R., & Gross, C. G. (1982). A new visual area in the parieto-occipital sulcus of the macaque. *Soc. Neurosci Abstrs., 8,* 681.

Cusick, C. G., & Kaas, J. H. (1988a). Cortical connections of area 18 and dorsolateral vision cortex in squirrel monkeys. *Visual Neurosci.*

Cusick, C. G., & Kaas, J. H. (1988b). Surface view patterns of intrinsic and extrinsic cortical connections of area 17 in a prosimian primate. *Brain Research.* Submitted.

Cusick, C. G., Gould, H. J. III, & Kaas, J. H. (1984). Interhemispheric connections of visual cortex in owl monkeys *(Aotus trivirgatus),* marmosets *(Callithrix jacchus),* and galagos *(Galago crassicaudatus). J. Comp. Neurol., 230,* 311–336.

Cragg, B. G. (1969). The topography of the afferent projections in circumstriate visual cortex of the monkey studied by the Nauta method. *Vision Res., 9,* 733–747.

Desimone, R., Albright, T. D., Gross, C. G., & Bruce, C. (1984). Stimulus-selective properties of inferior temporal neurons in the macaque. *J. Neurophysiol., 4,* 2051–2062.

Desimone, R., Schein, S. J., Moran, J., & Ungerleider, L. G. (1985). Contour, color and shape analysis beyond the striate cortex. *Vision Res., 25,* 441–452.

Desimone, R., & Ungerleider, L. G. (1986). Multiple visual areas in the caudal superior temporal sulcus of the macaque. *J. Comp. Neurol., 248,* 164–189.

DeYoe, E. A., & Van Essen, D. C. (1985). Segregation of efferent connections and receptive field properties in visual area V2 of the macaque. *Nature, 317,* 58–61.

Doty, R. W., Kimura, D. S., & Mogenson, G. P. (1964). Photically and electrically elicited responses in the central visual system of the squirrel monkey. *Exp. Neurol., 10,* 14–51.

Dow, B. M. (1974). Functional classes of cells and their laminar distribution in monkey visual cortex. *J. Neurophysiol., 37,* 927–946.

Dubner, R., & Zeki, S. M. (1971). Response properties and receptive fields of cells in an anatomically defined region of the superior temporal sulcus. *Brain Res., 35,* 528–532.

Ebbesson, S. O. E. (1984). Evolution and ontogeny of neural circuits. *The Behavioral and Brain Sciences, 7,* 321–366.

Economo, von C. (1929). *The cytoarchitectonics of the human cortex.* Oxford, England: Oxford University Press.

Felleman, D. J., & Kaas, J. H. (1984). Receptive-field properties of neurons in middle temporal visual area (MT) of owl monkeys. *J. Neurophysiol., 52,* 488–513.

Felleman, D. J., Knierim, J. J., & Van Essen, D. C. (1986). Multiple topographic and non-topographic subdivisions of the temporal lobe revealed by the connections of area V4 in macaques. *Soc. Neurosci. Abstrs., 12,* 1182.

Ferrier, D. (1874). The localization of function in the brain. *Proc. R. Soc. London Ser. B., 22,* 229–232.

Florence, S. L., Conley, M., & Casagrande, V. A. (1986). Ocular dominance columns and retinal projections in New World spider monkeys *(Ateles ater). J. Comp. Neurol., 243,* 234–248.

Fries, W., Keizer, K., & Kuypers, H. G. J. M. (1985). Large layer VI cells in macaque striate cortex (Meynert cells) project to both superior colliculus and prestriate visual area V5. *Experimental Brain Res., 58,* 613–616.

Gattass, R., & Gross, C. G. (1981). Visual topography of striate projection zone (MT) in posterior superior temporal sulcus of the macaque. *J. Neurophysiol., 46,* 621–638.

Gattass, R. Sousa, A. P. B., & Covey, E. (1985). Possible substrates for pattern recognition mechanisms. In C. Chagas, R. Gattass, & C. Gross (Eds.), *Pattern recognition Mechanisms* (pp. 1–20). Vatican City: Pontifical Academy of Sciences.

Gould, H. J., III, Cusick, C. G., Pons, T. P., & Kaas, J. H. (1986). The relationship of corpus callosum connections to electrical stimulation maps of motor, supplementary motor, and frontal eye fields in owl monkeys. *J. Comp. Neurol., 247,* 297–325.

Gross, C. G., Rocha-Miranda, C. E., Bender, D. B. (1972). Visual properties of neurons in the inferotemporal cortex of the macaque. *J. Neurophysiol., 35,* 96–111.

Hassler, R. (1966). Comparative anatomy of the central visual systems in day- and night-active primates. In R. Hassler & H. Stephen (Eds.), *Evolution of the forebrain* (pp. 419–434). Stuttgart: Thieme.

Horton, J. C. (1984). Cytochrome oxidase patches: A new cytoarchitectonic feature of monkey visual cortex. *Philos. Trans. R. Soc. Lond. (Biol)., 304,* 199–253.

Hubel, D. H., & Livingstone, M. S. (1985). Complex-unoriented cells in a subregion of primate area 18. *Nature, 315,* 325–327.

Hubel, D. H., & Wiesel, T. N. (1968). Receptive fields and functional architecture of monkey striate cortex. *J. Physiol.* (Lond.), *195,* 215–243.

Hubel, D. H., & Wiesel, T. N. (1977). Functional architecture of macaque monkey visual cortex. *Proc. R. Soc. London Ser. B, 198,* 1–59.

Huerta, M. F., Krubitzer, L. A., & Kaas, J. H. (1986). The frontal eye field as defined by intracortical microstimulation in squirrel monkeys, owl monkeys, and macaque monkeys. I. Subcortical connections. *J. Comp. Neurol., 253,* 415–439.

Huerta, M. F., Krubitzer, L. A., & Kaas, J. H. (1987). The frontal eye field as defined by intracortical microstimulation in squirrel monkeys, owl monkeys, and macaque monkeys. II. Cortical connections. *J. Comp. Neurol., 265,* 332–361.

Humphrey, A. L., Skeen, L. C., & Norton, T. T. (1980). Topographic organization of the orientation column system in the striate cortex of the tree shrew *(Tupaia glis)*. II. Deoxyglucose mapping. *J. Comp. Neurol., 192,* 549–566.

Hyvärinen, J. (1982). Posterior parietal lobe of the primate brain. *Physiol. Rev., 62,* 1060–1129.

Jones, E. G., & Powell, T. P. S. (1970). An anatomical study of converging sensory pathways within the cerebral cortex of the monkey. *Brain, 93,* 793–820.

Kaas, J. H. (1978). Organization of visual cortex in primates. In C. R. Noback (Ed.), *Sensory systems of primates* (pp. 151–179). New York: Plenum Press.

Kaas, J. H. (1980). A comparative study of visual cortex organization in mammals. In S. O. E. Ebbesson (Ed.), *Comparative neurology of the telencephalon* (pp. 483–502). New York: Plenum Press.

Kaas, J. H. (1982). The segregation of function in the nervous system: Why do sensory systems have so many subdivisions? In W. P. Neff (Ed.), *Contributions to sensory physiology* (Vol. 7, pp. 201–240). New York: Academic Press.

Kaas, J. H. (1986). The structural basis for information processing in the primate visual system. In J. P. Pettigrew, W. R. Levick, & K. J. Sanderson (Eds.), *Visual neuroscience* (pp. 315–340). Cambridge, England: Cambridge University Press.

Kaas, J. H. (1987). The organization of neocortex in mammals: Implications for theories of brain function. *Ann. Rev. Psychol., 38,* 129–151.

Kaas, J. H., & Huerta, M. F. (1988). Subcortical visual system of primates. In H. P. Steklis (Ed.), *Comparative primate biology, Vol. 4: Neurosciences* (pp. 327–391). New York: Alan R. Liss.

Klüver, H., & Bucy, P. C. (1939). Preliminary analysis of functions of the temporal lobes in monkeys. *Archives of Neurology and Psychiatry, 42,* 979–1000.

Krubitzer, L. A., & Kaas, J. H. (1987). Connections of modular subdivisions of cortical visual areas 17 and 18 with the middle temporal area, MT, in squirrel monkeys. *Soc. Neurosci. Abstrs.*

Kuypers, H. G. J. M., Szwarcbart, M. K., Mishkin, M., & Rosvold, H. E. (1965). Occipito-temporal cortico-cortical connections in the rhesus monkey. *Exp. Neurol., 11,* 245–262.

Livingstone, M. S., & Hubel, D. H. (1984a). Anatomy and physiology of a color system in the primate visual cortex. *J. Neurosci., 4,* 309–356.

Livingstone, M. S., & Hubel, D. H. (1984b). Specificity of intrinsic connections in primate visual cortex. *J. Neurosci. 4,* 2830–2835.

Maunsell, J. H. R., & Van Essen, D. C. (1983a). Functional properties of neurons in the middle temporal visual area (MT) of the macaque monkey: I. Selectivity for stimulus direction, speed and orientation. *J. Neurophysiol., 49,* 1127–1147.

Maunsell, J. H. R., & Van Essen, D. C. (1983b). Functional properties of neurons in the middle temporal visual area (MT) of the macaque monkey: II. Binocular interactions and the sensitivity to binocular disparity. *J. Neurophysiol., 49,* 1148–1167.

Maunsell, J. H. R., & Van Essen, D. C. (1983c). The connections of the middle temporal visual area (MT) and their relationship to a cortical hierarchy in the macaque monkey. *J. Neurophysiol., 3,* 2563–2586.

Maunsell, J. H. R., & Newsome, W. T. (1987). Visual processing in monkey extrastriate cortex. *Ann. Rev. Neurosci., 10,* 363–401.

Marrocco, R. T., & McClurkin, J. W. (1985). Evidence for spatial structure in the cortical input to the monkey lateral geniculate nucleus. *Exp. Brain Res., 59,* 50–56.

Merzenich, M. M., & Kaas, J. H. (1980). Principles of organization of sensory-perceptual systems in mammals. In J. M. Sprague & A. N. Epstein (Eds.), *Progress in psychobiology and physiological psychology* (pp. 1–42). New York: Academic Press.

Mishkin, M. (1966). Visual mechanisms beyond the striate cortex. In R. W. Russell (Ed.). *Frontiers in physiological psychology* (pp. 93–119). New York: Academic Press.

Mishkin, M., Ungerleider, L. G., & Macko, K. A. (1983). Object vision and spatial vision: Two cortical pathways. *Trends Neurosci., 6,* 414–417.

Mountcastle, V. B. (1957). Modality and topographic properties of single neurons of cats' somatic sensory cortex. *J. Neurophysiol., 2,* 408–434.

Mountcastle, V. B. (1975). The view from within: Pathways to the study of perception, *The Johns Hopkins Medical Journal, 136,* 109–131.

Newsome, W. T., & Allman, J. M. (1980). Interhemispheric connections of visual cortex in the owl monkey, *(Aotus trivirgatus),* and the bushbaby, *Galago seneglensis). J. Comp. Neurol., 194,* 209–233.

Newsome, W. T., & Pare, E. B. (1986). MT lesions impair discrimination of direction in a stochastic motion display. *Soc. Neurosci. Abstrs., 12,* 1183.

Newsome, W. T., Wurtz, R. H., Dursteler, M. R., & Mikami, A. (1985). Deficits in visual motion perception following ibotenic acid lesions of the middle temporal visual area of the macaque monkey. *J. Neurosci., 5,* 825–840.

Perrett, D. I., Smith, P. A. J., Potter, D. D., Mistlin, A. J., Head, A. S., Milner, A. D., & Jeeves, M. A. (1985). Visual cells in the temporal cortex sensitive to face view and gaze direction. *Proc. R. Soc. London Ser. B, 223,* 293–317.

Rockland, K. S., & Lund, J. S. (1983). Intrinsic laminar lattice connections in primate visual cortex. *J. Comp. Neurol., 216,* 303–318.

Rodieck, R. W. (1987). The primate retina. In H. P. Steklis (Ed.), *Comparative primate biology, Vol. III, Neurosciences.* New York: Alan R. Liss.

Rodieck, R. W., & Brening, R. K. (1983). Retinal ganglion cells: Properties, types, genera, pathways, and trans-species comparisons. *Brain Behav. Evol., 23,* 121–164.

Sesma, M. A., Casagrande, V. A., & Kaas, J. H. (1984). Cortical connections of area 17 in tree shrews. *J. Comp. Neurol., 230,* 337–351.

Sherk, H. (1986). The claustrum and the cerebral cortex. In E. G. Jones & A. Peters (Eds.), *Cerebral cortex* (Vol. 5). Sensory-motor areas and aspects of cortical connectivity (pp. 467–499). New York: Plenum Press.

Shipp, S., & Zeki, S. (1985). Segregation of pathways leading from area V2 to areas V4 and V5 of macaque monkey visual cortex. *Nature, 315,* 322–325.

Siegel, R. M., & Andersen, R. A. (1986). Motion perceptual deficits following ibotenic acid lesions of the middle temporal area (MT), in the behaving rhesus monkey. *Soc. Neurosci, Abstrs., 12,* 1183.

Smith, G. E. (1906). A new topographic survey of human cerebral cortex, being an account of the distribution of the anatomically distinct cortical areas and their relationship to the cerebral sulci. *J. Anat. Physiol., 42,* 237–254.

Spatz, W. B. (1977). Topographically organized reciprocal connections between area 17 and MT (visual area of superior temporal sulcus) in marmoset *(Callithrix jacchus.) Exp. Brain Res., 27,* 91–108.

Spatz, W. B., Tigges, J., & Tigges, M. (1970). Subcortical projections, cortical associations and some intrinsic interlaminar connections of the striate cortex in the squirrel monkey *(Saimiri). J. Comp. Neurol., 140,* 155–174.

Stone, J. (1983). *Parallel processing in the visual system.* New York: Plenum Press.

Sur, M., Wall, J. T., & Kaas, J. H. (1984). Modular distribution of neurons with slowly adapting and rapidly adapting responses in area 3b of somatosensory cortex in monkeys. *J. Neurophysiol., 51,* 724–744.

Talbot, S. A. (1941). A lateral localization in cat's visual cortex. *Fed. Proc., 1,* 84.

Tootell, R. B. H., Hamilton, S. L., & Silverman, M. S. (1985). Topography of cytochrome oxidase activity in owl monkey cortex. *J. Neurosci., 5,* 2786–2800.

Tootell, R. B. H., Silverman, M. S., Switkes, E., & DeValois, R. L. (1982). Deoxyglucose analysis of retinotopic organization in primate striate cortex. *Science, 218,* 902–904.

Ts'o, D. Y., Gilbert, C. D., & Wiesel, T. N. (1986). Relationships between color-specific cells in cytochrome oxidase rich patches of monkey striate cortex. *Soc. Neurosci. Abstrs., 12,* 1497.

Ungerleider, L. G., & Mishkin, M. (1982). Two cortical visual systems. In D. J. Ingle, J. W. Mansfield, & M. A. Goodale (Eds.), *Advances in the analysis of visual behavior* (pp. 549–596). Cambridge, MA: MIT press.

Van Essen, D. C. (1979). Visual areas of the mammalian cerebral cortex. *Ann. Rev. Neurosci., 2,* 227–263.

Van Essen, D. C. (1985). Functional organization of primate visual cortex. In A. Peters & E. G. Jones (Eds.), *Cerebral cortex* (vol. 3). New York: Plenum Press.

Van Essen, D. C., Maunsell, J. H. R., & Bixby, J. L. (1981). The middle temporal visual area in the macaque: Myeloarchitecture, connections, functional properties and topographic representation. *J. Comp. Neurol., 199,* 293–326.

Weller, R. E., & Kaas, J. H. (1981). Cortical and subcortical connections of visual cortex in primates. In C. N. Woolsey (Ed.), *Cortical sensory organization, Vol. 2: Multiple visual areas.* Clifton, NJ: Humana Press.

Weller, R. E., & Kaas, J. H. (1982). The organization of the visual system in Galago: Comparisons with monkeys. In D. E. Haines (Ed.), *The lesser bush baby (Galago) as an animal model: Selected topics* (pp. 107–135). CRC Press.

Weller, R. E., & Kaas, J. H. (1983). Retinotopic patterns of connections of area 17 with visual areas V-II and MT in macaque monkeys. *J. Comp. Neurol., 220,* 253–279.

Weller, R. E., & Kaas, J. H. (1985). Cortical projections of the dorsolateral visual area in owl monkeys: The prestriate relay to inferior temporal cortex. *J. Comp. Neurol., 234,* 35–59.

Weller, R. E., & Kaas, J. H. (1987). Subdivisions and connections of inferior temporal cortex in owl monkeys. *J. Comp. Neurol., 256,* 137–172.

Weller, R. E., Wall, J. T., & Kaas, J. H. (1984). Cortical connections of the middle temporal visual area (MT) and the superior temporal cortex in owl monkeys. *J. Comp. Neurol., 228,* 81–104.

Wong-Riley, M. T. T., & Carroll, E. W. (1984). Quantitative light and electron microscopic analysis of cytochrome oxidase-rich zones in V-II prestriate cortex of monkey. *Brain Res., 14,* 271–291.

Woolsey, C. N., Akert, K., Benjamin, R. M., Leibowitz, H., & Welker, W. I. (1955). Visual cortex of the marmoset. *Fed. Proc., 14,* 166.

Woolsey, C. N., & Fairman, D. (1946). Contralateral ipsilateral and bilateral representation of cutaneous receptors in somatic area I and II of the cerebral cortex of pig, sheep and other mammals. *Surgery, 19,* 684–702.

Zeki, S. M. (1969). Representation of central visual fields in prestriate cortex of monkey. *Brain Res., 14,* 271–291.

Zeki, S. M. (1971). Cortical projections from two prestriate areas in the monkey. *Brain Res., 34,* 19–35.

Zeki, S. M. (1973). Colour coding in rhesus monkey prestriate cortex. *Brain Res., 53,* 422–27.

Zeki, S. M. (1978). Functional specialization in the visual cortex of the rhesus monkey. *Nature, 274,* 423–428.

II
Disorders of Object Perception

2

Cerebral Disturbances of Elementary Visual Functions

J. Zihl

INTRODUCTION

Brain damage can lead to different visual perceptual disturbances ranging from visual field defects to gnostic disorders. Although modern human neuropsychology deals mainly with cognitive aspects of visual perception, disorders of "lower" visual functions should not be neglected since these disorders may affect "higher" visual abilities. The necessity of taking this into consideration has been examplarily shown by Siemerling in 1890. He described a patient who, on the basis of his difficulties with object perception and, as a consequence, recognition, could well have been classified as having visual agnosia. A detailed analysis of the underlying factor(s) revealed, however, that a combination of elementary visual disorders (visual field loss, reduced visual acuity, and disturbed color vision) adequately accounted for the severe deficits in object identification. Siemerling published his observations in the same issue of the "Archiv für Psychiatrie und Nervenkrankheiten" (Archives of Psychiatry and Nervous Diseases) in which Lissauer's classical paper appeared on "psychic blindness" in a patient suffering from bilateral "posterior" brain damage. Lissauer himself pointed out that his patient suffered from extensive visual field loss, severely restricted visual exploration, reduced visual acuity, and blurred vision, indicating that his case did not show a "pure" form of agnosia. Object perception may therefore have been additionally affected by disturbances of more elementary visual abilities. Siemerling (1890), whose contribution has been completely neglected in the neuropsychological literature, and later Poppelreuter (1917) discussed in detail the methodological and theoretical problems of Lissauer's concept of visual agnosia. However, most of the later authors did not refer to the critical question of how visual agnosia can be differentiated from secondary inpairments in object identification which are a result of disturbed elementary visual functions.

This chapter presents the elementary visual disorders after brain damage that are most frequently encountered in the clinic. These include visual field disorders and impairments in visual acuity and color vision. In addition, the disabilities of patients that result from these disorders are be discussed.

VISUAL FIELD DISORDERS

Disorders of the visual field are probably the most frequent type of visual impairment after brain damage. Since postchiasmatic damage always leads to impairment of vision in corresponding regions of the left or right hemifields of both eyes—except for the loss of the temporal crescent (see. p. 37)—the resulting field disorders are called homonymous. Two classes of homonymous visual field disorders exist: (1) complete loss of vision in the affected field region, and (2) loss of some visual functions while others may remain partially spared.

Visual field defects can be measured quantitatively by perimetric techniques (see e.g., Aulhorn & Harms, 1972; Ellenberger, 1974). In routine perimetry a target of a given size and luminance is moved from the periphery towards the center of the perimetric sphere. The task of the patient is to indicate the appearance of the target by, for example, pressing a buzzer-key while he is steadily fixating another stimulus in the center of the perimeter. The extent of the visual field is defined by those positions where the target is detected by the patient. Since a target of white light is usually used for field plotting, the resulting map indicates only the visual field extent for the detection of light. For the testing of other visual functions, like color or form vision, special targets and procedures are required (see Aulhorn & Harms, 1972).

Visual Field Loss

The most common types of visual field loss are hemianopias (loss of vision in one hemifield), quadranopias (loss of vision in one quadrant) and scotomata (regions of blindness occurring mainly in the central field region; see Figure 1). Table 1 shows the frequency and etiology of homonymous visual field defects in a group of 392 patients who were examined in our Department between 1978 and 1986. As can be seen, hemianopias predominate and were found in more than 75% of the patients, whereas quadranopias and especially paracentral scotomata occur rather rarely. This distribution is in agreement with that reported by Trobe, Lorber, and Schlezinger (1973) but is in contrast to the results of visual field studies with patients suffering gunshot injuries where many more cases are reported with irregular unilateral and especially bilateral field losses, in particular quadranopias or scotomata (see, e.g., Holmes, 1918; Poppelreuter, 1917;

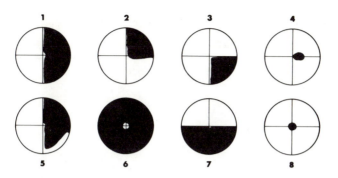

FIGURE 1 Schematic maps of homonymous visual field defects after unilateral left-sided (1–5) and bilateral brain damage (6–8). 1: hemianopia, 2: upper quadranopia, 3: lower quadranopia, 4: paracentral scotoma, 5: hemianopia with sparing of the temporal crescent (all field defects may also occur in the left hemifield); 6: bilateral homonymous hemianopia with preservation of the central visual field ("tunnel vision"), 7: bilateral lower (inferior) hemianopia, 8: central scotoma.

Teuber, Battersby, & Bender, 1960). It is likely that this disagreement reflects different aetiologies. Cerebrovascular damage, which was the most common cause of visual field loss in our group (79%) as well as that of Trobe et al. (89%), usually leads to larger and probably more regular brain damage than gunshot injuries, resulting in concomitantly larger and more regular field defects.

The degree of disability of the patient obviously depends on the extent of field sparing in the affected hemifield. As Table 1 shows, sparing is less than 4° of visual angle in about 70% of the patients. There is a long lasting controversy in the literature as to the minimal degree of visual field sparing after total unilateral postchiasmatic damage (cf. Polyak, 1957; Putnam & Liebman, 1942). Some authors deny that any portion of the visual field sparing at all, assuming that "foveal splitting" is the rule, and any sparing is either due to inaccurate perimetric testing or to unstable or eccentric fixation. Others agree, on the basis of their observations, that sparing must be present but dispute the extent of such sparing. Wilbrand (1890) for example assumed that minimal field sparing is only about 0.5 degrees of visual angle. Williams and Gassel (1962), however, found sparing in the range of 3 to 5 in their patients. Obviously inaccurate perimetric testing can "simulate" larger sparing but can also lead to an artificial shrinkage of the residual field (see Williams & Gassel, 1962). If for example patients respond slowly, which is commonly a nonspecific effect of brain damage (cf. Birch, Belmont, & Karp, 1967), than no field sparing may be found at all. In some cases the target may have just crossed the vertical axis when the patient indicates that it has been detected.

According to our observations field sparing can range from 0.5 degrees upwards, even though the majority of cases show a small residual field (cf. Table

TABLE 1

Frequency of Homonymous Visual Field Defects, Aetiology and Degree of Visual Field Sparing in a Group of 392 Patients

A. *Type of visual field loss*

–unilateral defects	370	94%
–bilateral defects	22	06%
–hemianopias	284	77%
–upper quadranopias	38	10%
–lower quadranopias	33	09%
–paracentral scotomata	15	04%

B. *Aetiology*

–infarctions: 66%
–haemorrhages: 13%
–closed-head-trauma: 11%
–tumours (operated): 04%
–chronic cerebral hypoxia: 03%
–other aetiologies: 03%

C. *Visual field sparing*

	<2	2–4	5–10	>10
–hemianopias (%)	30	46	16	08
–quadranopias (%)	13	37	34	16
–paracentral scotomata (%)	33	47	20	00
Total (in %)	24	45	21	10

1). Studies with hemidecorticated patients (Huber, 1962; Sharpe, Lo, & Rabinovitch, 1979) revealed that the foveal region (diameter: 1.5 degrees; see Putnam & Liebman, 1942) is always spared after unilateral brain damage. These clinical observations are supported by experimental results with monkeys, showing that the fovea and also a small strip along the vertical axis are bilaterally represented (Bunt, Minckler, & Johanson, 1977). One should therefore always indicate the extent of sparing in terms of degrees of visual angle, since this information is more useful in both scientific and clinical work. Obviously accuracy and reliability of perimetric testing and a perimeter allowing high spatial resolution are essential prerequisites for determining the visual field border and thus the amount of visual field sparing.

Patients with visual field loss usually complain of difficulties with reading and of detecting and finding objects in the space corresponding to the region of the lost visual field. If field sparing is rather small, and this is also true of cases with paracentral scotomata, (i.e., limited to about 2–3 degrees) then patients show marked difficulties with reading (the so-called hemianopic reading disorder; cf. Wilbrand, 1907). Reading disabilities in these cases may arise because the visual field sparing is too small to allow sufficient text to be simultaneously perceived. As a consequence, syllables may disappear at the beginning or at the end of words, and words may disappear at the left or right side of the line, depending on the side of the field loss. Patients then show both incorrect and slow reading (see Poppelreuter, 1917; Zihl, Krischer, & Meissen, 1984). About half of the patients (48%) summarized in Table 1 showed difficulties with reading when tested formally.

The other disability that patients with homonymous field loss complain of is the problem of finding objects in the space corresponding to the field loss and of avoiding obstacles appearing on the defective side. In contrast to the common belief that hemianopic patients invariably adjust themselves to this disability by *spontaneously* compensating for their visual field loss using eye and head movements, earlier and more recent studies have shown that the impairment in visual search associated with hemianopia may remain unchanged even over many months (Pfeifer, 1919; Poppelreuter, 1917; Zihl & von Cramon, 1986). As a rule these patients use rather small saccadic eye movements (Meienberg, Zangemeister, Rosenberg et al., 1981; see Figure 2). Using such an oculomotor strategy to overcome the field loss typically results in neglecting targets appearing in the far periphery, because the patient does not search there, and more often, in a marked increase in the time spent searching (Chedru, Leblanc, & Lhermitte, 1973; Zihl & Wohlfarth-Englert, 1986). After adaptation, either spontaneously or after treatment, to their field loss patients may use larger saccadic eye movements to glance quickly over the whole hemispace using 2 or 3 shifts of gaze (Gassel & Williams, 1963; Meienberg et al., 1981; Zihl & Werth, 1984; see also Figure 2). As a consequence the field of search becomes markedly

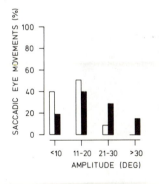

FIGURE 2 Distribution of amplitudes of saccadic eye movements (n = 80) in a 27-year-old patient exhibiting a left-sided homonymous hemianopia with field sparing of 2 deg of visual angle (field plot see Figure 3) before (4 months after right posterior cerebral artery infarction; white bars) and after adaptation to his field loss (6 months after occurrence of brain damage; black bars). Note the increase in the size of saccadic eye movements after the patient has been trained to use larger eye movements.

enlarged, even under spontaneous searching conditions (Figure 3). It should be added that, in contrast to patients suffering from visual hemineglect, patients showing a restricted field of search in association with hemianopia, search immediately and very effectively for targets in the whole hemispace after instruction or cuing.

Patients in whom the temporal crescent is preserved (cf. Figure 1) are able to detect visual stimuli appearing peripherally and show a greater tendency to explore the affected side. These patients are therefore much less disabled than patients without sparing of vision in the outer periphery of the visual field (Benton, Levy, & Swash, 1980; Meienberg, 1981; Poppelreuter, 1917).

It is interesting to note that patients who possess a small residual field on the affected side are well aware of their problems, especially those concerning reading, and can often report these problems in great detail. However, they do not describe them as a field loss but rather as some sort of "poor vision" in the eye ipsilateral to the field loss (see Critchley, 1949).

Bilateral posterior brain damage can lead either to bilateral field loss, sparing the central region or to almost total loss of vision. In cases suffering from chronic cerebral hypoxia the central visual field may be lost (the so-called central scotoma; Hoyt & Walsh, 1958). Patients with total cerebral blindness are, as a rule, not aware of their blindness and claim to "see" their surroundings (Anton, 1898). Even though in most of the cases some vision may return spontaneously in the central field region, visual acuity and thus form vision may remain markedly impaired (Gloning, Gloning, & Tschabitscher, 1962; Poppelreuter, 1917). The denial of blindness and the occurrence of both simple and complex visual pseudohallucinations make diagnosis of cerebral blindness difficult because one cannot rely on the responses of the patient (see, e.g., Brown, 1983).

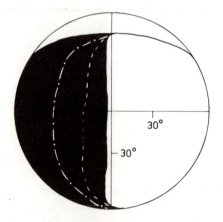

FIGURE 3 Extent of field of search in a patient with a left-sided hemianopia before (- - -) and after (—·—) increase of the amplitude of saccadic eye movements into the left hemifield (cf. Figure 2). Black area indicates field loss.

Similar problems arise in the investigation of vision, which may eventually recover. One possible way of avoiding these difficulties is to use the pattern-generated visually evoked potential (VEP) as an indicator of the presence or absence of vision in such cases. However, while the absence of any clear VEP undoubtedly indicates blindness (cf. Kooi & Sharbrough, 1966) a normal or nearly normal VEP may be found in some cases that fail to demonstrate any visual ability when their visual field or their visual acuity is tested (Bodis-Wollner, Atkin, Raab, & Wolkstein, 1977). As Celesia, Polcyn, Holden et al. (1982) have shown, VEPs may be preserved in cortically blind patients as long as "functional islands" of occipital cortex are present. This functional sparing may, however, not suffice for visual perception. Thus a normal or nearly normal VEP response in these patients cannot be used either as an unequivocal indicator of the presence of vision or as an index for the extent of the visual abilities a patient may possess.

Hemiachromatopsia and Hemiamblyopia

Another type of visual field disorder consists of impairment of visual functions rather than the complete loss of vision. Two types of such disorders have been reported in the literature, hemiachromatopsia and hemiamblyopia.

Hemiachromatopsia is probably a comparatively rare visual field disorder; Lenz (1905, 1909) found that about 6% of cases, in a group of 81 patients suffering from unilateral postchiasmatic brain damage, showed this symptom. Typically patients report a target appearing in the periphery and are able to identify the form of the target (e.g., a circle) at the respective eccentricity but cannot, however, perceive any color. As soon as the colored target appears in the intact field where color perception is spared the patient can identify and even name the color (Albert, Reches, & Silverberg, 1975; Damasio et al., 1980; Henderson, 1982; Samelsohn, 1881; Zihl & Mayer, 1981). Form vision and light sensitivity are, as a rule, not altered in the field region where color vision has been lost. The existence of a "hemianopia for colors" has been denied in principle by some authors, e.g., by Critchley who wrote in 1965 (p. 718): "No case has been described where a patient with intact visual fields has shown a color deficit of hemianopic distribution." However, the cases that have been reported of hemianopia for colors may be taken as evidence for the existence of this kind of homonymous visual field disorder. Cases with some sparing of the color visual field may notice their disorder, complaining that the world appears somehow changed on one side. When asked for more detail they may state that all objects appear greyish on this side and, therefore, somewhat strange and unfamiliar (Samelsohn, 1881). If one examined their visual field using routine perimetry one would map a quite normal visual field. The use of colored targets which the patient has to identify is therefore the method of choice in these cases (see Frisen, 1973; Zihl & Mayer, 1981).

Cases with *hemiamblyopia* (the term being introduced by Poppelreuter, 1917) show homonymous impairment of all visual functions in one hemifield (see Figure 4A). Light sensitivity may be only slightly depressed in some, but very severely depressed in other cases. Whether patients will detect targets or, especially when tested under conditions of double simultaneous stimulation, neglect targets appearing on their defective side, depends on the size and luminance of the target (i.e., on the degree of threshold increase). Moving targets can usually be detected better than stationary ones. In some cases mapping the hemifield with stationary targets results in a hemianopic field loss while the use of moving or flickering targets may reveal a near normal field extent (Poppelreuter, 1917; Riddoch, 1917; Teuber et al., 1960). Since patients cannot identify the direction of stimulus movement (Gloning et al., 1962; Poppelreuter, 1917) their residual vision should not be taken as evidence for some sort of selective sparing of movement vision as proposed by Riddoch (1917).

Various kinds of brain damage may lead to cerebral amblyopia. In a group of 161 cases who underwent a special screening for this field disorder in our Department within the last 2 years 33 patients (20%) showed cerebral amblyopia. In 6 cases (18%) both hemifields were affected, whereas in all other cases amblyopia was limited to one hemifield. If both hemifields are affected, patients may show visual disabilities that are similar to those seen with bilateral field loss ("tunnel vision") since form and color vision may be present only in the central

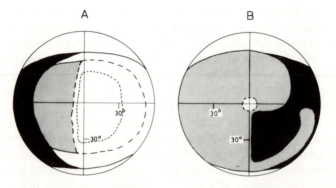

FIGURE 4 Unilateral (A; left-sided) and bilateral (B) cerebral hemiamblyopia (indicated by dotted area) in 2 patients, one suffering from closed head trauma (A; 28-years-old; time since damage: 26 months) and one from bilateral posterior cerebral artery infarction (B; 26-years-old; time since damage: 5 months). Field extent for color (— —) and form vision (- -) in A is restricted to 8 and 5 deg eccentricity respectively, in the left hemifield while in B only the inner visual field, up to about 5 degrees eccentricity on either side, shows preservation of form and color vision. Black area indicates visual field loss.

field region (cf. Figure 4B). Patients suffering from bilateral hemiamblyopia complain in particular of severe difficulties with reading, with identification of objects and with visual-spatial orientation because they can perceive only a small section of either the stimulus array or of their surroundings at any one time.

Regarding etiology of brain damage, 48% of the cases suffered from cerebrovascular, 39% from traumatic damage, and the rest (13%) from cerebral hypoxia. The sparing of color and form vision was less than 3 degrees in about 40% of the cases; they all complained of severe reading difficulties of the same sort as patients with left- or right-sided hemianopia. In the cases suffering severe hemiamblyopia the degree of disability should be considered equivalent to that of patients suffering from hemianopia, because these cases show a reading disorder which is similar to that reported in hemianopics (see p. 38). When they are examined properly, a relatively high number of cases with cerebral amblyopia may be found, and this indicates that color and form perimetry should be part of a routine clinical examination, at least for cases showing normal field extent for white light but nevertheless complaining of problems with reading or of avoiding obstacles on one side. For testing color and form vision the Tübinger perimeter is very useful since it allows, in addition, a precise determination of light difference threshold (Aulhorn & Harms, 1972; Johnson, Keltner, & Balestrery, 1979; Zihl & Mayer, 1981).

IMPAIRMENTS IN VISUAL ACUITY

Visual acuity does not seem to be impaired after unilateral brain damage except in cases with involvement of the optic tract. In these cases acuity may be reduced either in the eye ipsilateral to brain damage or even in both eyes (Savino, Paris, Schatz, & Corbett, 1978; but see Frisen, 1980). However, since the acuity of the patient prior to brain damage is frequently unknown, the effect of the damage on visual acuity is difficult to assess accurately. As a consequence, a relative acuity of for example 90% or even lower, evaluated as being within the normal range, may in fact be impaired because the acuity of the patient prior to brain damage was 100% or even higher. As Frisen (1980) stated, the lower limit for "normal" acuity should never be set below 100% or 20/20, and even these values are below the effective acuity in many subjects. Therefore, even unilateral brain damage could lead to an undetected change in visual acuity.

Another difficulty in evaluating acuity data after brain damage—and this also holds true in cases with bilateral brain damage (see below)—is that acuity is usually tested only for far vision (generally for a distance of 6 m). Since a high proportion of visual performance takes place, however, at near distances, i.e., between 30 and 50 cm, visual acuity should always be additionally tested for near vision.

Patients with bilateral brain damage may exhibit a marked reduction in visual acuity (Gloning et al., 1962; Pöppel, Brinkmann, von Cramon, & Singer,

1978), but in some cases normal acuity has been reported (Förster, 1890). Frisen (1980) suggested that acuity remains unaffected as long as foveal fibers are not involved in postchiasmatic damage. Bilateral postchiasmatic damage may affect not only acuity but also other foveal visual functions which probably represent essential prerequisites for acuity such as light sensitivity, contrast sensitivity, and light and dark adaptation. Other than existing as a primary impairment visual acuity can therefore also be reduced as a result of such secondary factors.

Visual Field Disorders.   Impairments in acuity per se are probably not the direct result of unilateral or bilateral visual field disorders. However, such disorders may well influence the testing of acuity. In particular, cases with rather small field sparing may show difficulties with finding single test targets and with perception of words or numbers as a whole when such material is used for acuity testing (see p. 38). As a consequence patients may not be able to identify these complex test items and will show an apparent reduction of visual acuity.

Another factor which may influence visual acuity more severely is "visual blurring," a visual disturbance which, of course, does not represent a unitary visual symptom. Patients complaining of visual blurring usually report that they are no longer able to read because letters appear to be indistinct. Letters, words and lines merge into one another and sometimes patients report that the whole page they are trying to read appears obscured by shadows. Patients become, as a rule, aware of visual blurring while reading but do not always report this phenomenon for far vision. Searching for an explanation for this symptom Bodis-Wollner and his coworkers (1972; Bodis-Wollner & Diamond, 1976) tested the spatial contrast sensitivity of brain-damaged patients who complained of "blurred" or "foggy" vision. They found a significant elevation of contrast thresholds. Visual acuity was normal or nearly normal for far vision; unfortunately, no acuity data are reported for near vision. This pathological reduction in spatial contrast sensitivity may represent one factor underlying blurred vision after brain damage.

Another factor may be an *instability* of visual function as suggested by Bender and Teuber (1946). These authors reported that brain-damaged patients experience fluctuation and even extinction of visual stimuli after prolonged inspection. These observations are in agreement with the complaints of some of our patients who claim that at the beginning of reading, vision is normal and clear but that it degrades shortly after. They can then no longer continue to read because letters become greyish and the whole page appears to be covered with a "dense fog." In contrast to the complaints of patients reported by Bodis-Wollner et al. (1972, 1976), "clear" vision is available at least for a short period of time before blurring takes place. Surprisingly, most of these patients show intact accommodation and convergence and normal acuity for both near and far vision. This is probably because the presentation of the single test item is sufficiently brief to prevent the occurrence of blurring during routine acuity testing. Again this symptom is mainly reported when reading and rarely for far vision. Closing the eyes leads to at least a brief period of recovery, unfortunately, however, without preventing further blurring. It could be hypothesized that visual capacity is highly reduced in these cases so that visual fatigue takes place rapidly. If this is true then one should find an electrophysiological correlate in recordings of pattern-generated visual evoked potentials (VEPs). Using a special sampling technique which allows averaging every 16 sec (reversal rate of the pattern: 2 Hz) we recorded the VEPs over a period of 4 minutes. Figure 5 shows a typical result in a case with normal visual acuity but who complained of visual blurring after about 1 minute when reading. There is marked fluctuation of the amplitude of the first positive wave (P1) while the latency of the same wave remains essentially unchanged. In contrast, no obvious fluctuation was present in the VEP of another brain-damaged case who did not complain of such visual blurring (Figure 6). Difficulties with binocular fusion can be excluded as being responsible for this type of visual blurring since VEPs were recorded under monocular conditions. It remains unclear whether impaired spatial contrast sensitivity can also account for this type of visual blurring or whether some kind of visual fatigue, as hypothesized by Bender and Teuber (1946), may cause this instability of vision over time. It is interesting to note that larger print or larger spatial separation of letters or numbers can reduce this visual disorder in that the latency of onset of blurring is greatly increased. This may support the hypothesis that an impairment in spatial contrast sensitivity may in fact represent one of the most prominent factors causing blurring of vision. Since routine acuity testing may not give sufficient information about spatial resolution, contrast sensitivity testing should therefore be included in visual screening of brain-damaged patients. Unfortunately no standardized test is yet available for such a screening. The "Cambridge Low Contrast-Gratings Test" (see Della Sala, Bertoni, Somazzi et al., 1985) may be useful in routine clinical examination because it allows a simple and rapid screening for contrast sensitivity. Unfortuntely, however, even this test has been constructed for far vision (at a distance of 6m) but not for near distances which would allow for measurement of contrast sensitivity at a typical reading distance. Finally, temporal instability of vision should be taken into account; tests including prolonged stimulus exposure may be of help in the search for an objective correlate of this type of blurred vision.

A third factor which also may cause or may at least be associated with blurred vision after brain damage is impairment of *light- and dark adaptation* (Gloning et al., 1962; Koerner & Teuber, 1973; Teuber et al., 1960; Ullrich, 1943; see Figure 7). Following disturbances of dark adaptation patients usually complain that their surroundings appear dark and that they need more light in order to see objects and persons "clearly," and print appears greyish so that they can no longer read. In contrast, cases with loss of light adaptation complain of a strong sensation of blinding even under low illumination. They find it very unpleasant to look, for example, at a sheet of white paper because the reflectance

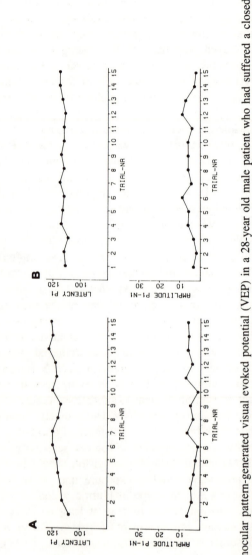

FIGURE 5 Monocular pattern-generated visual evoked potential (VEP) in a 28-year old male patient who had suffered a closed-head trauma 7 months before VEP-recording and complained of "blurred" vision. Total duration of recording was 4 min; each trial shows mean averaging of 32 single recordings (recording time: 16 sec). Note the large variability of amplitudes (in MV) of P1 for both left (A) and right eyes (B). Variability coefficients are 0.74 for the left and 0.90 for the right eye.

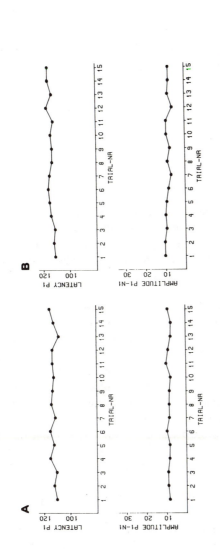
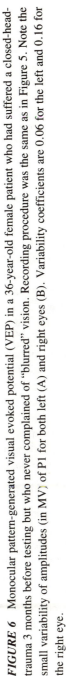

FIGURE 6 Monocular pattern-generated visual evoked potential (VEP) in a 36-year-old female patient who had suffered a closed-head-trauma 3 months before testing but who never complained of "blurred" vision. Recording procedure was the same as in Figure 5. Note the small variability of amplitudes (in MV) of P1 for both left (A) and right eyes (B). Variability coefficients are 0.06 for the left and 0.16 for the right eye.

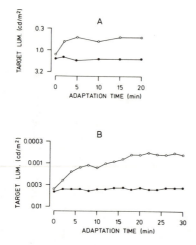

FIGURE 7 Foveal light (A) and dark adaptation (B) determined with the Tübingen perimeter in a 49-year-old patient suffering from right-sided posterior cerebral artery infarction (time since damage: 6 months) and complaining of blinding and "dark" vision (closed circles). Open circles show results from a normal subject for comparison. Note patient's loss of light- and dark adaptation.

of the paper causes immediate blinding and written words blur or may even fade. Since most of the cases show impairment of *both* light and dark adaptation the resulting disability is particularly severe. On the one hand, more illumination is required, on the other hand, however, any small increase in illumination immediately causes blinding (see Table 2). The consequences, especially for reading, are self-evident: patients either have problems in identifying letters and words, in particular when presented with small print. Letters do not contrast sufficiently with their background and appear greyish and indistinct. In addition, patients cannot read large print because the whole page looks as if it is "immersed in a glistening light." Obviously these phenomena occur for all types of visual stimuli in near vision but again patients are usually aware of them when reading.

It is not yet clear how frequently visual blurring may occur after brain damage. Blurred vision has been observed both in cases suffering from bilateral and unilateral damage. Gloning, Gloning, and Hoff (1968) reported about 30% of cases complaining of blurring of vision in a total of 241 cases with posterior damage. In a group of 215 cases with postgeniculate damage we found about 25% of patients complained of visual blurring. Even though blurred vision does not seem to be exclusively associated with a particular aetiology of brain damage (Gloning et al., 1968) we found this symptom in only about 10% of cases with cerebrovascular damage but, in contrast, in about half of the cases with traumatic

TABLE 2
Rating of Illumination (Median and Range, in Lux) by Normal Subjects (N) by Brain-
Damaged Patients with Disturbance of Light (L), Dark (D) or Light and Dark (LD)
Adaptation.

	"too dark"	"comfortable"	"too bright"
N (n=14)	190 (150–220)	590 (470–800)	780 (600–1000)
L (n=7)	170 (80–250)	380 (130–480)	390 (90–700)
D (n=3)	420 (400–500)	800 (700–1200)	1100 (1000–1300)
LD (n=27)	258 (4–260)	305 (30–680)	540 (700–900)

Brain damage was unilateral in 18 cases (13 left-, 8 right-sided) and bilateral in 8 cases. Regarding aetiology, 24 cases had suffered cerebrovascular damage, 7 patients closed-head trauma, and 6 cerebral hypoxia. The time between occurrence of brain damage and testing varied between 2 months and 6 years. Note the abrupt change in rating from "comfortable" to "too bright" in the L-group, and the small range between categories in the LD-group.

brain damage. In most of the cases in our group who complained of visual blurring (n = 56) it was found in association with either pathological fluctuation of the P1-amplitude in the VEP (65%) or impairment of light and dark adaptation (80%). Further detailed investigations are required to identify the different factors which cause this visual impairment. In conclusion, further investigations should distinguish between impairments of visual acuity per se and apparent disturbances in visual acuity which can be accounted for by impairments of sensitivity to contrast and of light and dark adaptation.

Color Vision Disorders Acquired After Brain Damage

This section deals with color vision disorders of central origin. Color impairments restricted to one hemifield have been briefly discussed above (see p. 41). It seems that achromatopsia extending throughout the visual field occurs rarely and predominantly after bilateral brain damage. Meadows (1974) reviewed 14 cases of cerebral achromatopsia and since then additional cases have been reported (Green & Lessel, 1977; Heywood, Wilson, & Cowey, 1987; Pearlman, Birch, & Meadows, 1979; Pöppel et al., 1978; Young & Fishman, 1980; Young, Fishman, & Chen, 1980). Patients with cerebral achromatopsia do not see their surroundings in color. They report that the world looks drained of color and even bright, saturated colors look pale. In contrast, such patients may be able to differentiate different shades of grey correctly (Heywood et al., 1987). Even though most of the cases with achromatopsia often show additional impairments of other visual functions, including light sensitivity and visual acuity, these deficits can hardly account for the color vision disorder (see Zihl & von Cramon, 1986).

As pointed out earlier, unilateral brain damage may result in achromatopsia in one hemifield but foveal color vision appears intact. In a task requiring the sorting of colored wools, Poppelreuter (1917) reported that unilateral brain damage can result in a mild impairment in hue discrimination. More recently the Farnsworth-Munsell 100-hue test (FM 100-hue test; Farnsworth, 1943) is most commonly used because it is sufficiently sensitive to detect small impairments even in the least severe cases (Meadows, 1974). Using this test Verriest, Van Laethem, & Uvijls (1982) published extensive data obtained from 232 normal subjects between 10- and 80-years-of-age. They found that subjects performed better under binocular than under monocular conditions and, in addition, that the error score depended on age. On the basis of these normative data Han and Thompson (1983) developed "nomograms" that permit a quick and easy determination of whether the test score of a given subject is normal compared with the age-matched normative group. Using the FM 100-hue test several authors have found an impairment in hue discrimination in cases with unilateral posterior damage (Lhermitte, Chain, & Aron, 1969; Scotti & Spinnler, 1970; Zihl & Mayer, 1981). While Lhermitte et al. (1969) and Zihl and Mayer (1981) did not find any significant difference in error scores between cases with left- and right-sided brain damage Scotti and Spinnler (1970) reported significantly higher error scores in those cases with right-sided brain damage. These authors interpreted this difference in terms of a right hemisphere advantage for color vision. Whether the apparent preponderance of color vision disorders in cases with right posterior brain damage really represents a functional difference between the two hemispheres remains an open question (see Damasio, 1985). One factor which may influence color vision testing—at least when the FM 100-hue test is used—is the occurrence of visual field disorders reaching the foveal region. Visual field disorders are of particular interest in this context because nearly all patients who were reported to be impaired in this color sorting test also suffered from homonymous visual field disorders. According to the original test constructed by Farnsworth (1943) colored chips have to be ordered from left to right. It could well be that left-sided field disorders may influence performance because only a few chips can be simultaneously compared and therefore only one or two chips may be used when ordering colors according to their hue. If this assumption is correct then reversing the direction of testing should lead to a better result in this group. Patients with right-sided field disorders should, on the other hand, perform worse if they are requested to arrange the colored chips from right to left. The comparison of the test scores between the two directions of testing would thus allow an evaluation of the influence of visual field disorders on the performance in hue discrimination as tested by the FM 100-hue test. Figure 8 shows the outcome of hue discrimination testing using the FM 100-hue test in a case with a complete left-sided homonymous hemianopia performing the

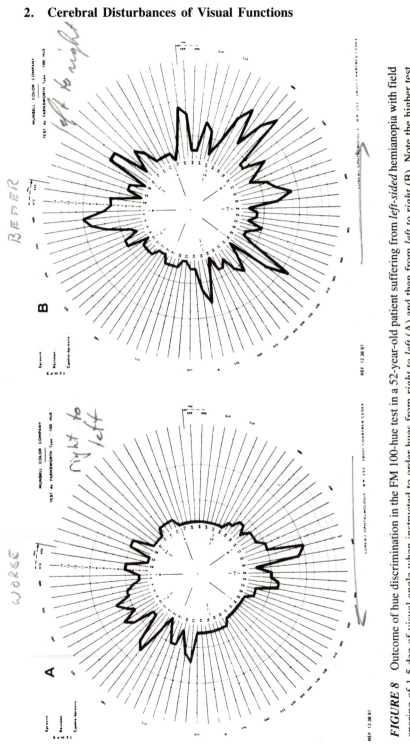

FIGURE 8 Outcome of hue discrimination in the FM 100-hue test in a 52-year-old patient suffering from *left-sided* hemianopia with field sparing of 1.5 deg of visual angle when instructed to order hues from *right to left* (A) and then from *left to right* (B). Note the higher test scores in condition B (410) as compared with condition A (309).

test (A) in the usual direction from left to right, and (B) in the reverse direction. As the profiles show, the patient performed much worse in the first condition while test scores were within normal limits in the second. Since the test was first administered in the reverse direction, the increase in error scores in the usual direction cannot be attributed to insufficient familiarity with the test or to problems with understanding the instruction. A similar picture emerged from a patient with a right-sided hemianopia who performed the FM 100-hue test first in the usual and afterwards in the reverse direction (see Figure 9). In cases with complete left-sided hemiamblyopia the test results may be quite similar to those obtained from cases with left-sided hemianopia. Finally, Figure 10 shows a case with a left-sided hemianopia whose error scores were equally high in each direction of testing. This suggests that performance was poor even if the influence of the hemianopia is taken into account.

These observations indicate that visual field disorders can significantly influence the outcome in the FM 100-hue test, in that cases with left-sided field disorders may show higher error scores than cases with right-sided disorders simply because of the direction of testing advocated by Farnsworth (1943) in the original test construction. One should therefore be cautious in interpreting impairments in such tests in terms of hemispheric differences or poor hue discrimination.

COMMENT

This chapter presents the most frequently occurring disorders of elementary visual functions in patients with brain damage and to show how disturbances of these "lower" visual abilities may affect more complex visual capacities. The emphasis has been placed on disturbances of the visual field, visual acuity, and color vision. From the detailed description of the impairments it becomes clear that a detailed investigation of these elementary visual functions is needed not only to evaluate the visual disabilities of patients but also to assess the influence of these disorders on "higher" visual abilities.

ACKNOWLEDGMENTS

I wish to acknowledge the help I received from the following people. Dr. Charles Heywood and Madeline Eacott from the Department of Experimental Psychology, Oxford, commented on and assisted in the final preparation of the manuscript. Christel Schmid recorded the VEPs, Georg Kerkhoff assisted in the testing of light and dark adaptation, and Gisela Gajewski prepared the figures.

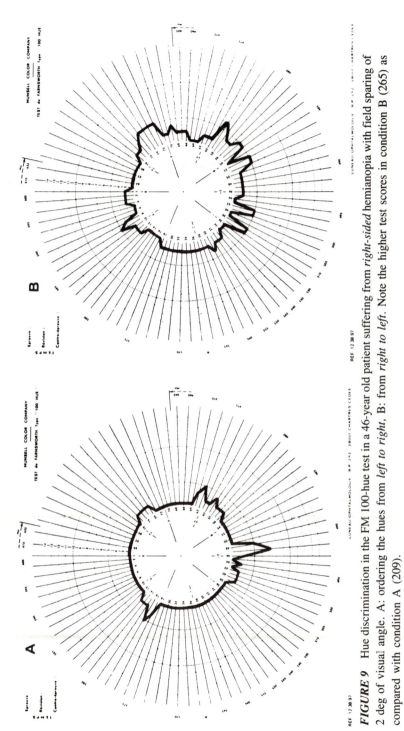

FIGURE 9 Hue discrimination in the FM 100-hue test in a 46-year old patient suffering from *right-sided* hemianopia with field sparing of 2 deg of visual angle. A: ordering the hues from *left to right*, B: from *right to left*. Note the higher test scores in condition B (265) as compared with condition A (209).

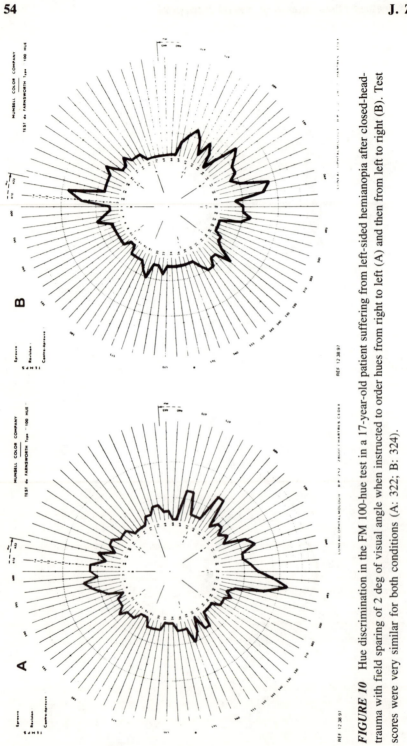

FIGURE 10 Hue discrimination in the FM 100-hue test in a 17-year-old patient suffering from left-sided hemianopia after closed-head-trauma with field sparing of 2 deg of visual angle when instructed to order hues from right to left (A) and then from left to right (B). Test scores were very similar for both conditions (A: 322; B: 324).

REFERENCES

Albert, M. L., Reches, A., & Silverberg, R. (1975). Hemianopic color blindness. *Journal of Neurology, Neurosurgery, and Psychiatry, 38,* 546–549.

Anton, D. G. (1898). Über Herderkrankungen des Gehirns, welche vom Patienten nicht wahrgenommen werden. *Wiener klinische Wochenschrift, 11,* 227–229.

Aulhorn, E., & Harms, H. (1972). Visual perimetry. In D. Jameson & L. Hurvich (Eds.), *Handbook of sensory physiology* (Vol. 7, pp. 102–145). Berlin and New York: Springer.

Bender, M. B., & Teuber, H.-L. (1946). Phenomena of fluctuation, extinction and completion in visual perception. *Archives of Neurology and Psychiatry, 55,* 627–658.

Benton, S., Levy, I., & Swash, M. (1980). Vision in the temporal crescent in occipital infarction. *Brain, 103,* 83–97.

Birch, H. G., Belmont, I., & Karp, E. (1967). Delayed processing and extinction following cerebral damage. *Brain, 90,* 113–130.

Bodis Wollner, I. (1972). Visual acuity and contrast sensitivity in patients with cerebral lesions. *Science, 178,* 769–771.

Bodis-Wollner, I., & Diamond, S. P. (1976). The measurement of spatial contrast sensitivity in cases of blurred vision associated with cerebral lesions. *Brain, 99,* 695–710.

Bodis-Wollner, I, Atkin, A., Raab, E., & Wolkstein, M. (1977). Visual association cortex and vision in man: Pattern-evoked occipital potentials in a blind boy. *Science, 198,* 629–631.

Brown, J. (1983). The microstructure of perception: Physiology and patterns of breakdown. *Cognition and Brain Theory, 6,* 145–184.

Bunt, A. H., Minckler, D. S., & Johanson, G. W. (1977). Demonstration of bilateral projection of the central retina of the monkey with horseradish peroxidase neuronography. *Journal of Comparative Neurology, 171,* 619–630.

Celesia, G. G., Polcyn, R. E., Holden, J. E. et al. (1982). Visual evoked potentials and positron tomographic mapping of regional cerebral blood flow and cerebral metabolism: Can the neuronal potential generators be visualized? Electroencephalography and clinical *Neurophysiology, 54,* 243–256.

Chedru, F., Leblanc, M., & Lhermitte, F. (1973). Visual searching in normal and brain-damaged subjects (Contributions to the study of unilateral inattention). *Cortex, 9,* 94–111.

Critchley, M. (1949). The problem of awareness or non-awareness of hemianopic field defects. *Transactions of the Ophthalmological Society UK, 69,* 95–109.

Critchley, M. (1965). Acquired anomalies of color perception of central origin. *Brain, 88,* 711–724.

Damasio, A. R. (1985). Disorders of complex visual processing: Agnosias, achromatopsia, Balint's syndrome, and related difficulties of orientation and construction. In M.-M. Mesulam (Ed.), Principles of behavioral neurology (pp. 259–288). Philadelphia, PA: F.A. Davis Company.

Damasio, A. R., McKee, J., & Damasio, H. (1980). Central achromatopsia: Behavioral, anatomic, physiological aspects. *Neurology, 30,* 1064–1071.

Della Sala, S., Bertoni, G., Somazzi, L. et al. (1985). Impaired contrast sensitivity in diabetic patients with and without retinopathy: A new technique for rapid assessment. *British Journal of Ophthalmology, 69,* 136–142.

Ellenberger, C. (1974). Modern perimetry in neuro-ophthalmic disease. *Archives of Neurology, 30,* 193–201.

Farnsworth, D. (1943). The Farnsworth-Munsell 100-hue and dichotomous tests for color vision. *Journal of the Optical Society of America, 33,* 568–578.

Förster, R. (1890). Über Rindenblindheit. *Von Graefes Archiv für Ophthalmologie, 36,* 94–108.

Frisen, L. (1973). A versatile color confrontation test for the central visual field. *Archives of Ophthalmology, 89,* 3–9.

Frisen, L. (1980). The neurology of visual acuity. *Brain, 103,* 639–670

Gassel, M. M., & Williams, D. (1963). Visual function in patients with homonymous hemianopia. Part II. Oculomotor mechanisms. *Brain, 86,* 1–63.

Gloning, I., Gloning, K., & Tschabitscher, H. (1962). Die occipitale Blindheit auf vaskulärer Basis. *Von Graefes Archiv für Ophthalmologie, 165,* 138–177.

Gloning, I., Gloning, K., & Hoff, H. (1968). *Neuropsychological symptoms and syndromes in lesions of the occipital lobe and the adjacent areas.* Paris: Gauthier-Villars.

Green, G. J., & Lessell, S. (1977). Acquired cerebral dyschromatopsia. *Archives of Ophthalmology, 95,* 121–128.

Han, D. P., & Thompson, H. S. (1983). Nomograms for the assessment of Farnsworth-Munsell 100-hue test scores. *American Journal of Ophthalmology, 95,* 622–625.

Henderson, V. W. (1982). Impaired hue discrimination in homonymous visual fields. *Archives of Neurology, 39,* 418–419.

Heywood, C. A., Wilson, B., & Cowey, A. (1987). A case study of cortical color "blindness" with relatively intact achromatic discrimination. *Journal of Neurology, Neurosurgery, and Psychiatry, 50,* 22–29.

Holmes, G. (1918). Disturbances of vision by cerebral lesions. *British Journal of Ophthalmology, 2,* 353–384.

Hoyt, W. F., & Walsh, F. B. (1958). Cortical blindness with partial recovery following cerebral anoxia from cardiac arrest. *Archives of Ophthalmology, 60,* 1061–1069.

Huber, A. (1962). Homonymous hemianopia after occipital lobectomy. *American Journal of Ophthalmology, 54,* 623–629.

Johnson, C. A., Keltner, J. L., & Balestrery, F. (1979). Acuity profile perimetry. *Archives of Ophthalmology, 97,* 684–689.

Koerner, F., & Teuber, H.-L. (1973). Visual field defects after missile injuries to the geniculo-striate pathway in man. *Experimental Brain Research, 18,* 88–113.

Kooi, K. A., & Sharbrough, III, F. W. (1966). Electrophysiological findings in cortical blindness. Report of a case. *Electroencephalography and clinical Neurophysiology, 20,* 260–263.

Lenz, G. (1905). Beiträge zur Hemianopsie. *Klinische Monatsblätter für Augenheilkunde, 43,* 263–326.

Lenz, G. (1909). *Zur Pathologie der zerebralen Sehbahn unter besonderer Berücksichtigung ihrer Ergebnisse für die Anatomie und Physiologie.* Leipzig: Verlag von W. Engelmann.

Lhermitte, F., Chain, F., Aron, D. et al. (1969). Les troubles de la vision des lesions posterieures du cerveau. *Revue Neurologique, 121,* 5–29.

Lissauer, H. (1890). Ein Fall von Seelenblindheit nebst einem Beitrag zur Theorie desselben. *Archiv für Psychiatrie und Nervenkrankheiten, 21,* 222–270.

Meadows, J. C. (1974). Disturbed perception of colors associated with localized cerebral lesions. *Brain, 97,* 615–632.

Meienberg, O. (1981). Sparing of the temporal crescent in homonymous hemianopia and its significance for visual orientation. *Neuro-ophthalmology, 2,* 129–134.

Meienberg, O., Zangemeister, W. H., Rosenberg, M. et al. (1981). Saccadic eye movement strategies in patients with homonymous hemianopia. *Annals of Neurology, 9,* 537–544.

Pearlman, A. L., Birch, J., & Meadows, J. C. (1979). Cerebral color blindness: An acquired defect in hue discrimination. *Annals of Neurology, 5,* 2153–261.

Pfeifer, R. A. (1919). Die Störungen des optischen Suchaktes bei Hirnverletzten. *Deutsche Zeitschrift für Nervenheilkunde, 64,* 140–152.

Polyak, S. (1957). *The vertebrate visual system.* Chicago: University of Chicago Press.

Poppelreuter, W. (1917). Die psychischen Schädigungen durch Kopfschuss in Kriege 1914/1916. Bd. I. Die Störungen der niederen und höheren Sehleistungen durch Verletzungen des Okzipitalhirns. Leipzig: L. Voss.

Pöppel, E., Brinkmann, R., von Cramon, D., & Singer, W. (1978). Association and dissociation of visual functions in a case of bilateral occipital lobe infarction. *Archiv für Psychiatrie und Nervenkrankheiten, 225,* 1–21.

Putnam, T. J., & Liebman, S. (1942). Cortical representation of the macula lutea. *Archives of Ophthalmology, 28,* 415–443.

Riddoch, G. (1917). Dissociations of visual perceptions due to occipital injuries, with especial reference to appreciation of movement. *Brain, 40,* 15–57.

Samelsohn, J. (1881). Zur Frage des Farbensinnzentrums. *Centralblatt für die medizinischen Wissenschaften, 19,* 850–853.

Savino, P. J., Paris, M., Schatz, N. J., & Corbett, J. J. (1978). Optic tract syndrome. *Archives of Ophthalmology, 96,* 656–663.

Scotti, G., & Spinnler, H. (1970). Color imperception in unilateral hemisphere-damaged patients. *Journal of Neurology, Neurosurgery, and Psychiatry, 33,* 22–28.

Sharpe, J. A., Lo, A. W., & Rabinovitch, H. E. (1979). Control of saccadic and smooth pursuit systems after cerebral hemidecortication. *Brain, 102,* 387–403.

Siemerling, E. (1890). Ein Fall von sogenannter Seelenblindheit nebst anderweitigen cerebralen Symptomen. *Archiv für Psychiatrie und Nervenkrankheiten, 49,* 63–88.

Teuber, H.-L., Battersby, W., & Bender, M. B. (1960). Visual field defects after penetrating missile wounds of the brain. Cambridge, MA: MIT Press.

58   J. Zihl

Trobe, J. D., Lorber, M. L., & Schlezinger, N. S. (1973). Isolated homonymous hemianopia. *Archives of Ophthalmology, 89*, 377–381.

Ullrich, N. (1943). Adaptationsstörungen bei Sehhirnverletzten. *Deutsche Zeitschrift für Nervenheilkunde, 155*, 1–31.

Verriest, G., Van Laethem, J., & Uvijls, A. (1982). A new assessment of the normal ranges of the Farnsworth-Munsell 100-hue test scores. *American Journal of Ophthalmology, 93*, 635–642.

Wilbrand, H. (1890). *Die hemianopischen Gesichtsfeldformen und das optischen Wahrnehmungszentrum*. Wiesbaden: J.F. Bergmann.

Wilbrand, H. (1907). Über die makulär-hemianopische Lesestörung und die von Monakow'sche Projektion der Makula auf die Sehsphäre. *Klinische Monatsblätter für Augenheilkunde, 45*, 1–39.

Williams, D., Gassel, M. M. (1962). Visual function in patients with homonymous hemianopia. Part I. Visual field defects. *Brain, 85*, 175–250.

Young, R. S. L., & Fishman, G. A. (1980). Loss of color vision and Stiles π-1 mechanism in a patient with cerebral infarction. *Journal of the Optical Society of America, 70*, 1301–1305.

Young, R. S. L., Fishman, G. A., & Chen, F. (1980). Traumatically acquired color vision defect. *Investigative Ophthalmology & Visual science, 19*, 545–549.

Zihl, J., & Mayer, J. (1981). Farbperimetrie: Methode und diagnostische Bedeutung. *Nervenarzt, 52*, 547–580.

Zihl, J., & Werth, R. (1984). Contributions to the study of "blindsight"-II. The role of specific practice for saccadic localization in patients with postgeniculate visual field defects. *Neuropsychologia, 22*, 13–22.

Zihl, J., & Wohlfarth-Englert, A. (1986). The influence of visual field disorders on visual identification tasks. *European Archives of Psychiatry and Neurological Sciences, 236*, 61–64.

Zihl, J., Krischer, C., & Meissen, R. (1984). Die hemianopische Lesestörung und ihre Behandlung. *Nervenarzt, 55*, 317–323.

Zihl, J., & von Cramon, D. (1986). *Zerebrale Sehstörungen*. Kohlhammer, Stuttgart.

3

Disorders of Visual Gnosis

D. Frank Benson, M. D.

In the past several decades a remarkable growth has occurred in two neurologic subspecialties that deal with vision—neuroophthalmology, and behavioral neurology. Both have advanced sufficiently in scope and depth to attain ranking as major subspecialties within neurology. Neuroophthalmologists have focused on "hardwiring" problems, variations in visual field disturbance, and disturbances of extraocular movement. Behavioral neurology originally focused on language and memory disturbances and, in recent years, the overall mental impairment called dementia. The interface, disturbances of visual recognition, have received relatively limited attention.

An ongoing controversy surrounds whether or not the disorders of visual gnosis reflect a problem in sensation, perception, recognition, or associative functions. Satisfactory distinctions are difficult to obtain but these elements need separation. The following definitions are presented as guides for discussion of the visual gnosis disorders:

1. *Sensation* indicates the conduction activity of the primary visual nervous system, the retina, optic nerves, chiasm and tracts, and lateral geniculate nucleus, and the geniculo-calcarine pathways to the primary visual cortex (Brodmann area 17). Disturbance in this circuit produces an abnormality of primary visual sensory function, best demonstrated as blindness in all or part of the visual fields.

2. *Perception* is difficult to define and has been used broadly (Hamburger, 1970). For discussion of disordered visual gnosis a narrow definition is needed. Efron (1968) presented a concise definition of perception as the "awareness of discriminated existents." For present purposes we shall consider perception to be the act of discriminating variables within the primary sensory input.

3. *Association* represents an additional step, one in which the variables discriminated by the perceptive process are compared to prior perceptions.

4. *Recognition* has been given broad and diverse meanings. Almost all disorders of visual knowledge, from sensory problems to associative disorders, can be called recognition problems. Obviously, such broad use restricts the

59

meaningfulness of the term. For present purposes recognition indicates the association of a freshly perceived stimulus with previously noted stimuli for the purpose of identification. At least some degree of memory retrieval is inherent in the recognition process.

5. *Agnosia* as a term, has passed through a variety of meanings. Once used to identify almost any disorder of recognition (Nielsen, 1936), there followed a period in which there was doubt that any "true" agnosia existed (Bay, 1953; Critchley, 1964). Classically two types of agnosia have been postulated, one dealing with disordered perception (apperceptive agnosia) and the other with disordered association (associative agnosia). Both remain controversial as distinct entities but both are now accepted as real entities by some investigators.

A number of additional terms have been used to identify various problems in visual gnosis. They are often used indiscriminately, the same term used to identify slightly or completely different problems. Many names have been given to a single problem. As far as possible, most terms are defined in context in this article.

Many other problems hinder the investigation of visual gnosis disorders. For instance, a variety of totally different pathologies can produce a single visual gnostic disorder coupled with widely divergent neighborhood signs (as an illustration, Table 1 presents a partial list of disorders known to produce cortical blindness). Although the anatomical location of pathology underlying a visual gnostic disorder may vary considerably, even minor anatomical variations tend to produce different overall clinical pictures. The educational/vocational background of the subject may be of consequence; a visual-spatial discrimination disturbance will be far more disabling to an individual with artistic or engineering background that one without developed visual-spatial skills. Finally, the disease processes underlying disorders of visual gnosis almost always produce additional, often dramatic, nonvisual symptoms that often overshadow the visual problems. Disorders of visual gnosis are often ignored in the evaluation of other serious behavioral disorders.

Despite the problems noted above, most studies of visual gnosis are based on human brain injury case material. Advantages for the use of human disease processes overcome the disadvantages. First, many of these abnormalities cannot be studied in any other manner. No animal has a system of higher associations like the human so that study of visual gnostic functions is often dependent on disease process investigation. If a sufficient number of cases are recorded, salient features stand out; responsible clinical/anatomical correlations can be made and pertinent cerebral connections implied. While difficult, visual gnosis can be investigated by current clinical/structural/functional correlation processes and offers a rich opportunity for understanding an important human mental mechanism.

To ease the problem of utilizing disease process material a classification has been suggested (Table 2). As with all classifications, this one must be considered

TABLE 1
Partial List of Causes of Cortical Blindness

Developmental	Congenital malformation
	Congenital hydrocephalus
Neoplastic	Tumor—both intra-and extracerebral
Trauma	Contusion and abrasion
	Gunshot wound
Toxic/metabolic	Methanol poisoning
	Lead or mercury intoxication
	Many others
Vascular	Cerebrovascular ischemia
	A-V malformation
	Status/post angiography (hypoperfusion)
Disease process	Migraine
	Epilepsy (post-ictal)
	Schilder's disease
	Jakob-Creutzfeldt disease
	Subacute sclerosing panencephalitis
Functional	Edema
	Anoxia

artificial, awkward, and potentially misleading. There is a considerable overlap; separation into sensation/perception and recognition/association is rarely exact. Most disorders that affect one aspect affect others also. Nonetheless, the two categories are sufficiently different that separation is often possible for the clinician. This classification omits two major visual sensory abnormalities—blindness and visual field defects. These problems are well handled in both neurologic and neuroophthalmology texts and need not be repeated here; we will concentrate on the more obscure disorders of visual gnosis.

VISUAL COLOR DISTURBANCES

Three distinct varieties of color vision disturbances are recognized (Meadows, 1974a; Oxbury, Oxbury & Humphrey, 1969)—achromatopsia (Damasio et al., 1980), color agnosia (Benson, 1982), and anomia for colors (Kinsbourne & Warrington, 1964). Clinical differences in the three are significant for understanding the processing of color identification.

TABLE 2
Disorders of Visual Gnosis

	Sensory/Perceptual	Associative/Recognition
COLOR	achromatopsia	color agnosia color naming disorder
LANGUAGE		alexia anomia
MEMORY		visual learning disorder
SPATIAL	amorphosynthesis (unilateral visual neglect) constructional disturbance	hemi-inattention (unilateral neglect) constructional disturbance dressing disturbance
GEOGRAPHICAL		topographagnosia environmental agnosia
OBJECT	apperceptive visual agnosia visual hallucinosis	associative visual agnosia visual hallucinosis visual allesthesia palinopsia
FACE	facial matching	prosopagnosia
MOTOR		Balint's syndrome ocular dysmetria sticky fixation simultanagnosia
GENERAL		Posterior cortical atrophy

Achromatopsia

In recent years considerable interest has been given to a syndrome with loss of color vision but preserved form vision called achromatopsia (Damasio et al., 1980; Meadows, 1974a). Most individuals with this disturbance have a visual field loss, either a hemianopic or quadrantic defect, and pathology involving the visual association cortex of the occipito-temporal portion of the brain is invariably present. The pathology is usually more posterior than anterior in the visual association cortex, often involving tissue at or near the occipital pole. An original suggestion that color disorder most often followed right hemisphere dysfunction has not been substantiated; either right or left hemisphere lesions can produce this disturbance (Damasio, 1985; Meadows, 1974a).

Color Agnosia

This term has been suggested for the two-way defect in which the patient can neither name a color on presentation nor point to a given color when the name is offered but color vision per se is intact as demonstrated by the ability to sort colored chips into groups correctly (color matching) and the problem is not a primary language disturbance as color names are readily associated with objects (e.g., red with fire engine). Most cases showing this two-way defect have an occipital alexia syndrome and a full right homonymous hemianopsia. The underlying lesion usually involves the left visual sensory pathways (producing the right visual field defect) and the splenium of the corpus callosum or tracts from the splenium as they traverse left hemisphere white matter (Geschwind & Fusillo, 1966). While color can be perceived correctly in the right hemisphere, this information cannot be passed to the left hemisphere for linguistic interpretation (naming). It should be noted that not all patients with the occipital alexia syndrome have a disturbance in color identification (Greenblatt, 1976; Stachowiak & Poeck, 1976).

Color Naming

This category is frequently combined with color agnosia, both being called color anomia or color naming defect (Damasio, 1985). There are differences, however, of considerable pertinence. First, the patient with color naming disorder will fail to name colors demonstrated but can point to the correct color when the name is given. The color naming defect is almost always associated with other evidence of aphasia which may range from a mild anomia to a well developed posterior aphasia. These patients will fail questions such as "What color is a fire engine?" but often can chose the correct color chip if a picture is demonstrated. Color matching is good. No specific locus of pathology or correlation with a specific field defect has been outlined for color naming disorder but its association with aphasia usually indicates abnormality affecting the posterior language area.

VISUAL LANGUAGE DISTURBANCES

At present, all disturbances of visually oriented language are considered associative. Nonetheless, any significant sensory loss and/or perceptual distortion will seriously interfere with reading capability. The underlying problems are so obvious that the consequent reading disorder is not honored with a specific term.

Alexia

One of the classic forms of reading impairment, called alexia without agraphia (Dejerine, 1892; Geschwind, 1962) or occipital alexia (Benson, 1985), is a pure visual language disturbance. The patient fails to read, or reads letters only (verbal alexia). Eventually the patient learns to spell words aloud and readily comprehends the spelled word. Only the visual presentation of a spelled word produces failure. Color agnosia (see above) and right visual field defect are frequent but not mandatory accompanying findings (Benson, 1982; Greenblatt, 1976). Patients with this disturbance also have the posterior interhemispheric pathway lesion that prevents the transfer of the visualized written word from the intact right visual cortex to the intact left language cortex. These patients can copy language (in a slow and slavish manner) and can write to dictation with facility, demonstrating that both visual sensation/perception and language are preserved. The most common cause is left posterior cerebral artery territory infarction but the syndrome has also been described with tumors, A-V malformations and intracerebral hemorrhages affecting the dominant hemisphere parietal-occipital areas.

Anomia

The presence of a word-finding problem is often overlooked in individuals with dramatic visual problems. If sought, the problem can be demonstrated both in spontaneous speech and in confrontation naming tasks. Anomia is common in dominant hemisphere posterior cerebral artery infarction (Benson, Marsden, & Meadows, 1974) that has produced a right visual field defect and an occipital alexia. There has long been a question as to whether the anomia is due to the occipital damage (Gloning, Gloning, & Hoff, 1968) or involvement of the inferior portion of the lateral aspect of the dominant temporal lobe (Benson & Tomlinson, 1971); both areas receive their blood supply from the posterior cerebral artery. In addition, it appears possible that the problem in visual identification represents a partial visual agnosia, insufficiently developed to warrant the term.

VISUAL-SPATIAL DISTURBANCES

In many ways, visual-spatial abnormality can be considered the key disturbance of visual gnosis. While common, visual-spatial problems are both multifactorial and complex. Three commonly recognized syndromes are described but many additional subcategorizations have been suggested (See Critchley, 1953 for an exhaustive list). Not infrequently a single visual-spatial disturbance has been described under several different names; on the other hand, truly different visual-spatial disorders are seen.

Unilateral Neglect

The common problem of unilateral inattention is best defined by double simultaneous stimulation tests. In the visual mode, fingers or other stimuli are presented simultaneously to the right and left visual fields. If the patient responds to stimuli in both visual fields when stimulated individually but from one side only with bilateral simultaneous stimulation, the extinction is called unilateral neglect or hemi-inattention. The defect may involve either the right or the left visual field and there is no recognized predilection for one hemisphere to be more affected. Denny-Brown and colleagues (Denny-Brown & Banker, 1952; Denny-Brown, Meyer, & Horenstein, 1954) suggested the term amorphosynthesis to describe a subtle, unilateral disturbance of single modality sensory or perceptual functions under bilateral stimulation.

If hemi-inattention involves all sensory modalities the possibility of thalamic, frontal, parietal or brainstem lesion deserves consideration (Heilman, Valenstein, & Watson, 1985; Mesulam, 1981). That this is not merely disordered sensation is clearly demonstrated by the cases of Bisiach and Luzzatti (1978). When told to imagine standing in a main square in Milan facing in one direction, their patients described only what would be viewed on their right side; when told to imagine facing in the opposite direction they omitted these items but described the left lying items not decribed originally. In these cases the unilateral inattention involved purely imagined (revisualized) scenes.

Unilateral neglect and inattention should not be overlooked as symptoms. They probably rank as the most common disorders of visual gnosis and can occur following pathology involving a diverse variety of areas. They are easily demonstrated disturbances of considerable importance in the investigation of visual function.

Constructional Disturbance

Most literature dealing with constructional disturbances use the term constructional apraxia; the disorder is not an apraxia, however. Constructional disturbance is defined as an impairment of the ability to reproduce a given visual-spatial array and may follow either right or left hemisphere damage (Arrigoni & DeRenzi, 1964; Hécaen & Assal, 1970; McFie, Piercy, & Zangwill, 1950; McFie & Zangwill, 1960); in addition, it has been described following frontal, parietal or occipital damage in either hemisphere (Luria & Tsvetkova, 1964; Nahor & Benson, 1970).

Constructional disturbance can be demonstrated by many tests; the most common is a request to copy two- and three-dimensional drawings; reproduction of block designs, three-dimensional block constructions, stick figures, hidden figures, and many other tests have been used.

One major constituent of constructional ability is visual-spatial discrimination, a perceptual function that is rarely investigated. Benson and Barton (1970), looking at relatively pure visual-spatial discrimination in patients with focal brain damage,demonstrated that the most severe disturbance occurred in patients with right posterior (parietal-occipital) pathology. In contrast, a more language dependent construction task (stick designs) proved most difficult for subjects with left parietal damage. As an elementary breakdown, constructional tasks can be divided into two major realms—a visual-spatial discrimination aspect, primarily a right hemisphere function, and an executive aspect (the constructing itself), more of a left hemisphere function. Construction, like most other higher behavioral functions, is complex and utilizes much of the brain for its accomplishment (Benson & Barton, 1970).

Dressing Disturbance

Often called dressing apraxia, this disorder is also misnamed as an apraxia. Two distinctly different types of dressing disturbance have been described (Benson & Geschwind, 1985). One is a unilateral neglect; the individual will dress or groom only one side of the body, failing to care for (ignoring) the other side. Thus, a suit coat will be correctly put on one side but no attempt will be made to put on the other half of the coat. Such individuals can fail to comb one side of their hair, fail to shave one side of the face, or fail to apply lipstick on one side while correctly grooming the other side. The locus of pathology for this unilateral neglect lies in the contralateral hemisphere.

The second type of dressing disturbance is a visual-spatial disturbance. In this situation the individual apparently fails to recognize the relationship in space of the body and the garment and incorrectly manipulates the garment in space so that it cannot be applied to the body. Most often a coat with a sleeve inverted is presented to the patient; with manipulation the patient produces only a rumpled mess. The visual-spatial type of dressing disturbance usually indicates damage in the right posterior hemisphere but an exact locus has not been specified.

VISUAL MEMORY DISTURBANCES

As with construction, memory is a complex, multifactorial function but among aspects of memory, visual learning deserves consideration. Unfortunately, it is rarely tested and only a small literature on this attribute exists

(Milner, 1966; Rausch, 1985). While visual memory would appear important for many aspects of visual gnosis, little attempt has been made to correlate disturbances in visual memory function with other disorders. One visual memory problem, visual learning disorder, is fairly well defined and deserves mention.

Visual Learning Disorder

Testing for this disturbance is similar to testing for verbal learning disorder; two or more unrelated (preferably unnameable) drawings are presented for copy and the patient is asked to redraw them as well as possible after a 5 to 15 minute delay. This function deteriorates significantly following right temporal lobectomy (Milner, 1968; Rausch, 1985). Rausch has also demonstrated that a right temporal epileptic focus may produce decreased visual learning ability. If visual learning is poorer than verbal learning, right temporal lobe malfunction is suggested.

VISUAL GEOGRAPHICAL DISORDERS

All disorders mentioned under this heading are categorized as associative or recognition disturbances. Primary sensory disturbance may alter visual geographical functions but not to the same degree seen with involvement of association cortex. Many terms and examples have been presented for geographical gnostic disorders (Critchley, 1953) but only two are presented.

Topographagnosia

This term is often used to denote all problems with visual geographic function but is used here to indicate problems in interpretation of maps, house plans, and other artificial demonstrations of topography. Individuals with topographagnosia often perform normally in real situations, driving long distances, navigating through complex city streets, etc. but cannot place themselves on a map (McCrae & Trolle, 1956). Although they have no problem getting about in their own houses, they can neither draw a plan of their house nor identify rooms on a plan drawn for them. Most individuals with topographagnosia have nondominant, right parietal lobe damage (Hécaen, Penfield, Bertrand, & Malmo, 1956). Topographagnosia is almost always associated with other nondominant parietal dysfunctions, particularly constructional disturbance, and may be overshadowed by these problems.

Environmental Agnosia

A disturbance characterized by "getting lost in familiar places" has been called environmental agnosia. In contrast to patients with topographagnosia, individuals with environmental agnosia may read maps and house plans well, but cannot find their way, even in familiar locales. They get lost in their own neighborhood, even in their own homes (DeRenzi, Faglioni, & Viller, 1977; Paterson & Zangwill, 1945). This problem comes to medical attention when a patient gets lost between his hospital bed and the bathroom. Patients with environmental agnosia *always* have pathology that involves the medial aspects of the right occipital lobe (Landis, Cummings, Benson, & Palmer, 1986). Although the causative lesion may be tumor, vascular infarction, AVM, etc., the location is consistent. As could be anticipated, other visual gnostic disturbances such as constructional disturbance, dressing apraxia, and prosopagnosia are present in some cases but are not consistent (Landis et al., 1986). Topographagnosia and environmental agnosia are clinically and anatomically discrete; it is not unusual to find a patient with one but not the other. It would appear that two separate visual associative systems exist for orienting oneself in space. One, a visual association cortex to parietal association cortex system, subserves artificial visual orientation (maps, etc.) The second, a visual association cortex to medial parietal-occipital junction dysconnection leads to impaired recollection of previously visualized enviromment.

VISUAL OBJECT DISTURBANCE

A dramatic disturbance of visual gnosis is the inability to recognize visualized objects, a disorder called visual agnosia or visual object agnosia. The visual agnosias have been separated into two major categories, apperceptive and associative, for almost a century (Lissauer, 1889). Visual hallucinations can also be categorized as visual object disturbances. In a somewhat similar manner, visual hallucinations appear to have both primary and secondary forms.

Apperceptive Visual Agnosia

Originally postulated by Lissauer (1889) as a failure to recognize due to distortion of the stimulus at sensory-perceptual levels (Critchley, 1953), individuals with apperceptive visual agnosia cannot name, copy, or recognize visually presented objects but immediately identify the item following tactile or auditory cues. They fail at all constructional tasks, cannot copy drawings or writing and cannot identify faces. In sharp contrast, they correctly identify color, light intensity, direction and dimension of visual stimuli; they only fail to recognize visual form (Benson & Greenberg, 1969). The etiology is usually a diffuse brain disorder such as hypoxia, cerebral edema or metabolic disturbance. Good neuropathological descriptions of apperceptive visual agnosia are rare, probably because diffuse rather than focal pathology underlies the dysfunction. Many investigators insist that apperceptive visual agnosia is not a true agnosia (Bender, Feldman, & Sobin, 1968; Critchley, 1964; Teuber, 1968) but, rather, represents a sensory pathway disorder. Others (Luria, 1966) consider this disorder to be the true visual agnosia.

Associative Visual Agnosia

Described by Lissauer (1889) and again by Head (1926), associative visual agnosia was rigidly defined by Teuber (1968) who demanded that there could be neither distortion of visual percept nor disorder of naming. Visual object agnosia is "in its purest form a normal percept that has somehow been stripped of its meaning." Teuber defined an agnosia in which both perception and language were intact but separated and felt the condition must be very rare. Bay (1953) totally denied the existence of visual agnosia; in his opinion all cases were based on a combination of visual sensory defect and dementia. A number of reported cases, however, fulfill the definition of Teuber (Lhermitte et al., 1972; Rubens & Benson, 1971; Taylor & Warrington, 1971). Patients with associative visual agnosia cannot name on visual stimulation but easily copy figures or written material. Tactile or auditory stimuli are named normally. Routine language testing shows no significant abnormality and the IQ is normal except for those test modalities demanding visual identification. Of significance, individuals with associative visual agnosia do well on many visual tests such as hidden figures, block designs, etc. (Rubens & Benson, 1971). Each autopsied case has had damage that disconnected the visual sensory area from the dominant hemisphere language area and each case has had bilateral pathology.

Visual Hallucinosis

Most physicians tend to consider hallucinations as psychogenic and the phenomenon has been far more remarked upon than studied. It has long been known, however, that organic disorders could produce hallucinations. The widespread use of hallucinogenic drugs (LSD, mescaline) demonstrated an artificial means of producing hallucinations; originally considered an artificial schizophrenia, additional study demonstrated that the major disturbance was a drug-induced alteration of perception, a hallucination (Bradley, Morley, Bacher, & Smythies,

1979; Freedman, 1969). Many organic causes of hallucinations are now recognized (Cummings, 1985; Davison & Bagley, 1969) and both perceptual disturbances and associative abnormalities may be seen.

Perceptual visual hallucinations range from simple distortions, flashing lights, jagged lines, glitter, scintillating scotomata, etc. to distortions of reality such as micropsia, macropsia, and metamorphopsia. Recognized causes include vascular ischemia, migraine, drugs (LSD, alcohol) and their withdrawal, mass lesions, structural disturbances, and seizure discharges. In cases allowing localization of causative pathology, the territory of the posterior cerebral artery, particularly the occipital visual areas and their major input systems, is the region most often involved.

Associative visual hallucinations may range from simple to complex scenes and be associated with pleasant, frightening or neutral affective tone. Peduncular hallucinosis (Lhermitte, 1951), a rare but frequently discussed disorder, most often indicates abnormal posterior artery circulation. Many etiologies for associative visual hallucinations are known including vascular, neoplastic, traumatic, toxic-metabolic, and epileptic. An old observation suggests that formed, complex visual hallucinations indicate anterior (temporal lobe) disorder, while simple distortions most frequently indicate occipital disturbance. At best this is inconsistent. Nonetheless, two distinct forms of visual hallucination exist and the difference probably represents a significant difference in the underlying anatomical/physiologic disorder.

Visual Allesthesia

The transposition of a perceived visual image from one quadrant or hemifield to another has been called visual or optic allesthesia (Jacobs, 1980). Often a distinct latency is present between the perception of a visual image and its appearance in the normally functioning visual field. Not infrequently a distortion of the displaced image is reported (Jacobs, 1980). Visual allesthesia is clearly related to palinopsia and is almost invariably associated with structural damage in posterior hemisphere structures.

Palinopsia

A form of visual hallucination in which an image persists or recurs after the stimulus is gone has been called palinopsia (Bender et al., 1968). Classically, an image appears in the blind half field of an homonymous hemianopsia. The image may recur or persist for up to several hours following removal of the stimulus and remains in the same position in the visual field when the eyes are moved (Cummings, 1985). Pathology almost invariably involves occipital and parietal areas but both right and left hemisphere lesions have been reported (Bender et al., 1968). Most often palinopsia appears following an acute change in brain structure (e.g., CVA, brain surgery) and disappears within weeks. Many consider palinopsia to be an ictal event but one recent case report suggests that, at least in some instances, it is a release phenomenon (Cummings, Syndulko, Goldberg, & Treiman, 1982).

VISUAL FACIAL DISTURBANCES

Human beings recognize a tremendous number of faces, a far greater capability than their ability to associate a name with the face. Abnormalities or disturbances of the ability to recognize faces has been intensively studied in recent years. Both perceptual and associative disturbances can be suggested.

Facial Matching

The face is made up of many prominent features (eyes, nose, mouth, jaws, brows, cheeks, ears, etc.); although visualized from many different angles and in many different degrees of lighting, the features can be identified as belonging to one individual. Matching of a face as the same or different from a previously seen face is easily performed despite considerable alterations in overall appearance. Many investigators have studied matching of subtle facial features, usually under the title of facial recognition (Benton & Van Allen, 1969; Bornstein, Sroka, & Munitz, 1969; De Renzi & Spinnler, 1966; Hécaen & Tzavaras, 1968–1969), and have clearly demonstrated that this function is seriously disturbed following structural damage to the right posterior brain. Damage to other areas of the brain may cause mild problems but patients with right posterior damage suffer considerably more problem in facial matching. Whether visual-spatial discrimination or visual memory is the cause remains unsettled but the right posterior brain appears essential for the matching of faces.

Prosopagnosia

Loss of the ability to recognize familiar faces (or well-known animals or automobiles, etc.) is a dramatic clinical situation called prosopagnosia (Bodamer, 1947; Bornstein et al., 1969; Damasio, Damasio, & Van Hoesen, 1982; Whiteley & Warrington, 1977). The striking disturbance in which one cannot recognize one's own spouse, children or even one's own face in a mirror and yet can successfully perform many other visual activities is one of the more dramatic human behavioral disorders. While failing to recognize familiar faces, patients with prosopagnosia demonstrate at least fair ability on facial matching tests (Hécaen & Tzavaras, 1968–1969; Rubens & Benson, 1971).

In his extensive review, Meadows (1974b) showed that most reported cases of prosopagnosia suffer a left visual field defect (either full hemianopsia or left upper quadrantopsia). Some exceptions were noted, however, and all cases of prosopagnosia that have come to postmortem had evidence of bilateral posterior cerebral damage. While prosopagnosia is often considered a right posterior hemisphere abnormality, it appears that bilateral damage is essential (Damasio et al., 1982). In several well studied cases, the pathology involved the inferior longitudinal fasciculus on the side of the brain with intact visual field (Benson et al., 1974; Lhermitte et al., 1972). It can be suggested that a connection between the visual association cortex and the infero-temporal cortex is essential for the recognition of familiar faces, but apparently either hemisphere can perform the task. Also, it appears that recognition of familiar faces is quite separate from facial matching, at least as performed in psychological test batteries. One (prosopagnosia) appears to demand considerable memory function; the other (facial recognition) is a more demanding visual-spatial discrimination task.

VISUAL MOTOR DISTURBANCES

Balint's Syndrome

Most visual motor disturbances are the product of dysfunction in the extraocular motor system. As such they are not considered disorders of visual gnosis. One combination of higher level visual motor disturbances is recognized and has been called Balint's syndrome (Damasio, 1985; Hecaen & de Ajuriaguerra, 1954). While described many years ago (Balint, 1909), disagreement as to the features comprising the syndrome has been persistent (Hécaen & Albert, 1978). Three major findings stand out and are now generally accepted as representative. Balint's syndrome consists of optic ataxia, sticky fixation, and simultanagnosia.

Optic Ataxia. This disorder, often called ocular dysmetria, is characterized by disturbance of the ability to reach out and touch an object in space. When reaching for an object in space, the hand will miss by several inches, most often on a horizontal plane but occasionally in the vertical plane also. With repeated trials the patient corrects to some degree but if distracted or following a rest period, the finding will again be present.

Sticky Fixation. Also called oculomotor apraxia (Cogan & Adams, 1953) and ocular apraxia (Damasio, 1985), sticky fixation is characterized by a subject's inability to change gaze volitionally from one fixed visual stimulus to another, as though the gaze was stuck to the original stimulus. Patients must often resort to artificial means such as closing their eyes and/or bobbing their head to break the fixation. In contrast, when following a moving visual stimulus, the eyes move from place to place.

Simultanagnosia. Although clearly described by Wolpert (1924), simultanagnosia is rarely noted. The patient appears to see and report only a portion of a complex scene, apparently unaware of the other features. Vision becomes fixed on one object so that other objects in the field of vision are not noted (Tyler, 1968). For instance, a person looking out a window may see a building but be unaware that snow is falling (Luria, 1959) or may pick one feature from a complex picture, ignoring the other features (Wolpert, 1924).

The three aspects of Balint's syndrome often co-occur but not always in equal degree. One or more element may not be easy to demonstrate and the presence of Balint's syndrome is easily overlooked. There is little firm data concerning location of the causative pathology but most reported cases suggest bilateral occipital lesions. In at least one case, however, Balint's syndrome occurred when occipital-frontal pathways were involved bilaterally (Hécaen & Albert, 1978) and purely frontal pathology has been suggested as a potential source (Hausser, Robert, & Giard, 1980). The latter would represent an indirect effect based on impaired attention (Stuss & Benson, 1986).

GENERAL VISUAL GNOSTIC DISTURBANCE

Posterior Cortical Atrophy

A few patients have been reported who show a progressive degenerative disorder that appears to start in the posterior cerebral hemispheres and progresses forward. Regional signs and symptoms include alexia, constructional disturbance, and visual agnosia. Balint's syndrome is eventually demonstrable and with progression a complete Gerstmann syndrome, transcortical sensory aphasia, and a verbal learning disorder can all be noted. To date there is no recognized pathology; no patients show evidence of either neoplastic or vascular disorder. The slowly progressive course suggests a degenerative disorder, a posterior lobar atrophy that is at least superficially similar to Pick's disease.

DISCUSSION

An attempt has been made to present and categorize the major disorders of visual gnosis. Entities selected or excluded, the terminology and the system of categorization can be criticized but the listing does offer a rational beginning to understanding a sizeable and complex group of visual abnormalities. It can be hoped that from this beginning a concept of the organization of the higher visual functions can be proposed.

Considerable evidence suggests that individual processes within visual gnosis, particularly the sensory, perceptual, and associative processes, can be differentiated to a greater or lesser degree. This is best exemplified by visual agnosia where the apperceptive and associative types of visual agnosia produce a superficially similar picture but are clinically distinct. Both visual hallucinations and the distinguishing of facial features also appear to have clearly separable categories.

Current evidence indicates that separable circuits underlie many of the higher level gnostic functions (Benson, 1979; Heilman et al., 1985; Mesulam, 1985). Similar examples in visual gnostic disturbances would include topographic agnosia and environmental agnosia, each a feature of the ability to utilize geographical location but each seen without the other. They are distinctly different in clinical manifestations and, apparently, reflect involvement of different portions of the right posterior hemisphere. Separate circuits are involved.

It must be admitted, however, that a considerable overlap of symptom pictures is common in visual gnostic disorders. Thus, constructional disturbance co-occurs with almost all, no matter where the pathology is located and even occurs with loci of pathology that apparently cause no other visual disorders. Facial matching, dressing disturbance, and topographagnosia may all be disturbed by lesions of the occipital-parietal junction area in the right hemisphere. Many distinctly different problems apparently emanate from a single lesion location. Thus, while a single phenomenon can occur with pathology in a variety of loci, quite different clinical features can follow lesions in a relatively restricted area.

In attempting to interpret these observations, the importance of the functional systems emerges. The circuitry interconnecting the areas appears crucial for the individual syndromes. Specific circuits apparently connect specific cortical sites to subserve a given gnostic task. Neuropathology affecting several different cortical sites or the interconnecting pathways may produce a single gnostic abnormality. Dependent upon the area involved other disorders may or may not be present. Damage to a single site or pathway may produce several visual gnostic disorders but a lesion slightly further downstream (or upstream?) on the circuit may produce one clinical syndrome but not the other. To study higher visual functions through visual gnostic disorders we must recognize that multiple, interconnected cerebral sites of pathology may produce a given syndrome. This information must be collated to establish the neurocircuitry essential for a given function.

The use of clinical material to study a complex interrelationship such as that of the visual gnostic disorders is difficult. At present, the entities are poorly characterized and only crude anatomical correlation is available. Nonetheless, it is hoped that with better delineation of the disorders, attention to the specific circuitry underlying a given gnostic task can be highlighted and the cerebral interrelationships allowing complex visual responses better understood.

REFERENCES

Arrigoni, G., & De Renzi, E. (1964). Constructional apraxia and hemispheric locus of lesion. *Cortex, 1,* 170–197.

Balint, R. (1909). Seelenlahmung des "Schauens," optische Ataxie, raumliche Storung der Auf merksamheit. *Monatsschrift für Psychiatrie und Neurologie, 25,* 51–81.

Bay, E. (1953). Disturbances of visual perception and their examination. *Brain, 76,* 515–550.

Bender, M. D., Feldman, M., & Sobin, A. J. (1968). Palinopsia. *Brain, 91,* 321–338.

Benson, D. F. (1979). Neurologic correlates of anomia. In H. Whitaker & H. A. Whitaker (Eds.), *Studies in neurolinguistics* (Vol. 4, pp. 293–328). New York: Academic Press.

Benson, D. F. (1982). The alexias: A guide to the neural basis of reading. In H. S. Kirshner & F. R. Freemon (Eds.), *The neurology of aphasia* (pp. 139–162). Amsterdam: Swets Publishing Service.

Benson, D. F. (1985). Alexia. In J. A. M. Fredericks (Ed.), *Handbook of clinical neurology, 2nd Ed., Vol. 45: Clinical neuropsychology* (pp. 433–455). Amsterdam: Elsevier Science Publishers.

Benson, D. F., & Barton, M. I. (1970). Disturbances in constructional apraxia. *Cortex, 6,* 19–46.

Benson, D. F., & Geschwind, N. (1985). The aphasias and related disturbances. In A. B. Baker & R. Joynt (Eds.), *Clinical neurology* (Chapter 10). Philadelphia: Harper & Row.

Benson, D. F., & Greenberg, J. P. (1969). Visual form agnosia. *Archives of Neurology, 20,* 82–89.

Benson, D. F., Marsden, C. D., & Meadows, J. C. (1974). The amnesic syndrome of posterior cerebral artery occlusion. *Acta Neurologica Scandinavica, 50,* 133–145.

Benson, D. F., & Tomlinson, E. B. (1971). Hemiplegic syndrome of the posterior cerebral artery. *Stroke, 2,* 559–564.

Benton, A. L., & Van Allen, M. W. (1969). Impairment in facial recognition in patients with cerebral disease. *Cortex, 4,* 344–358.

Bisiach, E., & Luzzatti, C. (1978). Unilateral neglect of representational space. *Cortex, 14,* 129–133.

Bodamer, J. (1947). Die Prosop-Agnosie. *Archiv für Psychiatrie und Nervenkrankheit, 179,* 6–53.

Bornstein, B., Sroka, H., & Munitz, H. (1969). Prosopagnosia with animal face agnosia. *Cortex, 5,* 164–170.

Bradley, R. J., Morley, B. J., Bacher, S. A., & Smythies, J. R. (1979). Hallucinogens. In P. J. Vinken & G. W. Bruyn (Eds.), *Handbook of clinical neurology, Vol. 37* (pp. 329–346). Amsterdam: North Holland Publishers.

Cogan, D. G., & Adams, R. D. (1953). A type of paralysis of conjugate gaze (ocular motor apraxia). *Archives of Ophthalmology, 50,* 434–442.

Critchley, M. (1953). *The parietal lobes.* London: Edward Arnold.

Critchley, M. (1964). The problem of visual agnosia. *Journal of Neurological Sciences, 1,* 274–290.

Cummings, J. L. (1985). *Clinical neuropsychiatry.* Orlando, FL: Grune & Stratton.

Cummings, J. L., Syndulko, K., Goldberg, Z., & Treiman, D. (1982). Palinopsia reconsidered. *Neurology, 32,* 444–447.

Damasio, A. R. (1985). Disorders of complex visual processing: Agnosias, achromatopsia, Balint's syndrome and related difficulties of orientation and construction. In M-M. Mesulam (Ed.), *Principles of behavioral neurology* (pp. 259–288). Philadelphia: Davis.

Damasio, A. R., Damasio, H., & Van Hoesen, G. W. (1982). Prosopagnosia: Anatomic basis and behavioral mechanisms. *Neurology, 32,* 331–341.

Damasio, A. R., Yamada, T., Damasio, H., Corbett, J., & McKee, J. (1980). Central achromatopsia: Behavioral, anatomic and physiologic aspects. *Neurology, 30,* 1064–1071.

Davison, K., & Bagley, C. R. (1969). Schizophrenia-like psychoses associated with organic disorders of the central nervous system: A review of the literature. In R. N. Harrington (Ed.), *Current problems in neuropsychiatry. British Journal of Psychiatry Special Publication No 4* (pp. 113–183). Ashford, Kent: Headley Brothers.

Dejerine, J. (1892). Contribution à l'étude anatomoclinique et clinique des differentes varieties de cécité verbale. *Memoires Societé Biologique, 4,* 61–90.

Denny-Brown, D., & Banker, B. Q. (1954). Amorphosynthesis from left parietal lesion. *Archives of Neurology and Psychiatry, 71,* 302–313.

Denny-Brown, D., Meyer, J. S., & Horenstein, S. (1952). The significance of perceptual rivalry resulting from parietal lesion. *Brain, 75,* 433–471.

De Renzi, E., Faglioni, P., & Viller, P. (1977). Topographical amnesia. *Journal of Neurology, Neurosurgery, and Psychiatry, 40,* 498–505.

De Renzi, E., & Spinnler, H. (1966). Facial recognition in brain damaged patients. *Neurology, 16,* 145–152.

Efron, R. (1968). What is perception? *Boston Studies in the Philosophy of Science, 4,* 137–173.

Freedman, D. X. (1969). The psychopharmocology of hallucinogenic agents. *Annual Review of Medicine, 20,* 409–418.

Geschwind, N. (1962). The anatomy of acquired disorders of reading. In J. Money (Ed.), *Reading disability* (pp. 115–129). Baltimore: Johns Hopkins Press.

Geschwind, N., & Fusillo, M. (1966). Color naming defects in association with alexia. *Archives of Neurology, 15,* 137–146.

Gloning, I., Gloning, K., & Hoff, H. (1968). *Neuropsychological symptoms and syndromes in lesions of the occipital lobe and the adjacent areas.* Paris: Gauthier-Villais.

Greenblatt, S. H. (1976). Subangular alexia without agraphia or hemianopsia. *Brain & Language, 3,* 229–245.

Hamburger, D. (Ed.). (1970). *Perception and its disorders. Research Publications-Association for Research in Nervous and Mental Disease,* Vol. 53.

Hausser, C. O., Robert, F., & Giard, N. (1980). Balint's syndrome. *Canadian Journal of Neurological Sciences, 7,* 157–161.

Head, H. (1926). *Aphasia and kindred disorders* (2 vols.). London: Cambridge University Press.

Hécaen, H., & Albert, M. L. (1978). *Human neuropsychology.* New York: Wiley.

Hécaen, H., & de Ajuriaguerra, J. (1954). Balint's syndrome. *Brain, 77,* 373–400.

Hécaen, H., & Assal, G. (1970). A comparison of constructive deficits following right and left hemispheric lesions. *Neuropsychologia, 8,* 289–303.

Hécaen, H., Penfield, W., Bertrand, C., & Malmo, R. (1956). The syndrome of apractagnosia due to lesions of the minor cerebral hemisphere. *Archives of Neurology and Psychiatry, 75,* 400–434.

Hécaen, H., & Tzavaras, A. (1968–1969). Etude neuropsychologique des troubles de la reconassaince des visages humains. *Bull. Psychol, 276,* 754–762.

Heilman, K. H., Valenstein, E., & Watson, R. T. (1985). Behavioral aspects of neurology: Attentional, intentional and emotional disorders. In A. B. Baker & R. J. Joynt (Eds.), *Clinical neurology* (Chapter 22). Philadelphia: Harper & Row.

Jacobs, L. (1980). Visual allesthesia. *Neurology, 30,* 1059–1063.

Kinsbourne, M., & Warrington, E. K. (1964). Observations on color agnosia. *Journal of Neurology, Neurosurgery, and Psychiatry, 27,* 296–299.

Landis, T., Cummings, J. L., Benson, D. F., & Palmer, E. P. (1986). Loss of topographic familiarity: An environmental agnosia. *Archives of Neurology, 43,* 132–136.

Lhermitte, F., Chain, F., Escourolle, R., Ducarne, B., & Pillon, B. (1972). Etude anatomo-clinique d'un cas de prosopagnosie. *Revue Neurologique, 126,* 329–346.

Lhermitte, J. (1951). *Les hallucinations.* Paris: G. Doin & Cie.

Lissauer, H. (1889). Ein Fall von Seelenblindheit nebst einem Beitrage zur Theorie derselben. *Archiv fur Psychiatrie, 21,* 2–50.

Luria, A. R. (1959). Disorders of simultaneous perception in a case of bilateral occipito-parietal brain injury. *Brain, 82,* 437–439.

Luria, A. R. (1966). *Higher cortical functions in man.* New York: Basic Books.

Luria, A. R., & Tsvetkova, L. S. (1964). The programming of constructive activity in local brain injuries. *Neurospychologia, 2,* 95–108.

McCrae, D., & Trolle, E. (1956). The defect of function in visual agnosia. *Brain, 79,* 94–110.

McFie, J., Piercy, M. F., & Zangwill, O. L. (1950). Visual-spatial agnosia. *Brain, 73,* 167–190.

McFie, J., & Zangwill, O. L. (1960). Visual constructive disabilities associated with lesions of the left cerebral hemisphere. *Brain, 83,* 243–260.

Meadows, J. C. (1974a). Disturbed perception of colours associated with localized cerebral lesions. *Brain, 97,* 615–632.

Meadows, J. C. (1974b). The anatomical basis of prosopagnosia. *Journal of Neurology, Neurosurgery, and Psychiatry, 37,* 489–501.

Mesulam, M-M. (1985). Attention, confusional states and neglect. In M-M. Mesulam (Ed.), *Principles of behavioral neurology* (pp. 125–168). Philadelphia: F. A. Davis.

Milner, B. (1966). Amnesia following operation on the temporal lobes. In C. W. M. Whitty & O. L. Zangwill (Eds.), *Amnesia* (pp. 109–133). London: Butterworths.

Milner, B. (1968). Visual recognition and recall after right temporal-lobe excision in man. *Neuropsychologia, 6,* 191–200.

Nahor, A., & Benson, D. F. (1970). A screening test for organic brain disease in emergency psychiatric evaluation. *Behavioral Psychiatry, 2,* 23–26.

Nielsen, J. M. (1936). *Agnosia, apraxia, aphasia: Their value in cerebral localization.* New York: Hafner.

Oxbury, J. M., Oxbury, S. M., & Humphrey, N. K. (1969). Varieties of color anomia. *Brain, 92,* 847–860.

Paterson, A., & Zangwill, O. L. (1945). A case of topographical disorientation associated with a unilateral cerebral lesion. *Brain, 68,* 188–211.

Rausch, H. R. (1985). Differences in cognitive function with left and right temporal lobe dysfunction. In D. F. Benson & E. Zaidel (Eds.), *The dual brain: Hemispheric specialization in the human* (pp. 257–261). New York: Guilford Press.

Rubens, A. B., & Benson, D. F. (1971). Associative visual agnosia. *Archives of Neurology, 24,* 305–315.

Stachowiak, F. J., & Poeck, K. (1976). Functional disconnection in pure alexia and color naming deficit demonstrated by deblocking methods. *Brain & Language, 3,* 135–143.

Stuss, D. T., & Benson, D. F. (1986). *The frontal lobes.* New York: Raven Press.

Taylor, A., & Warrington, E. K. (1971). Visual Agnosia: A single case report. *Cortex, 7,* 152–161.

Teuber, H. L. (1968). Alteration of perception and memory in man. In L. Weiskrantz (Ed.), *Analysis of behavioral change* (pp. 268–375). New York: Harper & Row.

Tyler, H. R. (1968). Abnormality of perception with defective eye movements (Balint's syndrome). *Cortex, 4,* 154–171.

Whiteley, A. M., & Warrington, E. K. (1977). Prosopagnosia: A clinical, psychological and anatomical study of three patients. *Journal of Neurology, Neurosurgery, and Psychiatry, 40,* 395–403.

Wolpert, I. (1924). Die Simultanagnosie: Storung der Gesamtauffassung. *Zeitschrift fur die gesamte Neurologie und Psychiatrie, 93,* 397–415.

4

Finding the Way Around Topographical Impairments

M. J. Riddoch
and
G. W. Humphreys

INTRODUCTION

Disorders of recognition and exploration of the environment have long been documented. For example, Jackson (1876) described a patient with a glioma of the right temporal lobe who had marked difficulties in route finding even though, in some instances, she was correctly able to describe some aspects of the topography of her native town.

One interpretation of topographical disorientation is that environmental recognition and exploration require a cognitive process independent of those involved in other apparently similar processes such as object recognition, drawing or construction tasks. For instance, Landis, Cummings, Benson, and Palmer (1986) summarize the cases of 16 patients who showed a loss of environmental familiarity. The 16 patients all complained of an inability to recognize familiar environments, although they could see and describe their situation. All 16 patients had right posteromedial hemispheric lesions and 3 had additional left sided lesions. In addition to defective environmental recognition the patients exhibited a variety of other deficits (e.g., prosopagnosia (7 cases), impaired nonverbal learning (6 cases), constructional deficits (5 cases), and alterations in brightness modulation, dressing disturbances and left sided neglect (4 cases)). Despite this heterogeneity of additional symptomatology and indeed, lesion site, Landis et al. (1986) propose a common underlying deficit to account for the loss of environmental familiarity: an impaired ability to associate intact percepts with completely or partially preserved visuospatial memories. They suggest that a loss of environmental familiarity is a class specific agnosia similar to prosopagnosia. Similarly, Whiteley and Warrington (1978) have also proposed that topographical memory loss may occur as a selective impairment of memory for one class of visual material. Whiteley and Warrington's (1978) claim is illustrated by the case of a patient with apparently preserved perceptual and spatial skills and with an impairment of topographical memory for *new* topographical information. We should note, however, that there is a distinction between Landis et al.'s (1986) account which essentially claims that there is an inability to *associate* intact percepts with memory concepts and Whiteley and Warrington's account which proposes a deficit *specific* to forming new topographical memories. Such a distinction suggests that possibly different causes may underlie the same general symptomatology. This possibility is supported by a brief perusal of cases in the literature. For example, Case 4 of Hécaen, Penfield, Bertrand, and Malmo (1956) appears to have a recognition problem. He states, "I get lost if I go downtown. I cannot find my way anyway if I get out from the seeing of my home. I am completely lost. I don't recognize where I am." On the other hand, Holmes' (1919) patients had no problems with recognition but were quite unable to appreciate how objects were related to each other in space. Holmes describes that "Each was at first unable to find his way directly to any point to which he was asked to go though he saw it, or succeeded only after taking a devious route. . . ."

The argument that there are different types of topographical disorientation is certainly not new. Brain (1941) proposes a classification of visual disorientation which involves 9 subsections each implicating a different causal factor for visual disorientation. In fact, these 9 subsections reflect 4 basic disorders:

1. The loss of awareness of the absolute and relative positions of objects, which, when not limited to one hemifield, results in a failure to orientate towards a seen object.
2. Inattention to the left half of space following a right hemisphere lesion leading to a tendancy to ignore left sided turns.
3. Visual object agnosia.
4. Loss of topographic memory.

There are also problems with this sort of classification. Disparate and unrelated factors are involved. Furthermore, these factors are not linked to some underlying view of the processes normally involved in the recognition and exploration of the environment. If we wish to relate the different forms of topographical impairment to each other, and if we wish to learn anything about the processes normally involved in topographical recognition and exploration, it is necessary to establish some sort of framework of the processes normally involved.

Such an approach was taken at the beginning of work on topographic disturbances. In 1919 Gordon Holmes presented a lecture in Trinity College, Dublin on disturbances of visual space perception. He started by enumerating the various abilities we have for space perception. He stated that these abilities included:

1. the ability to determine the position of an object in space and the ability to point to it (this latter ability requires that movements of the arm should be directed and controlled).

2. the ability to roughly estimate how far an object is from the body.

3. the ability to judge roughly how far apart two objects are from each other, and also their distances relative to the viewer; whether one of the two objects is nearer and/or higher and/or more to one side than the other.

4. the ability to focus the eyes on the object if it initially falls on the peripheral part of the retina (this may require convergence of the eyes and accommodation of the pupils).

5. the ability to estimate the size of an object both in absolute terms and also relative to other objects.

6. the ability to recognize that an object has thickness and depth (i.e., that it is three dimensional).

7. the ability to identify the object.

This provides us with a detailed analysis of the main abilities necessary to allow interaction with the environment. We should now like to consider what *processes* may underlie these abilities.

In order to interact with the environment (i.e., to reach appropriately for objects, to walk around objects etc.) and in order to recognize objects, we require an integrated *viewpoint-dependent* representation of the world. That is, we need a representation which preserves information about the positions of objects relative to the viewer (see Marr, 1982). Several processes underlie the generation of a viewpoint-dependent representation. For instance:

(i) adequate early processing of the dimensions of visual stimuli across the visual field (e.g., spatial frequency, length, orientation, color, size, and movement).

(ii) adequate depth perception and coding of forms in 3D.

(iii) adequate integration of information within the form domain.

Impairments to these processes could produce failure to recognize visual landmarks and routes, and impairments in negotiating the environment appropriately (e.g., the loss of 3D information will lead to difficulties in reaching for objects).

In addition to these visual processes, some form of spatial working memory is necessary in order to hold information about one's current position on a route, and in order to plan future movements. Attentional processes are also necessary in order to allow the initiation and coordination of actions in response to the appropriate environmental cues. Finally, we also require stored memories for previously experienced landmarks and for routes ("spatial maps," although how these maps may be stored is a matter of debate; see Anderson, 1978; Kosslyn, 1980; Pylyshyn, 1981).

Disorders of any of these processes might render recognition and exploration of the environment difficult. In what follows, we attempt to classify cases of patients with topographical impairments in terms of the above processes, thought to be normally involved in topographical recognition and exploration. Our approach, which attempts to link topographical disorders to a model of normal behavior, has not been undertaken hitherto. Unfortunately, this means that few patients have been described and/or tested in a way that is sensitive to some of the distinctions that we wish to make. This means that our discussion is limited to those cases where there are sufficient details to reclassify the patient in terms of a disruption to particular process(es) in the normal model. To this extent, our discussion is selective and not inclusive of all documented cases of topographical impairments. We also interpret the term topographical impairment quite broadly to include spatial processing problems which impinge on recognition and exploration of the environment.

We are aware that brain lesions do not necessarily respect the functional organization of behavior. Patients may therefore have lesions which are so placed, or are so large, as to implicate 2 or more processes. Nevertheless, we feel that particular forms of impaired behavior can be identified and related to a model of normal behavior. Our hope is that the framework we provide can serve as a starting point for future work, which should aim to analyze the particular processing components impaired in a given patient. Patients who seem to have 2 or more impaired processes will have their different impaired processes described separately.

IMPAIRMENTS IN VIEWPOINT-DEPENDENT REPRESENTATIONS

Early Visual Processing

Patients have been reported with various selective impairments in processing the dimensions of visual stimuli, including selective losses of spatial frequency information (Bodis-Wollner, 1972, 1976; Campion, 1987), orientation information (Campion, 1987; Campion & Latto, 1985), 2D size and length information (Holmes, 1919), color (Meadows, 1974) and movement (Zihl, von Cramon, & Mai, 1983). More commonly, brain lesions can also disrupt vision in various parts of the visual field (see Ratcliff & Ross, 1981). Selective loss of these different types of information, or of information from particular parts of the visual field, can obviously produce difficulties for patients in coping with their environment. Loss of information from one part of space could lead to patients bumping into "unseen" objects. Loss of movement could produce problems in judging the rate and direction from which objects approach. Loss of the ability to appreciate the 2D length and size of an object would lead to failures to reach to it appropriately etc. Loss of spatial frequency and orientation information will make objects difficult to recognize. However, it remains unclear the extent to which the selective loss of any of these different types of information disrupts topographical recognition and exploration.

In many instances, topographical impairments have been noted. For instance, a few cases have been documented where the patient's loss of spatial frequency and orientation information is so severe as to drastically impair visual object identification (Campion, 1987; Campion & Latto, 1985). Similarly, some patients have been documented with impaired perception of even the simplest aspects of shape (Adler, 1944; Benson & Greenberg, 1969). Such patients typically have severe problems in negotiating the environment, presumably because their visual discrimination is too poor to support the discrimination of routes and landmarks. Thus Campion (1987) reports that his patient "cannot go out of the house unaccompanied" and Adler (1950) reports that "she knew that her only way to find remote places was to memorize landmarks and street numbers, and that she could never follow her sense of direction. In spite of all these precautions she occasionally gets lost when visiting places where she has been frequently because of errors in memorizing." Poor shape discrimination produces both poor visual object recognition (so-called "shape agnosia"; Humphreys & Riddoch, 1987b) and topograhical impairments.

The patient described by Zihl et al. (1983) had disturbed perception of movement. For instance, tea being poured from a pot to a cup "appeared to be frozen like a glacier." She had no problems recognizing objects, no disturbance in color vision etc.; nevertheless problems did arise with her exploration of the environment. People walking in a room appeared to be "suddenly here or there, but I did not see them move," so she failed to plan her actions appropriately. Similarly, she found it difficult to cross the road because she could not judge the speed of cars. These problems reflected the loss of movement vision rather than inadequate depth perception as the patient had normal stereopsis (see below). Again, the loss of elementary visual information seems to give rise to the topographical impairment.

However, the relations between other early perceptual deficits and topographical impairments are more problematic. Meadows (1974), in his review of acquired color blindness (achromatopsia) noted that achromatopsia tends to be accompanied by other visual processing problems, including face recognition (prosopagnosia) and topographical impairments. Since we normally have no special difficulties dealing with black and white scenes (on the television, in the cinema, or in photographs) there is no reason to think that the loss of color information per se generates topographical problems. A more viable account is that the brain regions involved in color perception are anatomically close to those involved in processing form information. A lesion to the "color" region is therefore also likely to affect form discrimination, with the topographical problems being precipitated by the problem in form discrimination (see Humphreys & Riddoch, 1987a, 1987b for a fuller discussion of this point).

It is also difficult to asertain the extent to which problems in discriminating 2D length and size information may generate topograhical problems. The patients described by Holmes (1919) as having poor 2D length and size discrimination also had poor discrimination of the relative distances between objects (see following section on Depth Perception, in addition to difficulties negotiating their environments. It may have been that the poor representation of distances in 3D, rather than the poor 2D discriminations, underlay the topographical problems in these patients.

Visual field deficits are a fairly common accompanyment to brain damage. Although all of the patients we have so far discussed with early visual processing problems do tend to have field defects of one form or another (see Meadows, 1974), it is also generally true that other patients can have similar field defects and not experience topographical problems (this is certainly true of hemianopias, for instance). Field defects, per se, do not seem to cause topographical problems. However, there may be exceptions to this rule. At least three of the patients named shape agnosics because of their poor shape discrimination (see above), suffered carbon monoxide poisoning (Adler, 1944; Benson & Greenberg, 1969; Campion, 1987). One consequence of this can be the production of a multitude of small disseminated lesions of the cortex, resulting in many local visual field defects (see Campion, 1987). Such defects could prevent the patient from perceiving form information in a way that would be adequate for normal object recognition, and so those defects could be the cause of any associated topographical problems.

Bay (1950, 1953) also argued that specific visual field defects could underlie visual recognition (and presumably, topographical) problems. Bay proposed that after brain damage, some patients could experience rapid fading of visual information. This fading would take place across the visual field, but its effect would be most severe on peripheral regions of the field because the processing of information from these regions would ordinarily be less efficient. Such patients would have a kind of functional tunnel vision, making it difficult for them to perceive whole objects or scenes "at a glance." However, it is not the case that all cases of agnosia suffer from the kind of field defect proposed by Bay (Humphreys & Riddoch, 1987b), and this is also true of patients with topographical impairments (see the section on Lesion Sites below). Nevertheless, there is some evidence for such defects in patients suffering from Balint's syndrome. There are considered to be 3 essential elements in Balint's syndrome: disturbance of visual attention, disturbance of gaze, and optic ataxia. The disturbance of visual attention involves the restriction of attention to one object at a time. For instance, a patient described by Luria, Pravdena-Vinarskaya, and Yarbus (1963) was normally capable of perceiving objects and geometric figures when presented singly but he could not perceive several objects presented simultaneously. If two objects were presented tachistoscopically, he perceived one or the other but not both at the same time unless they were identical objects or were fused into a single structure. Balint's (1909) original patient noted that "when I see one object, I do not see the other and it takes me time to find where it is." and Holmes (1919) notes that "while sitting in the ward, it was noticeable that the patients usually saw only what their eyes were directed on and that they took little interest in what was happening around them, unless their attention was called to it by sounds or other sense impressions. In walking, too, they frequently passed, without observing them, things that would have excited the notice of normal persons."

These accounts suggest that the attentional capacity of patients with Balint's syndrome is dramatically reduced. There appears to be no problem with focal attention—once an object has been fixated it can be identified. However, peripheral vision, which normally acts to signal focal attention to switch to areas of interest is functionally inoperative (see Holmes, 1919). This limitation results in marked problems for the patient when attempts are made to negotiate the environment. Successful negotiation of the environment requires the determination of the positions of objects in space both relative to themselves and to the viewer. Patients with Balint's syndrome may be unable to do this because they apparently cannot code information about a second object when identifying a first. Thus Holmes (1919) reports that "One man who was in the same small ward for 3 months, could not, even at the end of this time, go directly to his bed, though he could see and identify it, if he had to make two or three turns on the way. Another was tested day after day in an open space divided by a partition in which there was a gate, but even after weeks of training he could rarely go straight through the gate to a point in the other division which he knew." Thus, the magnitude of this disturbance of visual attention is such as to impair the recognition and exploration of the environment in its own right. Such problems will then be exacerbated if patients also have problems in the control of gaze and optic ataxia.[1]

In summary, there is evidence that patients can suffer "early" visual processing deficits after brain damage, and, at least in some cases (particularly those with deficits in the perception of form and movement), these deficits can give rise to topographical problems.

[1]The disturbance in gaze and the problem of visual attention in Balint's syndrome can both be attributed to the same cause: namely, the functional impairment in peripheral vision. Without peripheral vision, the eye movement system has few cues available to guide shifts in gaze. The third aspect of Balint's syndrome, optic ataxia, seems less related—particularly as ataxia in some cases is limited to homonymous half fields (Hécaen & Ajuriaguerra, 1954; Riddoch, 1935) and to either one hand (Balint, 1909; Hécaen et al., 1950; Hécaen & Ajuriaguerra, 1954) or to both hands (Pick, 1898; Holmes, 1918; Michel, Jeanerrod, & Devic, 1965). One might therefore suspect that problems in visual attention and gaze control might dissociate from cases of optic ataxia.

Depth Perception

There are also cases where patients appear to have intact "early" visual processes, but have impaired perception of depth and the distances between objects. In some cases, patients appear to lose the experience of 3D vision altogether. These effects can be quite striking. To the patient, people appear as moving cardboard cutouts, spheres as circles, a landscape as a painted picture or a piece of stage scenery (Riddoch, 1917). Holmes and Horrax's (1919) patient described a box as a piece of flat cardboard, no matter at what angle he saw it, while stairs appeared as a number of straight lines on the floor. Both Riddoch's patient and Holmes and Horrax's patient were able to appreciate light and shade in both left and right eyes. Holmes and Horrax's patient had a bilateral inferior altitudinal defect while Riddoch's patient was hemianopic in the left half fields. Both patients had received bullet wounds; in the Holmes and Horrax case the bullet entered through the posterior portion of the right angular gyrus and left through the upper part of the corresponding gyrus of the left side. In Riddoch's case the bullet entered in the left frontal region and became lodged near the right occipital pole. Holmes and Horrax's patient had impaired accommodation and convergence when these were required automatically; however, he was able to perform these operations if he was aware of the distance of the object from him.

The effect of a loss of stereoscopic vision is disorientation within a visual environment—the direct cause of this disorientation being the failure to appreciate relative distances or lengths between objects. This results in patients being unable to reach out for or to grasp objects and may also hinder their ability to plan and coordinate effective actions during route finding. Riddoch (1917) describes the problem in his patient thus: "This loss of appreciation of the relative position of things that he sees quite well has been the means of giving him many a fright. Two vehicles approaching each other in the street always seem about to collide. A person who is crossing the street is sure, he thinks, to be run over by a taxi which is really yards away. He used to stand and stare aghast till he found he was registering wrong impressions and that the accidents that he expected to occur every minute did not come off." Holmes and Horrax's (1919) patient experienced similar problems: "When asked to go across the ward he invariably walked into any obstacle in his way even though it was large and prominent and he had observed it before he started; he walked with considerable force into a wall, collided with a large red screen that stood in his path, and when asked to come to the observer, he continued on his course until he bumped heavily into him. When told to sit down on a chair some yards away he proceeded till he knocked it over with his knees, but immediately on touching it he righted it and placed himself correctly on it. On colliding with such obstacles he showed great surprise and considerable discomforture, and generally explained that he had not realized he was so near to them."

However, depth perception need not be impaired so drastically. 3D vision depends on a number of independent cues, both monocular (motion parallax, linear perspective, motion perspective, texture scale gradients etc.) and binocular (stereopsis: i.e., the creation of 3D information from the disparities present between the images present in the left and right eyes). Patients with complete loss of 3D vision seem to lose the ability to use all these different cues. But it is also the case that patients can selectively lose the ability to use only some of the cues. For instance, the loss of stereopsis may occur following brain damage. Here we may distinguish between global stereopsis, involving the integration of information from the two eyes across broad spatial areas, and local stereopsis, involving the ability to distinguish which one of two stereoscopically presented lines is the nearer (Julesz, 1971). It has been reported that patients can have impaired global stereopsis along with intact local stereopsis (Hamsher, 1978), although in other studies both local and global stereopsis have both been shown to be affected (e.g., Danta, Hilton, & O'Boyle, 1978; Ross, 1983). Such impairments in stereopsis tend to be associated with lesions to the right cerebral hemisphere (Ross, 1983). The loss of stereopsis ought to have the same effect on a patient as losing an eye: depth perception should be impaired, but information about the 3D form of objects should still be conveyed by monocular depth cues. Such patients should not be grossly disturbed in their interactions with the environment. Thus the marked problems experienced by Holmes and Horrax's (1919) and by Riddoch's (1917) patients, and the marked change in the phenomenal visual world of these patients, suggest that they suffered ancillary deficits concerning the representation of visual information in 3D space. One question that follows from this conclusion is whether a problem in representing visual information in 3D is itself contingent on an *earlier* processing problem, concerning the elementary dimensions of visual stimuli. The patient of Holmes and Horrax did experience problems matching the 2D length and size of objects, so it is possible that this (presumably) earlier problem generated the patient's 3D impairments. Against this, Holmes (1918) also reported other cases with severe problems in judging the 2D length and size of objects, but who could perceive the 3D forms of objects. Also, Riddoch reported that his patient could match 2D line lengths (at least on some occasions), and that the patient had no agnosic symptoms. These last two pieces of evidence suggest that the problem in representing form in 3D is *separable* from any early problems in processing the elementary dimensions of visual stimuli.

Other interesting disturbances in depth perception, affecting interactions with the environment, have been documented by Brain (1941). These patients had all suffered unilateral lesions, and their impairments were all confined to visual stimuli presented on the side of space contralateral to the site of lesion. One patient had a left upper parietal lesion, one a right upper parietal lesion, and the third had a right posterior temporal lesion. All patients apparently had full visual fields. Unlike the patients of Holmes and Horrax and Riddoch (above),

Brain's patients did not experience difficulty in perceiving objects in 3D; rather, his patients had problems coding the relative distances between objects in the environment. These problems are illustrated by Brain's second patient, who stated that people walking toward him on the left at first seemed a long way away and then "suddenly they are on top of me." A patient in a bed on the opposite side of the ward (about 18 feet away) was judged nearer than a vase of flowers (about 8 feet away) etc. These errors were not made when he judged relative distances on his right hand side. This suggests that, in addition to coding single objects in 3D space, we also code the spatial relations between objects. This coding might take the form of an environmentally based representation in which the spatial relations between objects in the environment are coded. Brain's patients had no apparent difficulties in coding single objects correctly; their difficulty appeared to lie in constructing an appropriate environmental-based representation. Such a selective deficit would occur if the environmental-based representation is constructed at a further processing stage, following the coding of single objects. Since Brain's patients all experienced unilateral problems (confined to the side contralateral to the lesion), his report also suggests that separate environmental-based codings might be constructed in each cerebral hemisphere.

Brain's (1941) patients 2 and 3 were also interesting because their spatial-coding problems apparently varied as a function of the distance of the objects from the patients (see also Whitty & Newcombe, 1973). Patient 2 was poor at estimating the relative distances of objects held within arms' reach. In contrast, Brain notes that patient 3 had problems at judging the relative distance of objects held close-to, but, because the patient did not walk into objects, Brain concludes that he had fewer problems with judging the relative distances between objects which were further away. From this (unfortunately) weak empirical base, Brain proposed that different brain areas may be concerned with coding different aspects of external space. Patient 2's lesion was in the upper part of the parietal lobe. Brain suggested that this brain region was concerned with coding the relative "walking distance" between objects, so that lesions here would only produce difficulties with judging the distances of objects far from the body. Patient 3's lesion was in the posterior part of the temporal lobe. Brain according- ly suggested that this region coded objects in terms of "manual space," an area of space capable of being explored by one or both hands. Thus lesions of the latter brain region would produce selective difficulties in estimating the distances between objects which are close to the body. Following Brain's suggestions, we can speculate that environmental-based codings are nonunitary in nature, and that there may be separate codings for objects according to the type of motor action required to negotiate objects in different parts of space. We are reminded here of the work conducted by Rizzolatti and his colleagues (e.g., Rizzolatti, Gentilucci, & Matelli, 1985; Rizzolatti, Matelli, & Pavesi, 1983) on the effects of lesions to the inferior parietal lobe and to area 8 (the frontal eye fields) in the postarcuate cortex of the monkey. After lesions to the inferior parietal lobe, monkeys display unilateral neglect (a failure to orient) almost exclusively to stimuli presented to the space around the body. Such monkeys do orient to stimuli presented far from the body, and they do make exploratory eye-movements to the contralateral field. After lesions to area 8, monkeys display neglect almost exclusively to stimuli presented far from the animal, and not to close stimuli. Such monkeys also do not make exploratory eye movements to the side contralateral to the lesion. Rizzolatti interprets these findings in terms of a distinction between the coding of "peripersonal" space and that of more distant spatial areas. Again, the suggestion is that different brain areas are concerned with coding different aspects of external space. Rizzolatti's distinction relates solely to the distances of objects from the observer, and not to the types of motor actions required for objects at different distances (as suggested by Brain). Also, the monkeys studied by Rizzolatti and his colleagues manifest unilateral neglect, so they may have different problems to those of Brain's patients (e.g., the monkeys may have problems only in effecting the appropriate orienting responses to stimuli in different parts of space, and they may not be impaired in *coding* the different parts of space per se). Nevertheless, both Rizzolatti's and Brain's work concurs with the argument that different parts of environmental space may be coded in different ways and by different brain regions. From this we would expect patients to be selectively impaired at particular aspects of distance-coding, so that the class of patients with problems in constructing environmentally based representations may need to be further subdivided according to the area of the environment they experience difficulty with.

Impaired Perceptual Integration

We have argued that our ability to recognize our visual environment requires the integration of the various types of form and depth information extracted "early-on" during visual processing (see the earlier section on Early Visual Processing and Depth Perception). It is possible that brain damage could selectively impair this integration process, while leaving other visual processes intact. Indeed, some agnosic patients appear to be impaired in just this way. We have documented the case of one such "integrative agnosic" patient, H.J.A. (Humphreys & Riddoch, in 1987; Riddoch & Humphreys, 1987). H.J.A. shows good discrimination of various dimensions of form, such as orientation and line length (Humphreys & Riddoch, 1984), but he is poor at all tasks which require that form information be integrated in parallel across various regions of the visual field (e.g., Humphreys, Riddoch, & Quinlan, 1985). For instance, he finds overlapping figures difficult to identify because the solution concerning how two lines relate together at one part of the figure can constrain the solution at other parts of the figure (Riddoch & Humphreys, 1987). Such mutual constraints can be most easily effected if the solutions to different parts of the figure are sought in parallel, and this is likely to be the way that the visual system normally carries out perceptual organization (e.g., Ballard, Hinton, & Sejnowski, 1983).

H.J.A. is impaired in this process. Because of this impairment, he typically attempts to identify objects by first identifying their salient local features. For instance, he recognized a pig "because of the curly tail." However, with more complex visual items the identification of individual features is often not sufficient to identify the whole item. A patient described by Pallis (1955) but who appears similar to H.J.A. in many respects, stated of faces that "I can see the eyes, nose and mouth quite clearly but they just don't add up." It is particularly necessary to be able to relate local parts of a figure with its global form in order to recognize and distinguish between items which are visually similar to other items from the same category. For instance, the various local parts of one face are very similar to those of many others (the nose, eyes, ears etc. considered in isolation), as is the general global shape of each face. Face recognition appears to be dependent on some *emergent* property which arises out of the specific combination of global and local features; it is this specific combination that defines the individual's facial identity. Patients who are poor at combining and integrating visual features in a spatially parallel fashion will be especially poor at recognizing stimuli such as faces. Our proposal concerning faces will also generalize to other stimuli from categories with visually similar exemplars, such as buildings. Consequently, such patients should show poor recognition and exploration of the environment because they either fail to identify or incorrectly identify visual landmarks (Humphreys & Riddoch, 1987a). In fact, there is a strong correlation between the inability of brain damaged patients to recognize familiar faces and the occurrence of topographical impairments (e.g., see Hécaen, Ajuriguerra, & Chiarelli, 1957; Meadows, 1974), and in many cases patients with topographical problems seem reliant on using local cues to orient themselves and to identify their surroundings. In both these respects, the pattern of impairment conforms to what we might expect if the patient has difficulty in integrating visual information. A good illustration of the feature-by-feature identification strategy used in such cases is given by Whitty and Newcombe's account of the patient studied by Oldfield (1939; see Whitty & Newcombe, 1973). They state that "he learnt small detailed landmarks for any route rather than making use of larger and more outstanding visual cues. For instance, he recognized a path by a post at one side and three on the other, rather than by a striking church on one side and a graveyard on the other; and he found the hospital by identifying a small street sign rather than recognizing the large building itself, prominent on the skyline. When watched in his perambulations he appeared to get no help from a sense of direction: at each turn there was a pause and the need to recognize some detail of a landmark before he could proceed. Until he learnt such cues he would invariably get lost."

However, the cooccurrence of topographical and face-recognition problems is not inevitable. The patient described by Whiteley and Warrington (1978) reported only a minor difficulty in recognizing people's faces, especially people he had met recently, though he had a marked difficulty in recognizing streets, buildings, and other landmarks. Similarly, a few other patients have been described who appear to have no particular problem with face recognition, despite being profoundly impaired in topographical orientation (De Renzi, Faglioni, & Villa, 1977; Hécaen, Tzortzis, & Rondot, 1980; Paterson & Zangwill, 1945).[2] Nevertheless, in Whiteley and Warrington's (1978) and Paterson and Zangwill's (1945) cases, the patients again seemed to rely on identifying local cues such as street names and house numbers in order to get about. Paterson and Zangwill (1945) state that "His ability to recognize rooms appeared to depend . . . on the presence of conspicuous individual detail. Thus recognition of a room in which he was regularly interviewed was found to depend on a small notice labelled 'A.C. Plugs.' If this notice were concealed recognition at once broke down." Because of the preservation of feature-by-feature identification of scenes by these patients, one might be tempted to conclude that the patients have a residual impairment in perceptual integration (even if they also have additional problems, see the Section on Early Visual Processing). The problem here is that patients with topographical impairments have typically not been tested to check whether they have intact perceptual integration.[3]

Recently we have had the opportunity to test the prosopagnosic patient described by Bauer (1982, 1984; Bauer & Trobe, 1984), who has, in addition, topographical memory problems. For instance, Bauer (1984) reported that "on leaving the clinic he became disoriented and could find his way back only by the concentrated use of verbal directional signs. On returning from breaks in testing, he twice entered the clinic reception area and sat in the chair next to the secretary's desk. Failing to notice that this room was completely unlike the examination room in which he had spent the last several hours, he patiently waited for the secretary, rather than the psychologist, to resume testing." As well as having face and scene recognition problems, this patient also finds some classes of material difficult to identify (e.g., fruits and vegetables), particularly when shown as line drawings. It is also of interest that his object and scene recognition is conducted using a "feature-by-feature" strategy (see Bauer & Trobe, 1984). From these latter problems, one might suspect that this patient too has some residual perceptual impairment. However, he performed quite normally on the tests used to estblish perceptual integration problems in H.J.A. (Humphreys et al., 1985, see above). It remains possible that the patient has some further, subtle deficit in perceptual integration which could be revealed by more extensive testing. For the time being, though, the most reliable conclusion is that patients with problems with perceptual integration, such as H.J.A., do show topographical impairments. Other patients (such as the patient described by

[2]Though Paterson and Zangwill's (1945) patient did initially have face recognition problems, and Whiteley and Warrington's (1978) patient did show relatively poor memory for faces relative to his good memory for other stimuli such as words.

[3]For instance, there is some suspicion of perceptual problems in Whitely and Warrington's (1978) patient. This patient performed below the normal range on the "fragmented letters" test, which is sometimes used to assess the patient's ability to carry out figure-ground operations (Warrington, 1982).

Bauer, 1982, 1984) show some of the ancillary problems that ought to cooccur with topographical impairments if there is poor perceptual integration, but it is also likely that these ancillary problems could stem from other causes.[4] More detailed testing is required on the majority of such patients before any firmer conclusions can be made about the functional problem producing their difficulty in recognizing and exploring the environment.

Two final, and interesting points concerning patients with perceptual integration problems should also be mentioned. One is that, although such patients use feature-by-feature identification strategies to recognize their environment, this does not mean that they only process local features. For instance, H.J.A. has information about the global shapes of objects available (Humphreys et al., 1985); it's just that his global shape descriptions are not elaborated by local feature information (due to his visual integration problem). He also has intact stereopsis (Riddoch & Humphreys, 1987). Thus he can reach appropriately to objects, and he does not bump into them etc. He can negotiate his way around the environment because he has some of the relevent cues to depth, and local and global form. He cannot *recognize* his environment, however, because these cues are not integrated correctly.

The second point is that such patients can also have intact memory for routes, so the patient can draw routes from memory, and can also describe routes from memory with all their attendant detail. Pallis's (1955) patient describes this ability thus: "In my mind's eye I know exactly where places are, what they look like. I can visualise T. . . . . Square without difficulty and the streets that come into it." "I know the order of the shops." "I can draw you a plan of the roads from Cardiff to the Rhondda Valley." "It's when I am out that the trouble starts. My reason tells me that I must be in a certain place and yet I don't realize it. It all has to be worked out each time" (see also Humphreys & Riddoch, 1987a). Thus the perceptual processes involved in constructing appropriate viewpoint-dependent representations of the world can be separated from those mediating long-term memory for objects, scenes, and routes (Riddoch & Humphreys, 1987).

PROBLEMS IN REPRESENTING AND USING SPATIAL INFORMATION IN WORKING MEMORY

According to the model in the introduction, patients may have completely intact perceptual processes and yet still have problems in recognizing and exploring the environment. For instance, patients might be unable to maintain a "spatial map" concerning their current and possibly also their future movements,

---

[4]For instance, a patient whose problem resides solely in accessing stored visual knowledge, and who has intact perceptual processes, could still manifest the effects of visual similarity on his recognition performance. This would occur because visually similar objects have more retrieval cues in common; adding noise to the retrieval process would selectively affect objects from visually similar categories (see Humphreys, Riddoch, & Quinlan, 1988).

or they might be unable to initate action on the basis of information represented in a spatial working memory.

One relatively common phenomenon associated with damage to the right parietal lobe is unilateral visuospatial neglect, where patients fail to initiate action to stimuli presented on the side of space contralateral to the site of the lesion (Brain, 1941; Critchley, 1966; although other brain areas can be implicated, see Kertesz & Dobrowlski, 1981; Heilman & Valenstein, 1972; Watson & Heilman, 1979). Patients with unilateral neglect may experience problems in negotiating their environment because of their difficulty in initiating action to their affected side of space. For instance, McFie, Piercy, and Zangwill (1950) describe a patient with unilateral neglect who complained of losing his way: "twice he missed his house on returning home and had great trouble finding it. He would become lost while driving his lorry along familiar routes and on occasion actually lost himself in his own house, finding himself in the "wrong room" " . . . . . "he thought most of the turnings he missed when he became lost were on the left" (McFie et al., 1950, Case 4).

An even stronger case for a direct relation between topographical disorientation and unilateral neglect has been made by Brain (1941). He documented 3 patients with right occipito-parietal lesions, each with a complete left homonymous hemianopia. These patients did not suffer from a loss of topographical memory or an inability to describe familiar routes but they nevertheless got lost in going from one room to another in their own homes, always making the same error of choosing a right turning instead of a left or a door on the right instead of one on the left. For example, one patient "did not always recognize her room and it was noticed that she could not find her way about the flat. When she set out for the bathroom she arrived at the lavatory, which was a door on the right, and when she tried to go to the lavatory she made a similar mistake, took a turning to the right and got lost again. Yet when she was asked how she would find her way to the bathroom, the door of which was at right angles outside her bedroom door, she replied "I should go first to the cupboard in which my husband keeps his clothes". (This was near the bedroom door). "Then I should open the bedroom door and outside would be where the coats are hung up. I should then look for the electric light switch which is outside the bathroom, because the Borough Council won't allow it inside, and then I should find the bathroom and the bath would be in it." Thus she clearly visualized the landmarks of the correct route. Similarly, when asked to describe how she would find the way from the tube station to her flat she described this in detail correctly and apparently visualized the landmarks, but she consistently said right instead of left for the turnings except on one occasion." This case of Brain's is of interest because the patient appears able to represent spatial information internally. However, when carrying out or visualizing her progress along a route she consistently turned to the right instead of the left, as if she was "drawn" to the right-side stimuli. Recently, Posner and his colleagues (e.g., Posner, Cohen, & Rafal, 1982; Posner, Walker, Friedrich, & Rafal, 1984) have argued that parietal damage produces neglect because patients cannot "disengage" their attention from stimuli on the side of space ipsilateral to the lesion. This problem may be particularly associated with damage to the right parietal lobe because the right hemisphere is dominant for mediating the attentional arousal response (see Heilman & Van den Abel, 1980). The right hemisphere may produce orienting responses (i.e., it may engage attention) to both ipsilateral and contralateral stimuli. The left hemisphere may only produce orienting responses to contralateral (right-side) stimuli. After right brain damage, orienting will only take place to right sided stimuli (contralateral to the left hemisphere). After left brain damage, orienting responses to both sides of space may still be produced by the intact (right) hemisphere. According to Posner's account, Brain's patients may have had difficulty in disengaging attention from right side stimuli in order to initiate actions on the left side of space.

In other neglect patients this problem seems even worse, in that the patients apparently fail even to visualize the left side of space. This is formalized in Bisiach's test requiring patients to describe familiar scenes from memory, where patients omit left sided detail from their descriptions (e.g., Bisiach & Luzzati, 1978). It is not the case that these patients have lost their long-term memory for particular scenes, since, when asked to describe the scene from the opposite perspective, they will then report the previously omitted details (now on the right side of the scene) and omit the previously reported details (now on the left of the scene) (Bisiach & Luzatti, 1978). Also, cuing the patients to attend to the left of their visualized scenes improves the recall of detail from that side (Bisiach, Capitani, Luzzati, & Perani, 1981). This suggests that the patients can construct representations of the whole scene in working memory, although they do not seem to have access to the information on the left side unless their attention is cued to that location. In this case, the problem does not seem confined to initiating actions to left-side stimuli, it generalizes to having any access to the left-side of internal spatial representations. Clearly, the ability to negotiate the environment will be affected in both cases, and tests of memory for routes, and for detail along the routes, are needed to tease apart the different problems suffered by neglect patients.

We have argued that patients with unilateral neglect have difficulty either accessing or initiating action to information represented on one side of an internal spatial working memory. To date, there have been no detailed studies of patients with acquired impairments to the spatial working memory system itself. However, one case of a developmental working memory problem, with whom we are currently working, is relevant. The normal working memory system is thought to have three separate components: a spatial "scratchpad" representation, an articulatory rehearsal system, and a central executive system (e.g., Baddeley, 1981, 1983). The central executive system controls and coordinates the processes conducted upon the information represented in the "slave" spatial and articulatory systems. Thus the process of maintaining one's current position on a route, updating and planning future movements will be a joint function of the spatial sketch pad and the central executive systems. The central executive is thought to have limited processing capacity, so that performance should decrease if the subject is engaged on a concurrent task which demands this limited capacity. In some cases, the capacity of the executive might even be pathologically small, so that engagement on any secondary task dramatically impairs performance. This appears to be true of our patient. Because of this impairment, she is abnormally poor at route learning and planning. The patient, H.S., is able to maintain new visual information. For instance, she shows normal decay functions on tests of pattern span (Wilson, Scott, & Power, 1987) and Posner letter matching (cf.Posner, 1978). However, she is poor at *working out* problems on the basis of this maintained visual information. She finds it difficult to trace around a letter in her mind to indicate which corners face in and which face out (cf. Brooks, 1968), and this task is made effectively impossible for her if she has to signal her responses by a pointing sequence which is incompatible with the spatial form of the letter. Such a pointing task can be presumed to compete for the spatial representation required to maintain the visualized letter, and coordination of the visualized stimulus with the response planning process may normally be a function of the central executive. H.S. seems to be very impaired at coordinating information in this way, suggesting that the executive component of her working memory is impaired. This problem may underlie her poor route learning and planning, and she typically finds her way about solely by identifying familiar landmarks.

DISORDERS OF LONG-TERM TOPOGRAPHICAL MEMORY

Benton (1969) has defined topographical memory failure as the difficulty of retrieving former geographical knowledge and long established visual memories concerning the spatial characteristics of familiar surroundings and routes. Such a retrieval problem might reflect a difficulty in gaining access to intact stored topographical knowledge when patients view the world, or it could reflect loss of this knowledge itself. To separate these possibly different problems, patients must be assessed to see whether they can draw scenes or routes from memory (indicating intact knowledge) even when they fail to access this knowledge when looking at scenes. The possible involvement of earlier perceptual problems must also be excluded.

In respect of these criteria, one of the most careful studies of a patient (A.R.) with a selective problem in retrieving stored topographical knowledge was reported by Hécaen et al. (1980). This study is of interest since it suggests a role for spatial working memory coding in the retrieval of long-term topographical knowledge: Hécaen et al.'s patient showed no impairment on a variety of perceptual tests, and he could discriminate stimuli from categories with visually similiar exemplars. For instance, he "could recognize famous persons from their photographs, readily identify his doctors and nurses and even find one of the examiners in a group photograph taken 20 years ago." Such good performance suggests that his topographical problem was not due to some underlying perceptual impairment. The patient described his difficulty thus: "On a street I have to take note of the landmarks, the immediate impression has disappeared, it's as if the physiogomy of the place has changed. The trees, the houses, I can see them all but I couldn't tell you whether I know them or not. I have them in my memory but when I see them they no longer seem the same, it's no longer the image I have of them, it's different." Hécaen et al. state that there appears to be a lack of correspondence between what the patient perceives and what he remembers. The problem appears particularly acute as regards routes rather than the buildings themselves. There was little difference between A.R.'s performance and two normal control subjects in recognizing photographs of various districts of Paris (even photographs of those districts as they appeared in the 19th century). However, A.R.'s performance was very hesitant, suggesting some residual problem also in recognizing buildings. In these respects, A.R.'s performance seems qualitatively similar to the patient reported by Whiteley and Warrington (1978). This patient also noted that formerly well-known buildings no longer looked as he remembered, although he fell at the bottom of the normal range on a test requiring identification of famous buildings. Most interestingly, Hécaen et al.'s patient showed a good ability to describe known routes from memory. This ability is not present in all patients with topographic impairments (e.g., Paterson & Zangwill, 1945; Whiteley & Warrington, 1978), suggesting that, in these patients, stored topographic knowledge is disrupted. Hécaen's case, however, indicates that patients can have a problem in *retrieving* topographic knowledge, along with apparently intact perceptual processes and intact stored knowledge.

In other tests conducted with A.R., Hécaen et al. showed that he was very poor at learning a route through a maze (cf. Milner, 1965) and at following a route in which the landmarks could not be verbalized. He was much better at following a route where the landmarks could be verbalized. These latter findings indicate that A.R.'s problem was pronounced even when he had only to encode and find his way between the locations of landmarks—visual recognition of the landmarks and the route was not required. The route-following task of Hécaen et al. seems to demand spatial working memory rather than long-term topographical memory, so A.R.'s problem suggests a deficit in encoding location information in spatial working memory. It could be that the representation mediating access to stored knowledge about scenes involves the tempory coding of the spatial relations between visual landmarks.[5] Further, this coding of the spatial relations between landmarks could contribute to sensing the familiarity of a scene

---

[5]A.R. also had problems learning both verbal and non-verbal paired associates. It could be that his impairment included the temporary coding of new relations, in addition to the spatial locations of landmarks.

or even a building—hence A.R.'s feeling of unfamiliarity with scenes. Also, because coding the spatial relations between landmarks will be less important for recognizing buildings than for recognizing scenes and routes, we can account for A.R.'s lesser problem in identifying buildings. If A.R. did have a spatial working memory deficit, then it seems to be different from that of H.S. (see the Section on Representing and using Spatial Information in Working Memory). H.S. is able to code the spatial relations between objects, her problem is in using the representation so coded to coordinate her current and future actions along a route. We identify H.S.'s problem with the executive component of the working memory system, and A.R.'s with the spatial scratchpad.

The patient described by De Renzi et al. (1977) also bears some similarities to A.R.. De Renzi's patient had suffered a right temporal-parietal lesion. As a result of this, "she showed spatial disorientation in her own apartment, where she had been living for many years, and she lost her bearings whenever she went out alone." The patient had no difficulties with object or face recognition. She performed normally on some fairly simple tests of visual perception (copying, orientation discrimination), and she showed good verbal memory. Like A.R., she also experienced great difficulties in learning a route through a maze. However, there are also some interesting contrasts with A.R., in that De Renzi's patient apparently had an intact spatial working memory. She showed good memory for the positions of visual stimuli, and good performance on Corsi's blocks (where the subject must point to those of a set of cubes tapped by an examiner). It remains possible that, like our own patient H.S., De Renzi's patient has some problem with executive working memory functions, which selectively prohibit her learning new routes (in the maze learning task). To assess this, we need to have information about the processing load imposed in the maze learning task, and whether their patient could succeed on a maze with fewer turns etc.. Alternatively, this patient appears to have a specific anterograde amnesia for route-learning. Unfortunely, insufficient information is given to learn much about the nature of this amnesia. For instance, we do not know whether the patient can learn new routes but does not have access to this knowledge (cf. Weiskrantz, 1980). We also do not know the extent to which the patient had retrograde amnesia for previously learned routes. Thus, although the case does suggest that patients might have a specific problem in storing, and possibly gaining access to, topographical knowledge, this argument is far from proven.

LESION SITES

We began this chapter with a critique of accounts that attribute all topographic impairments to a single cause, and which fail to relate topographical impairments to the processes normally involved in the recognition and the exploration of the environment. Accordingly, we sketched a framework of the processes normally involved in recognizing and exploring the environment. This framework suggests that topographic impairments could arise in a number of different ways—from poor registration and coding of visual information, to impaired long-term memory of scenes. To some extent the distinctions we are making map onto those in the field of object recognition, where distinctions can be drawn between patients whose object agnosia is due to a perceptual disturbance and patients whose problems are due to an inability to associate new input with stored knowledge (Humphreys & Riddoch, 1987b). Our review of the literature on topographical impairments indicates that patients can be classified on the basis of the normal framework. The broad distinctions concern disorders of perception, disorders of spatial working memory, and disorders of long-term retrieval—although further subdivisions exist within each of these broad areas. Given these distinctions, it also follows that topographical impairments of different varieties could result from lesions to any of a number of different brain regions. Early problems in shape discrimination could stem from multiple, small occipital lesions (Campion, 1987). Problems in stereopsis are associated with lesions to the right hemisphere (Ross, 1983), although lesions to area V2 in the prestriate cortex may also be important in the loss of stereopsis (see Humphreys & Riddoch, 1987). The patient described by Holmes and Horrax (1919), with apparently complete loss of 3D vision, had bilateral lesions to both angular gyri—though the similar patient described by Riddoch (1917) had only a left homonymous hemianopia and, presumably, a unilateral lesion of the right occipital lobe. Problems of perceptual integration have been found in cases with bilateral lesions in the occipital-temporal region, while unilateral neglect, and any related spatial disorientations, is associated with right parietal lesions. Those few patients with apparently selective problems in the retrieval of long term topographic knowledge have also generally had right hemisphere damage. De Renzi et al.'s (1977) patient suffered damage to the right temporal lobe, and Hécaen et al.'s patient had damage to the right occipital lobe. In two other patients, who, like De Renzi's patient, have problems in learning new routes, right hemisphere involvement has also been documented (though both suffered bilateral occipital lesions; Bauer, 1982; Bauer & Trobe 1984; Ross, 1980).[6] Whitely and Warrington's (1978) patient had no apparent neurological abnormalities. Hécaen et al. (1980) also noted the relation between their patient, who had problems retaining the spatial locations of landmarks, and animal work on spatial working memory. Lesions of the hippocampus or its pathways impair spatial memory in the rat (Olton, 1977, 1978), and activity in hippocampal cells is observed during the performance of conditioned spatial learning tasks (O'Keefe & Conway, 1978). Such work suggests that the hippocampus is

---

[6]Neither of these patients have been discussed in the section dealing with long-term memory deficits because their problems were not confined to route learning but included problems with faces, amongst other things.

particularly important in coding spatial information, and may be implicated in spatial working memory. Although hippocampal damage was not recorded in their patient, Hécaen et al. note that such damage would be consistent with damage in the region of the posterior cerebral artery.

Scanning across patients, there is a general tendency for an association between right hemisphere lesions and the topographical impairments we have documented. We can also distinguish between patients with spatial disorientation, who tend to have parietal lesions, and patients with poor recognition of the environment, who tend to have occipito-temporal lesions. The latter distinctions fit with the idea of a occipito-parietal pathway concerned with the representation of space (knowing *where* objects are) and an occipito-temporal pathway concerned with visual recognition (knowing *what* objects are; see Ungerleider, 1985). In general, our review indicates the heterogeneity of both the functional deficits and lesion sites found in patients with topographical impairments. There is no reason to think that the complex behaviors involved in exploring and recognizing the environment should be affected in any single way by brain damage. We suggest that it is only by specifying the nature of various functional deficits that we will come to understand the topographical problems experienced by patients and how these problems relate to normal behavior.

ACKNOWLEDGMENTS

The work reported in this chapter was supported by a grant from the MRC to both authors, and by a grant from the ESRC to the second author.

REFERENCES

Adler, A. (1944). Disintegration and restoration of optic recognition in visual agnosia. *Archives of Neurology and Psychiatry, 51,* 243–259.

Adler, A. (1950). Course and outcome of visual agnosia. *Journal of Nervous and Mental Diseases, 111,* 41–51.

Anderson, J. R. (1978). Arguments concerning representations for mental imagery. *Psychological Review, 85,* 249–277.

Baddeley, A. D. (1981). The concept of working memory: A view of its current state and probable future development. *Cognition, 10,* 17–23.

Baddeley, A. D. (1983). Working memory. *Philosophical Transactions of the Royal Society, B302,* 311–324.

Balint, R. (1909). Die seelenlahmung des "Schauens", *Mtschr. fur Psych. und Neur., 1,* 51–81.

Ballard, D. H., Hinton, G. E., & Sejnowski, T. J. (1983). Parallel vision computation. *Nature, 306,* 21–26.

Bauer, R. M. (1982). Visual hypoemotionality as a symptom of visual-limbic disconnection in man. *Archives of Neurology, 39*, 702–707.

Bauer, R. M. (1984). Autonomic recognition of names and faces in prosopagnosia: A neuropsychological application of the guilty knowledge test. *Neuropsychologia, 22*, 457–469.

Bauer, R. M., & Trobe, J. T. (1984). Visual memory and perceptual impairments in prosopagnosia. *Journal of Clinical Neuro-opthalmology, 4*, 39–46.

Bay, E. (1950). Agnosie und functionswandel. *Monogr. Gesamtgeb. Neurol. Psychiatr., 73*, 1–94.

Bay, E. (1953). Disturbances of visual perception and their examination. *Brain, 76*, 515–551.

Benson, D. F., & Greenberg, J. P. (1969). Visual form agnosia: Specific deficit in visual recognition. *Archives of Neurology, 20*, 82–89.

Benton, A. L. (1969). Disorders of spatial orientation. In J. P. Vinken & G. N. Bruyn (Eds.), *Handbook of clinical neurology III*. Amsterdam: North Holland.

Bisiach, E., & Luzzatti, C. (1978). Unilateral neglect for representational space. *Cortex, 14*, 129–133.

Bisiach, E., Capitani, E., Luzzatti, C., & Perani, D. (1981). Brain and conscious representation of outside reality. *Neuropsychologia, 19*, 543–551.

Bodis-Wollner, I. (1972). Visual acuity and contrast sensitivity in patients with cerebral lesions. *Science, 178* 769–771.

Bodis-Wollner, I. (1976). Vulnerability of spatial frequency channels in cerebral lesions. *Nature, 261*, 309–311.

Brain, R. (1941). Visual disorientation with special reference to lesions of the right hemisphere. *Brain, 64*, 244–272.

Brooks, L. R. (1968). Spatial and verbal components of the act of recall. *Canadian Journal of Psychology, 22*, 349–368.

Campion, J. (1987). Apperceptive agnosia: The specification of constructs and their use. In G. W. Humphreys & M. J. Riddoch (Eds.), *Visual object processing: A cognitive neurosychological approach*. Hillsdale, NJ: Lawrence Erlbaum Associates.

Campion, J., & Latto, R. (1985). Apperceptive agnosia due to carbon monoxide poisoning. An interpretation based on critical band masking from disseminated lesions. *Behavioral Brain Science, 15*, 227–240.

Critchley, M. (1966). *The parietal lobes*, New York: Hafner.

Danta, G., Hilton, R. C., & O'Boyle, D. J. (1978). Hemisphere function and binocular depth perception. *Brain, 101*, 569–589.

De Renzi, E., Faglioni, P., & Villa, P. (1977). Topographical amnesia. *Journal of Neurology, Neurosurgery and Psychiatry, 40*, 498–505.

Hamsher, K. de S. (1978). Stereopsis and unilateral brain disease. *Invest. Opthalmol. Visual Sciences, 17*, 336–342

Hécaen, H., & de Ajuriaguerra, J. (1954). Balint's syndrome (Psychic paralysis of visual fixation and its minor forms). *Brain, 77*, 373–400.

Hécaen, H., de Ajuriaguerra, J., David, M., Rouques, L., & Dell, R. (1950). Paralysie psychique du regard de Balint au cours de l'evolution d'une leuco-encephalite type Balo. *Rev Neurol, 83,* 81–104.

Hécaen, H., Angelerques, R., Bernhard, C., & Chiarelli, J. (1957). Essai de distinction des modalitees cliniques de l'agnosie des physionomies. *Rev. Neurol., 96,* 125–144.

Hécaen, H., Penfield, W., Bertrand, C., & Malmo, R. (1956). The syndrome of apractognosia due to lesions of the minor cerebral hemishere. *Archives of Neurology, Neurosurgery and Psychiatry, 75,* 400–434.

Hécaen, H., Tzortzis C., & Rondot, P. (1980). Loss of topographical memory with learning deficits. *Cortex, 16,* 525–542.

Heilman, K., & Valenstein, E. (1972). Frontal lobe neglect in man. *Neurology, 22,* 660–664.

Heilman, K., & Van den Abel, T. (1980). Right hemisphere dominance for attention: The mechanism underlying hemisphereic asymmetries of attention (neglect). *Neurology, 30,* 327–330.

Holmes, G. (1918). Disturbances of visual orientation. *British Journal of Opthalmology, 2,* 449–468, 506–516.

Holmes, G. (1919). Disturbances of visual space perception. *British Medical Journal, 2,* 230–233.

Holmes, G., & Horrax, G. (1919). Disturbances of spatial orientation and visual attention with loss of stereoscopic vision. *Archives of Neurology and Psychiatry, 1,* 385–407.

Humphreys, G. W., & Riddoch, M. J. (1984). Routes to object constancy: Implications from neurological impairments of object constancy. *Quarterly Journal of Experimental Psychology, 36A,* 385–415.

Humphreys, G. W., & Riddoch, M. J. (1987a). *To see but not to see: A case of visual agnosia.* Hillsdale, NJ: Lawrence Erlbaum Associates.

Humphreys, G. W., & Riddoch, M. J. (1987b). The fractionation of visual agnosia. In G. W. Humphreys & M. J. Riddoch (Eds.), *Visual object processing: A cognitive neuropsychological approach.* Hillsdale, NJ: Lawrence Erlbaum Associates.

Humphreys, G. W., Riddoch, M. J., & Quinlan, P. T. (1985). Interactive processes in visual organisation: Evidence from visual agnosia. In M. I. Posner & O. S. M. Marin (Eds.), *Attention and Performance XI.* Hillsdale, NJ: Lawrence Erlbaum Associates.

Humphreys, G. W., Riddoch, M. J., & Quinlan, P. T. (1988). Cascade processes in picture identification: Data and implications. *Cognitive Neuropsychology, 5,* 67–103.

Jackson, J. H. (1876). Case of a large cerebral tumour without optic neuritis and with left hemiplegia and imperception. In *Selected Writings, 2,* 146–152, London: Taylor. (Reprinted 1932).

Julesz, B. (1971). *Foundations of cyclopean perception.* Chicago, IL: University of Chicago Press.

Kertesz, A., & Dobrowolski, S. (1981). Right hemisphere deficits, lesion size and location. *Journal of Clinical Neuropsychology, 3,* 283–299.

Kosslyn, S. M. (1980). *Image and mind*. Cambridge, MA: Havard University Press.

Landis, T., Cummings, J. L., Benson, D. F., & Palmer, E. P. (1986). Loss of topographic Familiarity. *Archives of Neurology, 43*, 132–136.

Luria, A. R., Pravdina-Vinarskaya, E. N., & Yarbus, A. L. (1963). Disorders of ocular movement in a case of simultanagnosia. *Brain, 86*, 219–228.

McFie, J., Piercy, M. F., & Zangwill, O. L. (1950). Visual spatial agnosia associated with lesions of the right cerebral hemisphere. *Brain, 73*, 167–190.

Marr, D. (1982). *Vision*. San Francisco: W.H. Freeman.

Meadows, J. C. (1974). Disturbed perception of colours associated with localised cerebral lesions. *Brain, 97*, 615–632.

Michel, F., Jeannerod, M., & Devic, M. (1965). Trouble de l'orientation visuelle dans les trois dimensions de l'espace (a propos d'un cas anatomique), *Cortex, 1*, 441–446.

Milner, B. (1965). Visually-guided maze learning in man: Effects of bilateral frontal and unilateral cerebral lesions. *Neuropsychologia, 3*, 317–338.

O'Keefe J., & Conway, D. H. (1978). Hippocampal place units in the freely moving rat: Why do they fire, where they fire? *Experimental Brain Research, 31*, 573–590.

Olton, D. S. (1977). Spatial memory. *Scientific American, 236*, 82–99.

Olton, D. S. (1978). The function of septo-hippocampal connections in spatially organized behaviour. In *Function of the Septo-hippocampal System*, Ciba Foundation Symposium, Elsevier-Excerpta Medica, North Holland: Amsterdam.

Pallis, C. A. (1955). Impaired identification of faces and places with agnosia for colours. *Journal of Neurology, Neurosurgery and Psychiatry, 18*, 218–224.

Paterson, A., & Zangwill, O. L. (1945). A case of topographical disorientation associated with a unilateral cerebral lesion. *Brain, 68*, 188–211.

Pick, A. (1898). Ueber storungen der tienfenlocalisation in folge cereberaler Herderkrankung. In *Beitrage zur pathologie und pathologischen Anatomie des entralnervensystems, mit Bemerkungen zur normalen Anatomie desselben*, Berlin: Karger.

Posner, M. A. (1978). *Chronometric explorations of mind*. Hillsdale, NJ: Lawrence Erlbaum Associates.

Posner, M. I., Cohen, Y., & Rafal, R. D. (1982). Neural systems control of spatial orienting. *Philosophical Transactions of the Royal Society, B298*, 187–198.

Posner, M. I., Walker, J., Friedrich, F. J., & Rafal, R. D. (1984). Effects of parietal injury on covert orienting of visual attention. *Journal of Neuroscience, 4*, 1863–1874.

Pylyshen, Z. W. (1981). The imagery debate: Analogue media versus tacit knowledge. *Psychological Bulletin, 87*, 16–45.

Ratcliff, G., & Ross, J. E. (1981). Visual perception and perceptual disorders. *British Medical Bulletin, 37*, 181–186.

Riddoch, G. (1917). Dissociation of visual perception due to occipital injuries, with especial reference to appreciation of movements. *Brain, 40*, 15–57.

Riddoch, G. (1935). Visual disorientation in homonymous half-fields. *Brain, 58*, 376–382.

Riddoch, M. J., & Humphreys, G. W. (1987). A case of integrative agnosia. *Brain, 110,* 1431–1462.

Rizzolatti, G., Matelli, M., & Pavesi, G. (1983). Deficits in attention and movement following removal of the postarcuate (area 6) and prearcuate (area 8) cortex in macaque monkey. *Brain, 106,* 655–673.

Rizzolatti, G., Gentilucci, M., & Matelli, M. (1985). Selective spatial attention: One centre, one circuit or many circuits? In M. I. Posner & O. S. M. Marin (Eds.), *Attention and performance XI.* Hillsdale, NJ: Lawrence Erlbaum Associates.

Ross, E. D. (1980). Sensory-specific and fractional disorders of recent memory in man: I. Isolated loss of recent visual memory. *Archives of Neurology, 1980,* 193–200.

Ross, J. E. (1983). Disturbance of stereoscopic vision in patients with unilateral stroke. *Behavioral Brain Research, 7,* 99–112.

Ungerleider, L. G. (1985). The corticocortical pathways for object recognition and spatial perception. In C. Chagas (Ed.), *Pattern Recognition Mechanisms.* Pontificiae Acadamiae Scientiarum Scripta Varia.

Watson, R. T., & Heilman, K. M. (1979). Thalamic neglect. *Neurology, 29,* 290–294.

Warrington, E. K. (1982). Neuropsychological studies of object recognition. *Philosophical Transactions of the Royal Society, B298,* 15–33.

Weiskrantz, L. (1980). Varieties of residual experience. *Quarterly Journal of Experimental Psychology, 32,* 365–386.

Whiteley, A. M., & Warrington, E. K. (1978). Selective impairment of topographical memory: A single case study. *Journal of Neurology, Neurosurgery and Psychiatry, 41,* 575–578.

Whitty, C. W. M., & Newcombe, F. (1973). R. C. Oldfield's study of visual and topographic disturbances in a right occipito-parietal lesion of 30 years duration. *Neuropsychologia, 11,* 471–475.

Wilson, J. T. L., Scott, J. H., & Power, K. G. (1987). Developmental differences in the span of visual memory for pattern. *British Journal of Developmental Psychology, 5,* 249–255.

Zihl, J., Von Cramon, D., & Mai, N. (1983). Selective disturbance of movement vision after bilateral brain damage. *Brain, 106,* 313–340.

5

Visuomotor Ataxia

Pierre Rondot

Elective defects in grasping objects under visual control can occur even in the absence of paralysis or defects in visual acuity. The origin of this mysterious difficulty has long stimulated the curiosity of clinical practioners. As early as 1888, Badal, ophtalmologist at Bordeaux, reported the case of a 31-year-old woman who had eclampsia and hemorrhage of the afterbirth followed by curious visual difficulties, although there was a total absence of paralysis. "She experienced difficulty trying to find objects which she needed and was awkward in grasping objects which were presented to her. She groped along. . . . She had completely lost the ability to find her way even in surroundings she knew well. . . ." In this patient, who had inferior vertical hemianopsia, difficulty in grasping objects under visual control was combined with alexia with agraphia and loss of topographical memory, without doubt the first such case ever reported. Badal insisted on the fact that "loss of the sense of space" (inability to locate objects) concerned not only vision, but also hearing, thus rendering the patient unable to situate the source of a noise she had just heard either in front of or behind her. The lesion responsible was evidently bilateral occipital ischemia spreading to the parieto occipital borders which accounts for the loss of topographical memory (Hecaen, Tzortzis, & Rondot, 1980). But the syndrome was very complex and the difficulty in grasping, although clearly individualized by Badal, was not specifically mentioned and was included as part of the loss of sense of space. Difficulty in depth perception (Tiefenlocalization) was invoked by Pick (1898) several years after to explain difficulties in grasping in two patients, one of whom was aphasic and demented. Van Valkenburg (1908) referring to Pick, Anton, and Westphall, also reported poor localization of objects in space, along with problems in grasping which made it so difficult for the patient to evaluate distances that he walked with his arms held out like a blind person.

In an extremely complicated case, Balint masterfully isolated what he called "optic ataxia" associated with oculomotor paralysis and neglect of the space to the left (though the term had yet to be invented). Comparing the difficulty experienced by his patient in seizing objects with the incoordination of the tabetic deprived of the information furnished by deep sensation, Balint attributed the optic ataxia to "sensory incoordination."

Six injured war veterans gave Smith and Holmes (1916) and later Holmes (1918) the opportunity to reexamine this question on another level. For Holmes, "visual orientation," which provides the ability to situate objects in space, depends on two factors: the related points stimulated on the retina and the proprioceptive information received from the ocular and cervical muscles. In the problem of visual orientation "it is evident that both factors were involved, or more correctly, their combination which represents the physiological correlate of the psychological judgment, on which spatial localization depends". Here it is no longer a question of visual incoordination and Holmes makes no allusion to the interpretation of Balint.

He rather invoked a dysfunction of the associative centers, thus situating the problem on a more sophisticated level than in the hypothesis of Balint. It should be noted in all these cases that the difficulty in grasping was never isolated. In particular, Holmes' wounded men had great difficulty in correctly locating an object by sight and walked only with great care, often bumping into obstacles. The cerebral lesions were bilateral. The same thing was noted in the observations reported by Hecaen et al. (1950, 1954). However, the optic ataxia was, in one case, confined to the left hand.

An observation of Riddoch (1935) had already shown that the disorder in prehension could be localized to one visual half-field and similar results were obtained by Stenvers (1961).

Thus, optic ataxia has progressively been singled out from among the other accompanying signs which are due to the lesion of surrounding tissue. Furthermore, it sometimes appears as a localized disorder affecting only one hand in a single visual field which may or may not be homologous to the hand (Table 1). The five case reported by Rondot, de Recondo, and Ribadeau Dumas (1977) as three new cases (Table 2) were also localized and based on this fragmentary nature, they proposed a classification according to the supposed site of the lesion. They likewise suggested a process of visuomotor disconnection as the origin of certain varieties of optic ataxia. Indeed, the experimental work of Brinkman, and Kuypers (1973) had previously corroborated the possible role of disconnection.

That is only one of the processes implicated in disorders of prehension under visual control. Other mechanisms can be involved, linked to the integration of different sensory data, Hyvärinen and Poranen (1974), Mountcastle et al. (1975) have demonstrated the presence of neurons in area 7 that are stimulated by objects placed in the space immediately surrounding the person. It is conceivable that a lesion on this level can lead to important disorders in grasping. Thus, it would seem to us to be just as naive to deny the existence of a visuomotor disconnection as it would be to reject the idea of a disorder of sensory integration in accounting for certain visuo-motor ataxias.

TABLE 1
Visuomotor Ataxia (V.M.A.) Localization of Lesions

Authors		Sex	V.M.A. Eye field	V.M.A. Limbs	Site of lesion	Etiology
Pick, 1898		M	R	R + L	bilat.inf.pariet.	Vascular
Balint, 1908		M	R + L	R + L	bilat.18–19 areas angular gyrus	Vascular
Holmes, 1918	2	M	L	?	R.occ+L.angular gyrus	Gunshot wound
	5	M	R	?	R.angular gyrus + L.supramarginalis gyrus	
Riddoch, 1935		M	R	?	L. parietal	Glioblastoma
Hecaen et al. 1950		M	?	R	L.R. multiple	Leuco-Encephalitis
Hecaen, de Ajuriaguerra 1954	3	F	R + L	R + L	bilat.pariet.occ.	Astrocytoma
	4	M	?	L	bilat.pariet.occ.	Metastasis + Vascular
Michel et al. 1965		M	R + L	?	bilat.pariet.occ.	Vascular
Glonning, 1968	1, 2, 4	F, F, M	?	?	bilat.pariet.occ.	Glioblastoma
	5	M	?	?	posterior pariet.	Metastasis
	3	M	?	?	L. parieto-occ. + R. parietal	Vascular
Ferro et al., 1983		F	L	R	bilat.cuneus,pre-cuneus, post.part of the sup.pariet gyrus +post.third of the splenium	Vascular

As is the case for many other cerebral syndromes, optic ataxia has benefitted from the progress in cerebral imagery. Thanks to CT-scans among others, many more cases have been detected, permitting a better comparison between clinical symptoms and the site of the lesion.

The term optic ataxia makes the disorder sound too peripheral; I rather prefer that of visuomotor ataxia (VMA) the term that is used hereafter in this report.

VISUOMOTOR ATAXIA—CLINICAL SYNDROME

Patients often complain specifically about it; they are awkward when seizing objects, often overreaching the goal, less frequently underreaching it. When eating, patient will stick his fork beside the food. When the disorder is severe, the problem exists even with previous ocular fixation. But often, the disorder is more moderate and only shows up if one does not use the facility provided by ocular fixation to ensure proper grasp of an object. It is thus necessary to explore the ability to grasp in the peripheral visual fields by asking the patient to keep his gaze fixed on one point.

Certain rigorous conditions must be fulfilled before the disorder in manual seizure can be interpreted as VMA. On the sensory side, that is correct apprehension of the object by the eyes, as well as on the motor side, that is execution of the movement, no obstacle to the reception of the object nor to the accomplishment of the movement should be present.

The correct reception of visual information by the occipital cortex assumes that the retina be intact, thus normal visual acuity, and no amputation of the visual field in the sector explored. It is also important that there be no diplopia and that the object be recognized in the absence of any visual agnosia.

The accomplishment of the gesture should not be hindered by paralysis nor modified by an cerebellar syndrome which might give dysmetria. It is necessary to exclude any ideational or ideomotor apraxia as well as deep sensory disorders, which might otherwise cause ataxia that could be mistaken for VMA. In presence of such disorders, only difficulties in seizing objects in a single visual half-field can be retained on the condition that the same hand be able to grasp without difficulty an object in the other half-field.

Such rigorous conditions account for the relative rarity of VMA or at least of the cases which can be diagnosed with certainly.

Method of Examination

After the preceding conditions have been satisfied, the patient must fixate a point on the median line in front of him and maintain this fixed gaze throughout the examination. An object is then presented at various distances and heights, successively in the right visual field and then in the left. It is preferable that the object be held by an observer situated behind the patient so that the latter cannot use the direction of the arm of the observer as an aid. Then, in each of these positions, the patient is required to grasp the object with his right hand and then with his left, in each of the half-fields. If the disorder is pronounced, this examination can be completed after exploring the two half-fields with pre-hensions of objects in the central visual field. The different trials are recorded and noted as: (1) Normal prehension, (2) Faulty grasp subsequently corrected, (3) Grasp impossible.

In order to make this examination more sensitive and to better explore the posture of the hand during grasping, Tzavaras and Masure (1976) have adapted for human use the test used by Haaxma and Kuypers (1975) in monkeys. A groove leading to a central depression in a disk containing the object to be grasped is hollowed out along the disk's diameter. The object is seized between the thumb and the index finger which have been previously introduced into the groove, whose orientation is changed during the test in order to cause the hand to approach the object along varying axes. The position of the fingers is thus easy to observe.

It is also possible to explore the role of visual information concerning the hand which is seizing the object by studying prehension in the same patient in conditions of "open loop or closed loop" (Tzavaras and Masure, 1976). The apparatus allows the patient to grasp a given object by looking at its mirror image of the open loop condition, while in the closed loop condition the image of the object is seen through a see-through mirror which allows the eye to follow the hand.

Clinical Types

From the results of such an examination, the VMA's can be classified as unilateral or bilateral depending upon whether the disorder is localized in one visual half-field or in both (Figure 1). When the disorder in grasping affects the hand on the same side as the affected half-field, the VMA is called direct. It is called crossed if it is the hand opposite the affected visual half-field which seizes poorly. If both hands are affected in the same visual field, the ataxia is called mixed. Crossed prehension alone can be affected on both sides, giving what is called bilateral crossed VMA.

Functional Tests

Should a distinction be made between VMA's with lesions in the right and left hemispheres? Patients with lesions on the left differ from those with lesions on the right, according to the results of the test by Haaxma and Kuypers

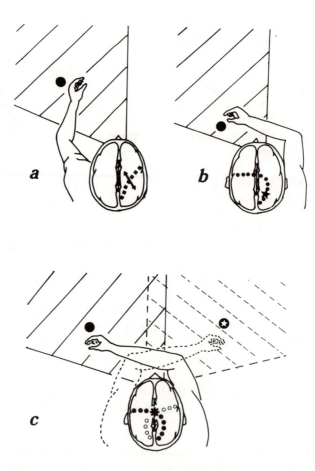

FIGURE 1 (a) unilateral direct visuomotor ataxia; this is localized to one hand in the homonymous field. (b) unilateral crossed visuomotor ataxia; this is localized to one hand in the visual field of the opposite side. (c) bilateral crossed visuomotor ataxia; this affects each hand in opposite visual fields. (From *Brain*, 1977, *100*, 355–376)

(Tzavaras & Masure, 1976). During such testing, lesions in the right hemisphere responsible for difficulties in seizing an object in the left visual field did not disturb the posture of the hand and fingers in the approach of the target. On the other hand, in the case of lesions in the left hemisphere, the right hand not only commits errors in grasping, but also places its fingers incorrectly when seizing the object. The final adjustment of the gesture is faulty, thus distinguishing these patients from those with right-side lesions. This disorder was interpreted as being apraxic by Tzavaras and Masure (1976).

This test is useful because it shows whether the VMA is aggravated in the open loop condition, that is to say, in the absence of visual information. In such a case, this test has the advantage of sensitizing the usual clinical examination. It can also specify if, on the contrary, (and we have had the opportunity to observe this once), the sight of the hand worsens performances. In such a case, it demonstrates poor interpretation of incoming visual information, a factor, which can aggravate, if not cause, VMA.

In the great majority of the preceding cases, the lesions were bilateral, thus corresponding to Balint's syndrome, implicating bi-hemispheric involvement. Nevertheless, in all these observations one area was consistently involved, that of the parieto-occipital junction. This zone corresponds to the confluence of the middle and posterior cerebral vascular territories, one of the fragile zones in the case of systemic circulatory insufficiency. Although a frontal lesion is sometimes mentioned (Hécaen et al., 1950; Hécaen & de Ajuriaguerra, 1954), it is only occasional and never occurs by itself. We return to this point later on.

The various anatomical examinations do not give any very precise data about the topography of the lesions responsible for VMA. However, in the case of Ferro, Bravo-Marques, Castro-Caldas, and Lobo Antunes (1983), in addition to crossed and direct VMA in the right half-space, there was a difficulty in grasping in the left half-space using the right hand. Now, since the right hemisphere was undamaged, the disorder in seizure of objects presented in the left half-space with the right hand could perhaps be attributed to a lesion of the corpus callosum, that is defective transfer of information from the right occipital cortex to the left motor areas.

In the five cases we reported in 1977 (Rondot et al., 1977), two were due to a very circumscribed lesion: surgical incision in the anterior part of the area 19, at the parieto-occipital junction, which was the approach used for the removal of an intraventricular tumor in one case (case 3) and for the ablation of an arterial anevrysm in the other (case 2). These two procedures were not followed by any symptoms other than VMA, which allowed us to conclude that the actual cerebral lesion was limited to the site of incision. In one case, VMA was direct and crossed, and in the other, it was direct.

Thus, a relatively isolated and unilateral lesion at the parieto-occipital junction is capable of provoking visuomotor incoordination in the contro-lateral visual field, either in one or both hands. In both these cases we find the same parieto-occipital topography of the lesion, which was common to the preceeding clinical observations.

EXPERIMENTAL DATA

Correct visuomotor coordination implies that the systems responsible for gathering visual and proprioceptive information, then for integrating it and transmitting it to the corresponding motor area, are all functioning properly. Thus, schematically, three phases can be distinguished during which a dysfunction of these systems can provoke VMA.

— an initial period in which visual and proprioceptive information is gathered;
— a phase of data integration;
— the transfer of data from the associative areas to the motor centers.

1. Information Gathering.   The information required for good visuomotor coordination comes from varied sources: proprioceptive input from the limbs, the eye muscles, the muscles, the tendons, and the joints of the cervical regions.

Visual experience is necessary for the development of good visuomotor coordination: A kitten kept in darkness does not develop righting reactions when approaching a plane (Hein, 1972). In order to grasp an object, it needs to have the visual experience of its front paws. One does not find examples of comparable sensory deprivation in humans which could cause VMA. Moreover, it is mainly during the development of coordination that visual experience intervenes the most. Proprioception from the limbs seems sufficient in adults to overcome lack of visual input. However, if the visual information is false, which sometimes happens in the case of oculomotor paralysis, then grasping could be disturbed.

Besides the visual experience of the limbs, good motor coordination also requires proprioceptive information concerning the ocular muscles, as well as the cervical muscles and tendons. After section of the ophthalmic branch of the trigeminal nerve, which carries proprioceptive information, kittens raised in darkness and then exposed to the light develop normal guiding behavior much later than to normal kittens. Here again ocular proprioception is essential for acquiring types of behavior which are guided by vision. In adults, it can easily be made up for by other sources of information. The proprioception of the ocular muscles is essentially necessary during the development of the guidance function of vision, later, it can be replaced by experience or by input from other sources. If either of these becomes defective, however, motor incoordination could result. That is what comes out of the studies done on commisurotomized monkeys with section of the optic chiasma and patches over one eye (Downer, 1959; Lund, Downer, & Lumley, 1970); Lehman, 1968; Gazzaniga, 1966): the monkey feels around with the hand ipsilateral to the open eye; he is awkward, imprecise, spreading out his hand fan-shaped without ever trying to use the opposition of thumb and index finger.

2. Integration of Sensory Data.   The parietal areas are responsible for integrating visual messages and proprioceptive information, thus permitting coordinated command of the gesture towards the target. Hyvarinen and Poranen (1974) located a large population of neurons in area 7, activated by both visual fixation and prehension. However, these authors could not determine if this activation was not exclusively related to ocular movements. In the same zone, area 7, Mountcastle et al. (1975, 1981) recognized neurons "functionally related to the coordination of the visual fixation of an arm-projection towards desired objects in immediate extrapersonal space." If the object was placed outside manual reach, the neurons were no longer stimulated.

Actually, the neurons in area 7, can be divided into several groups (Lynch, Mountcastle, Talbot, & Yin, 1977) of which only one is not related to ocular movements but rather to animal-relevant stimuli of weak intensity in the contralateral field. The ablation of areas 5 and 7 (Lamotte & Acuna, 1978) or of area 7 alone (Faugier-Grimaud, Frenois & Stein, 1978) causes visuomotor incoordination. Thus it is possible that a lesion in this superior parietal area can cause VMA in the controlateral visual field by disorganizing the integration of visual and proprioceptive input.

3. Visuomotor Transfer. Originating in the associative visual areas or the primary visual cortex, these connections run to the arcuate gyrus and the premotor and supplementary motor areas. In a series of studies in rhesus monkeys, Kuypers was able to localize the site of lesion capable of causing visuomotor incoordination in the animals. Thus, after section of the posterior parietal white matter, Haaxma and Kuypers (1975) caused the same grasping disorders as after occipital lobotomy. These disorders were slight, only affecting delicate and finalized movements and thus were overlooked by Myers.

In another series of studies, Moll and Kuypers (1977) analyzed the effects of cortectomy of the prefrontal area where the fibers coming from the occipital cortex and the parieto-occipital area arrive. The behavior of the animal more closely resembled apraxia than a lack of visual input. Thus, when he was supposed to go around a transparent piece of plastic through a hole to get an object, the animal attempted to grasp the object directly with the hand controlateral to the lesion and knocked into the plastic.

Interhemispheric connections have been explored in commissurotomized monkeys with sectioned optic chiasmas and one eye covered. The hand ipsilateral to the open eye feels around like the hand of blind person (Lehman, 1968). The animal attempts to make up for this deficit by a rotation of the eye, along with movements of the head and neck in the direction of the object, thus gathering a maximum of cinesthetic information (Gazzaniga, 1966, 1969).

PHYSIOPATHOLOGY

Based on the preceeding experimental data and the site of the lesions, one can specify the nature of the physiopathological mechanisms responsible for VMA.

*Lack of proprioceptive information?

Faulty reception of visual or proprioceptive information is one of the first mechanisms to be considered. In fact, although proprioceptive input appears to be useful in the learning of visuomotor coordination, it is nevertheless certain that this information can be replaced by other auxillary systems when defective. Holmes (1918) mentioned that in a case of quasi-total ophtalmoplegia due to a tumor of the pons, he did not observe any motor incoordination. Moreover, although VMA has often been reported in the past in cases of Balint's syndrome showing gaze paralysis, more recent observations (Gloning, Gloning, & Hoff, 1968; Rondot et al., 1977; Hirayama et al., 1983; Ferro et al., 1983; Hirose et al., 1985) have reported cases of VMA in the absence of any ocular involvement. Fixation can aid in partially compensating for VMA, but inability to fixate is not an important element in VMA.

It has been previously mentioned that the absence of proprioceptive information of muscular origin, whether from ocular muscles, limb muscles or those of the cervical region, does not affect visuomotor coordination once it has been acquired. Whereas development of such coordination is delayed in young animals raised in visual deprivation, in adult human beings there are no examples of visuomotor ataxia of such an origin.

It appears that the multitude of proprioceptive information available preserves visuomotor coordination. Thus, it is on the level of integration of sensory messages or of their transfer to the motor areas that lesions can produce VMA.

*Visual disorientation?

The importance of "visual disorientation" discussed in certain reports (Holmes, 1918; Hécaen & de Ajuriaguerra, 1954) as well as the inability to find adequate substitutes, are both perfectly compatible with a lesion of the centers of integration demonstrated by the works of Hyvarinen and of Mountcastle. Moreover, this visual disorientation is accompanied by considerable disorders in ocular motility, disorders in fixation, and in pursuit. Although oculomotility disorders are most probably not causally related to VMA, one must nevertheless keep in mind that Lynch et al. (1977) found a very heterogeneous neuron population in area 7, certain neurons being stimulated during ocular fixation, others during pursuit, and a third category being modulated by the interest provoked by an object place within reach of the hand. Involvement of these different neurons, whose situation in area 7 is not clearly defined, could cause such visual disorientation syndromes with gaze disorders.

*Visuomotor transfer disorder?

On the other hand, such involvement cannot explain other types of VMA which are clinically isolated and sometimes very localized either from the start or after the other symptoms have regressed (Rondot et al., 1977, cases 2 and 3;

Guard et al., 1984). In such cases, the incoordination sometimes only affects one half-field, in total absence of any oculomotor disorders. The neurons of area 7 are tightly interwined, whatever their function, and it is not conceivable that a tumor or a stroke could injure in a selective manner the population activated during the movement of the hand. Furthermore, no somatotopic organization of these associative areas has been reported could account for the cases in which the incoordination is restricted to a single hand in a single half-space. We must add to these reservations the fact that certain VMAs have been seen after section of the corpus callosum: Gazzaniga (1969) recognized their existence, and Tzavaras (personal communication) was also able to record two cases with the cooperation of R. W. Sperry. In the case of Ferro et al. (1983) the posterior two-thirds of the corpus callosum were involved and the patient suffered from incoordination of the right hand in the left visual field, a disorder which can be easily explained by the interruption of the connections between the parieto-occipital region and the left motor cortex. The existence of VMA due to transfer disorders seems to be a reality which nevertheless takes nothing away from the work consecrated to the parietal associative areas.

The various cases of VMA published as well as the eight cases shown in Table 2, are in favor of the hypothesis formulated (Rondot, 1975) concerning the existence of direct and crossed visuomotor connections.

The interruption of intrahemispheric connections between associative visual areas and motor areas causes direct homolateral VMA, whereas disconnections between associative visual areas of one side and motor areas of the other side gives crossed VMA. If we designate the type of VMA by the side of the visual field where the incoordination is located, a left-sided VMA by interruption of intra and interhemispheric motor connections would be both direct and crossed.

* * *

Visuomotor coordination develops using multiple and varied means of information gathering and of gesture execution. Proprioceptive information is an indispensable element during the period of development of visuomotor coordination. Later, the possibility of replacement makes it possible to eliminate one of the sources of proprioceptive information without creating visuomotor ataxia. On the other hand, VMA can be caused by involvement of either the associative visual centers or the transfer circuits from these associative areas to the motor centers. The result is two principal types of VMA, depending on the nature of the involved structure.

1. VMA due to damage of the associative centers is sometimes accompanied by major visual disorientation which can make even walking difficult,

TABLE 2
Visuomotor Ataxia (VMA) Personal Cases

Pt, sex age of onset	V.M.A.		Site of Lesion	Aetiology
	Eyefield	Limb		
1, F, 46	L	R	?	Vascular
2, F, 36	L	R + L	R. parieto-occipital	Aneurysm
3, F, 47	L	L	R. parieto-occipital	Tumor
4, F, 67	L	R	R. parieto-occipital	Hematoma
5, F, 74	L	R + L	R. parieto-occipital	Vascular
6, M, 79	L	R + L	R. parieto-occipital	Tumor
7, M, 59	L + R	R + L	?	Metastasis
8, M, 67	R	R	L. parieto-occipital	Hematoma

since the visual space is poorly defined in relation to the body. Added to this, in some cases, are disorders in ocular motility such as wandering gaze. The corresponding lesions are bilateral and located in the parietal lobes.

2. Opposed to this type of incoordination, are visuomotor ataxias caused by visuomotor disconnection. They correspond to the classification previously defined: uni or bilateral, direct and/or crossed ataxias, depending upon the topography of the lesion. The most demonstrative of such VMA is bilateral crossed ataxia related to a lesion in the corpus callosum which interrupts the crossed visuomotor connections. Such ataxias can appear as isolated symptoms or can be mixed signs of parietal or corpus callosum damage, usually without any disorders in ocular motility. The actual lesions are often located in the parietal region, but can sometimes be situated in the corpus callosum.

In the absence of associated symptoms, it can be difficult to distinguish between the two major types of VMA. VMA due to damage in the associative areas is generally more severe than VMA due to disconnection. It is likely that the mechanisms of substitution can develop in cases of visuomotor disconnection as has been shown by Haaxma and Kuypers (1975) in animals.

REFERENCES

Badal, J. (1888). Contribution à l'étude des Cécités Psychiques. Alexie-agraphie, hémianopsie inférieure, trouble du sens de l'espace. *Gazette hebdomadaire des Sciences Médicales, 25,* 294–295; *26,* 307–310, *27,* 320–322.

Balint, R. (1909). Seelenlähmung des "Schauens", optische Ataxie, räumliche Störung der Aufmerksamkeit. *Monatsschr. f. Psych. Neurolog., 25,* 51–81.

Brinkman, J., & Kuypers, H. G. J. M. (1973). Cerebral control of controlateral and ipsilateral arm, hand and finger movements in the split-brain rhesus monkey. *Brain, 96,* 653–674.

Downer, J. L de C. (1959). Changes in visually guided behavior following midsagittal division of the optic chiasma and corpus callosum in monkey (macacca mulatta). *Brain, 82,* 241–259.

Faugier-Grimaud, S., Frenois, C., & Stein D. L. (1978). Effects of posterior-parietal lesions on visually guided behaviour in monkeys. *Neuropsychologia, 14,* 151–168.

Ferro, J. M., Bravo-Marques, J. M., Castro-Caldas, A., & Lobo Antunes, (1983). Crossed optic ataxia: possible role of the dorsal splenium. *J. Neurol. Neurosurg. Psychiatry, 46,* 533–539.

Gazzaniga, M. S. (1966). Visuomotor integration in split-brain monkeys with other cerebral lesions. *Exp. Neurol., 16,* 289–298.

Gazzaniga M. S. (1969). Eye position and visual motor coordination. *Neuropsychologia, 7,* 379–382.

Gloning, I., Gloning, K., & Hoff, H. (1968). *Neuropsychological symptoms and syndromes in lesions of the occipital lobe and the adjacent areas.* Paris: Gauthier-Villars.

Guard, O., Perenin, M. T., Vighetto, A., Giroud, M., Tommasi, M., & Dumas, R. (1984). Syndrome pariétal bilatéral proche d'un syndrome de Balint. *Rev. Neurol., 140,* 358–367.

Haaxma, R., & Kuypers, H. G. J. M. (1975). Intrahemispheric cortical connexions and visual guidance of hand and finger movements in the rhesus monkey. *Brain, 98,* 239–260.

Hécaen, H., & de Ajuriaguerra, J. (1954). Balint's syndrome (psychic paralysis of visual fixation) and its minor form. *Brain, 77,* 373–400.

Hécaen, H., de Ajuriaguerra, J., Rouques, L., David, M., & Dell, R. B. (1950). Paralysie psychique du regard de Balint au cours de l'évolution d'une leucoencéphalite type Balo. *Rev. Neurol. 83,* 81–104.

Hécaen, H., Tzortzis, C., & Rondot, P. (1980). Loss of topographic memory with learning deficits. *Cortex, 16,* 525–542.

Hein, A. (1972). L'acquisition de la coordination perceptivo-motrice et sa réacquisition après lésion du cortex visuel (pp. 123–136). In H. Hecaen (Ed.), *Neuropsychologie de la perception visuelle.* Paris: Masson.

Hirayama, K., Toma, S., Hiyama, Y., Kita, K., & Kawamura, M. (1983). Semeiological analysis of optic ataxia (ataxie optique de Garcin) and its possible mechanism. *Clin. Neurol. 23*, 605–612.

Hirose, G., Kawada, J., Oda, R., Kitagawa, Y., & Kosoegawa, H. (1985). Visuomotor ataxie. Clinical and CT scan studies in three cases. *Clin. Neurol., 25*, 342–350.

Holmes, G. (1918). Disturbances of visual orientation. *Brit. J. of Ophtalmol., 2*, 449–468; 506–516.

Hyvärinen, J., Poranen, A. (1974). Function of the parietal associative area 7 as revealed from cellular discharge in alert monkeys. *Brain, 97*, 673–692.

Lamotte, R. H., & Acuna, C. (1978). Defects in accuracy of reading after removal of posterior parietal cortex in monkeys. *Brain Res., 139*, 309–326.

Lehman, R. A. W. (1968). Motor co-ordination and hand preference after lesions of the visual pathways and corpus callosum. *Brain, 91*, 525–538.

Levine, D. N., Kaufman, K. J., & Mohr, J. P. (1978). Inaccurate reaching associated with a superior parietal lobe tumor. *Neurology, 28*, 556–561.

Lund, J. S., Downer, J. L. de C., & Lumley, J. S. P. (1970). Visual control of limb movement following section of optic chiasma and corpus callosum in the monkey. *Cortex, 6*, 323–346.

Lynch, J. C., Mountcastle, V. B., Talbot, W. H., & Yin, T. C. T. (1977). Parietal lobe mechanisms for directed visual attention. *J. Neurophysiol., 40*, 362–388.

Michel, F., Jeannerod, M., & Devic, M. (1965). Trouble de l'orientation visuelle dans les trois dimensions de l'espace (A propos d'un cas anatomique). *Cortex, 1*, 441–466.

Moll, L., & Kuypers, H. G. J. M. (1977). Premotor cortical ablations in monkeys: Contralateral changes in visually guided reaching behavior. *Science, 198*, 317–319.

Mountcastle, V. B., Andersen, R. A., & Motter, B. C. (1981). The influence of attentive fixation upon the excitability of the light-sensitive neurons of the posterior parietal cortex. *J. Neurosci., 1*, 1218–1235.

Mountcastle, V. B., Lynch, J. C., Georgopoulos, A., Sakata, H., & Acuna, C. (1975). Posterior parietal association cortex of the monkey: Command functions for operations within extrapersonal space. *J. Neurophysiol., 38*, 871–908.

Myers, R. E., Sperry, R. W., & Mc Curdy, N. M. (1962). Neural mechanisms in visual guidance of limb movement. *Arch. Neurol., 7*, 195–202.

Pick, A. (1898). Beiträge zur Pathologie und pathologischen Anatomie des Centralnerven Systems. XIV Ueber Störungen der Tiefen localisation (in Folge cerebralen Herderkrankung). pp. 185–207. Berlin: Karger.

Porowski, S. (1985). Observations on Balints syndrom. 8ème Congrès International de Neurologie. Vienne. *Proceedings Rapports Berichte. Tome III*—Verlag der Wiener Medijinschen Akedemie.

Riddoch, G. (1935). Visual disorientation in homonymous half-field. *Brain, 58*, 376–382.

Rondot, P. (1975). Visuomotor disconnexion. Optical ataxia. *Brain and Nerve*. (Tokyo), *27*, 933–940.

Rondot, P., de Recondo, J., & Ribadeau Dumas, J. L. (1977). Visuomotor ataxia. *Brain, 100,* 355–376.

Smith, S., & Holmes, G. (1916). A case of bilateral motor apraxia with disturbance of visual orientation. *Brit. Med. J., I,* 437–441.

Stenvers, H. W. (1961). Les réactions opto-motrices. Contribution à l'étude des fonctions du cerveau (pp. 83–107). Paris: Masson.

Tzavaras, A., & Masure, M. C. (1976). Aspects différents de l'ataxie optique selon la latéralisation hémisphérique de la lésion. *Lyon Médical, 236,* 673–683.

Valkenburg, C. T., Van (1908). Zur Kenntnis der gestörten Tiefenwahrnehmung. *Deutsche Zeitschrift f. Nervenheilk., 34,* 322–337.

III

Neglect

6

Components of Visual Attention Disrupted in Unilateral Neglect

Guido Gainotti,
Patrizia D'Erme,
and Caterina De Bonis

Although some features of unilateral spatial neglect had been previously described by Poppelreuter (1917) and by Scheller and Seideman (1931), the merit of having isolated the syndrome of unilateral spatial neglect and of having emphasized its most important aspects is rightly attributed to Brain (1941). This author stressed, in fact, the striking behavioral consequences of neglecting one half of space and called attention to the relationships between unilateral neglect and right hemisphere damage. These two aspects of the syndrome and in particular the demonstration that hemi-neglect represents one of the most important signs of right hemisphere lesion account for most of the interest that neuropsychologists have since then continuously payed to the unilateral neglect syndrome. It must be acknowledged, however, that if a large agreement exists as for phenomenology, clinical context, and time course of unilateral spatial neglect, the problem of the mechanisms underlying this syndrome remains very controversial.

It is also surprising that most theories advanced to explain hemi-neglect have failed to account for the prevalence of this syndrome in right brain-damaged patients, which can be considered as one of the most characteristic aspects of unilateral neglect. Our discussion of the unilateral neglect syndrome is, therefore, focused on the problem of the mechanisms underlying hemi-neglect, trying in particular to evaluate if the prevalence of this pattern of behavior in right brain-damaged patients can help to elucidate the nature of the underlying mechanisms. On the other hand, because it would be absurd to discuss the meaning of clinical phenomena which have not been previously described, our discussion of hemi-neglect is introduced by a short description of the most characteristic features of this syndrome. Particular stress is put on those clinical features which are of greater interest from the pathophysiological point of view. We then pass to a survey of the most important theories advanced to explain hemi-neglect and of the main objections addressed to each of them. We then ask if the prevalence of neglect in patients with right hemisphere lesions is consistent across various types of visual-spatial tasks or if the occurrence of hemi-neglect in right and left brain-damaged patients varies according to the nature of the task. This problem has important implications for theories of hemi-neglect, since it should be logical to expect that, if specific as well as nonspecific components are usually included under the heading of unilateral spatial neglect, only the most specific components of the syndrome should be strongly lateralized to the right hemisphere. Finally, results of a recent study following this line of reasoning are reported and their implications as for theories of hemi-neglect discussed, with reference both to clinical data and to theories of spatial orienting of attention recently proposed by Posner and coworkers (Posner, 1980; Posner, Cohen, & Rafal, 1982; Posner & Cohen, 1984; Posner, Walker, Friedrich, & Rafal, 1984).

CLINICAL FEATURES AND TIME COURSE OF UNILATERAL SPATIAL NEGLECT

The most severe forms of hemi-neglect are usually observed in the acute stages of the evolution of extensive vascular disorders in the territory of the middle cerebral artery. The patient lies in bed with eyes and head rotated toward the half space ipsilateral to the damaged hemisphere and may fail to look to the contralateral half space if he is addressed from that side. Neuropsychological tests cannot be administered in this stage, as the patient's attention systematically orients toward stimuli lying on the extreme part of the nonneglected side. Some days later, the tendency to deviate head and eyes to the good side may be less apparent, or even disappear, and manifestations of neglect can be observed both during everyday activities and during the neuropsychological assessment. During daily activities the patient can fail to pick up food from one half plate, or neglect to lock the wheelchair on the side contralateral to the lesion. During the neuro-psychological examination, he may attend only to stimuli lying on the half space ipsilateral to the damaged hemisphere and typically omits on drawing tasks one half of models having a symmetrical configuration, such as a daisy, a human face, a clock or a house. Hemianopia is usually, although not necessarily, present but a formal tangent screen visual field examination is generally impossible and only the confrontation technique allows one to detect the presence of visual field defects. During the confrontation test, it is common to observe a conjugate deviation of the eyeballs toward the good side, which appears as soon as the examiner presents his hands simultaneously in both visual fields (Cohn, 1972).

In a further stage of evolution of the disability (in general some weeks after the onset of the disease) the most striking signs of hemi-neglect tend to disappear and only mild signs of unilateral neglect can be detected. Patients do not show, for example, a severe contralateral inattention on perceptual-motor tasks, but still omit lines lying on the extreme part of the contralateral half space on cancellation tests (Albert, 1973), bisect asymmetrically a line (Schenkenberg, Bradford, & Ajax, 1980) and may show a preference for responses lying on the good half space on difficult multiple-choice tasks requiring the patient to select the correct response from among a spatial display (Costa, Vaughan, Horowitz, & Ritter, 1969; Gainotti, 1968; Leicester, Sidman, Stoddard, & Mohr, 1969). Patients may also show an asymmetry of space exploration on visual searching tasks, as they tend to begin exploration from the side ipsilateral to the lesion, so that the searching time for items lying on the contralateral half space is usually lengthened (Chain, Leblanc, Chedru, & Lhermitte, 1979; Chedru, Leblanc, & Lhermitte, 1973; De Renzi, Faglioni, & Scotti, 1970). During visual field evaluation with the confrontation technique, these patients usually detect stimuli presented in isolation to the side opposite to the lesion, but fail to notice the same stimuli if a competing stimulus is simultaneously applied to the nonaffected half field.

THEORIES ADVANCED TO EXPLAIN THE UNILATERAL NEGLECT SYNDROME

Sensorimotor Theories

Because the most striking manifestations of neglect occur in patients showing a conjugate deviation of head and eyes toward the side of lesion and because hemi-neglect is often associated with visual field defects, some authors have assumed that unilateral neglect may be but a consequence of these elementary sensorimotor disturbances.

The *sensory defect hypothesis* has been most explicitly put forward by Battersby, Bender, Pollack, & Kahn (1956), who claimed that hemi-neglect is due to the interaction between a sensory defect and a background of widespread mental deterioration. A similar mechanism was proposed in an animal model of the syndrome by Sprague, Chambers, and Steller (1961) when they induced neglect in the cat by interrupting the lateral portion of the mesencephalon. As this part of the mesencephalon contains ascending sensory pathways, Sprague et al. concluded that neglect was due to a loss of sensory input to the cortex.

Several important objections have been addressed to the *sensory defect hypothesis:*

(a) the visual field can be unaffected in cases of unilateral spatial neglect (McFie, Piercy, & Zangwill, 1950);

(b) most hemianopic patients overcome their visual field defects with compensatory movements of the eyes and of the neck, whereas no such compensatory activity is shown by unilateral neglect patients (Gainotti, 1968; Meienberg, Zangemeister, Rosenberg, Hoyt, & Stark, 1981; Meienberg, Harrer, & Wehren, 1986);

(c) unilateral spatial neglect is not limited to the visual modality. Manifestations of neglect for one half space have also been observed during tasks of space exploration through the tactile modality (De Renzi et al., 1970) and during representative tasks based on description from memory of familiar surroundings (Bisiach & Luzzatti, 1978).

The *defective exploration hypothesis* stems from the observation that head and eye deviations toward the side of lesion are frequently associated with the most severe forms of unilateral spatial neglect. It has been, therefore, proposed by Schott, Jeannerod, and Zahin (1966) that hemi-neglect might be a consequence of the oculomotor disorder, preventing the patient from fully exploring the contralateral half space. Furthermore, the hypothesis viewing unilateral neglect as a byproduct of disrupted oculomotor mechanisms has been strengthened by the observation that conjugate gaze paresis, like hemispatial neglect, is more frequent and lasting following right than left hemispheric lesions (De Renzi, Colombo, Faglioni, & Gibertoni, 1982). Even more recently, data strongly supporting the same hypothesis have been obtained by Rubens (1985). This author, drawing on previous unsystematic observations by Silberpfennig (1941), Marshall and Maynard (1983) and Brown (personal communication) studied the effect of caloric vestibular stimulation on gaze direction and on tests of visual neglect in 18 patients with left sided visual neglect, observed during the acute postictal period. He reasoned that, if unilateral neglect is partly due to bias of gaze and postural turning, then caloric vestibular stimulation, producing eye deviation in the direction opposite to the pathologically acquired bias, might reduce signs of visual neglect. His results confirmed the hypothesis, since, as a result of the experimentally induced leftward eye deviation, unilateral neglect improved in all but one patients during vestibular caloric stimulation. It must be acknowledged, however, that if in the acute postictal periods the head and eye deviation toward the side of lesion certainly prevents the patient from paying attention to the contralateral half space, the role of oculomotor disorders seems less clear in further stages of evolution of the disease, when a severe neglect may persist even in the absence of conjugate gaze disorders. It is probably for this reason that Hécaen and Angelergues (1963), Gainotti (1968) and Chedru et al. (1973) have consistently shown that only a subset of patients with unilateral neglect exhibit conjugate eye disorders, whereas most neglect patients present no evidence of oculomotor disturbances.

Interhemispheric Imbalance Theories

A more complex model aiming to explain on the basis of an oculomotor imbalance mechanism not only the clinical manifestations of neglect, but also their prevalence in patients with right sided lesions, has been proposed by Kinsbourne (1970, 1973, 1974, 1977). Kinsbourne's model is based on the following assumptions:

1. each hemisphere subserves orientation to the contralateral half space and tends, when activated, to orient the gaze toward the contralateral spatial field;
2. cognitive activities determining the prevalent activation of one cerebral hemisphere favor the overflow of excitation of the corresponding orienting apparatus, causing the gaze to shift to the contralateral side;
3. in the intact brain the balance between the two sides is maintained through reciprocal transcallosal inhibitory influences.

According to this model, a unilateral brain lesion should reduce the orientation tendencies of the damaged hemisphere by decreasing hemispheric activation and by increasing the transcallosal inhibition exerted by the normal contralateral hemisphere.

Kinsbourne explains the prevalence of neglect in patients with right sided lesions by assuming that the verbal intercourse between doctor and patient may result in an overall activation of the patient's left hemisphere. This left hemisphere activation would cause a further rightward shift of attention in patients with right hemisphere lesions, but counteract the opposite neglect for the right half space, which might follow a left hemisphere lesion. Unfortunately, there is no convincing evidence that the severity of neglect is increased by tasks (or situations) that preferentially activate the normal hemisphere and reduced by tasks that preferentially engage the damaged hemisphere.

Caplan (1985) has shown, for example, that patients who exhibit neglect do so to a comparable degree on both verbal and visual-spatial tasks and other authors (e.g., Leicester et al., 1969, and Chain et al., 1979) have even shown that neglect is more severe when the abilities requested by the task are preferentially carried out by the damaged hemisphere.

Representational Theories

Because sensorimotor disorders are neither necessary nor sufficient to account for unilateral spatial neglect, some authors have assumed that this syndrome might be due to disruption of supra-modal integrative structures, designed with terms, such as "schema," "map," or "representation" and viewed as inner models against which external events should be matched. The first proponent of this kind of theory was Brain (1941) who emphasized the importance of the parietal lobe for the maintenance of the integrity of the "body schema." The same author, observing the fact that manifestations of neglect for the left half of the body and of extrapersonal space often coexist, attributed this association to the links existing between "body schema" and "scheme of the external world." A disruption of the former should, therefore, provoke both a defective experience of the contralateral half of the body and a disturbed perception of the corresponding part of extrapersonal space.

The theoretical objections raised to the construct of the "body schema" and the empirical observations showing that manifestations of neglect for the left half of the body and of extrapersonal space are often dissociated have discredited interpretations of unilateral spatial neglect based on the body schema hypothesis.

Representational theories, however, have recently raised new interest thanks to the work of Bisiach et al. (Bisiach, Capitani, Luzzatti, & Perani, 1981; Bisiach & Luzzatti, 1978; Bisiach, Luzzatti, & Perani, 1979). These authors have shown that manifestations of neglect can be observed even in tasks (such as the description from memory of familiar surroundings) which require neither an analysis of sensory information nor an active scanning of the external world by means of saccadic eye movements.

They have, therefore, argued that the inner representation of the outside reality is topologically structured across the two hemispheres and that unilateral spatial neglect is due to a disruption of one half of this internal map. Unfortunately, this theory too is not free from objections, since (a) patients who show unilateral neglect during perceptual-motor tasks do not necessarily present hemi-neglect during representation tasks, and (b) a marked decrease in neglect is observed in imagery tasks when patients are cued to direct attention to the neglected side (Bisiach et al., 1981). This finding suggests that the part of the internal map that is neglected during representation tasks has not disappeared from the internal network of the patient, but is simply not activated, owing perhaps to disorders in the internal movements of attention.

Attentional Theories

The term "visual inattention" was coined by Poppelreuter (1917) to designate the phenomenon of visual extinction during double simultaneous stimulation, which is considered by many authors as an important component of the unilateral neglect syndrome. Critchley (1949, 1953) was also a proponent of the same hypothesis, considering extinction as an instance of local inattention and maintaining that "the brain-injured individual cannot "attend" to two simultaneous claimant stimuli." Bender and Furlow (1944, 1945) objected, however, to the attentional theory of extinction stating that inattention cannot be a major determinant of this pattern of behavior, since the defect is not abolished by asking the patient to "concentrate" on the extinguished side. More recently, the hypothesis that an attentional disorder may subsume not only the visual extinction phenomenon, but also other behavioral components of the unilateral neglect syndrome has been advanced from very different points of view by Heilman and coworkers and, respectively, by Posner and coworkers. Heilman and coworkers, considering hemi-neglect as an attention-arousal disorder, aimed above all to discover the anatomical bases of this attention-arousal defect, whereas Posner et al., studying hemi-neglect from a more strictly cognitivist point of view, were more interested in discovering the components of the visual orienting of attention selectively disrupted in unilateral spatial neglect.

Heilman & his associates have maintained that arousal and attention are subsumed by a complex cortico-limbic-reticular loop and have proposed that neglect phenomena may be provoked by disruption of each component of this loop. Among the most important anatomical structures included in this loop, Heilman et al. list cortical areas, such as the posterior parietal cortex (Heilman, Pandya, & Geschwind, 1970; Heilman, Valenstein, & Watson, 1983) and the frontal premotor cortex (Watson, Miller, & Heilman, 1978), limbic areas, such as the cingulate gyrus (Heilman & Valenstein, 1972; Watson, Heilman, Cauthen, & King, 1973) and subcortical areas, such as the mesencephalic reticularis formation (Watson, Heilman, Miller, & King, 1974) and the nucleus reticularis thalami (Heilman, Valenstein, & Watson, 1985).

A very similar model has been more recently proposed by Mesulam (1981), who has suggested the existence of a cortical network for the modulation of directed attention within extrapersonal space. According to Mesulam (1981) four cerebral regions, each having a peculiar functional role, participate in this network and can give rise to different types of neglect when damaged. These regions are: (a) the posterior parietal cortex, providing an internal sensory map; (b) the frontal eye fields, containing an inner representation of motor programs for exploring the environment; (c) the cingulate cortex, regulating the spatial distribution of motivational drive, and (d) reticular structures, providing the underlying level of arousal and vigilance. Being very similar, the models proposed by Heilman and by Mesulam have in common important advantages, but also some disadvantages. The main advantage consists in the effort to root normal and pathological behavior into anatomo-physiological terms and to provide neurologically detailed and stimulating models. The disadvantage consists in a shared difficulty to selectively account for the main anatomical and for the main psychological aspects of the syndrome. Both the loop proposed by Heilman and the network described by Mesulam include, indeed, many cortical and subcortical structures, but in man the only structure that consistently produces neglect when damaged is the posterior parietal lobe (De Renzi, 1982). Now, the critical importance of the parietal region is not clearly explained by either the "loop" or the "network" theory. Similar difficulties have the two models to account for the specific psychological aspects of the unilateral neglect syndrome, since neither the "attention-arousal" function stressed by Heilman, nor the sensory, motor, motivational, and arousal components of attention described by Mesulam seem to correspond to the components of visual attention specifically impaired in unilateral neglect. In our opinion, a more analytical study of the components of attention specifically impaired in hemi-neglect is a prerequisite to better understand the nature of this syndrome. As this enterprise has been recently undertaken by Posner and coworkers and their findings are very relevant as for results obtained in our experimental research, we discuss in some detail Posner's data in a later section of this chapter.

UNILATERAL SPATIAL NEGLECT AND RIGHT HEMISPHERE DAMAGE

Since the classical work of Brain (1941) several authors have emphasized the relationships between unilateral neglect and lateralization of damage to the right hemisphere (Critchley, 1953; De Renzi, 1982; Gainotti, 1968; Hécaen & Angelergues, 1963; Piercy, Hécaen, & Ajuriaguerra, 1960; Oxbury, Campbell, & Oxbury, 1974; Weinstein & Friedland, 1977).

Most theories advanced to explain hemi-neglect, however, either ignore the prevalence of this syndrome in patients with right hemisphere lesions or explain it on the basis of poorly established assumptions.

One of these assumptions is that the function critically involved in unilateral spatial neglect might have a different organization at the level of the right and of the left hemisphere, being bilaterally represented in one parietal lobe, but unilaterally represented in the other parietal lobe. Disagreement, however, exists both about the nature of this critical function and about the side of its unilateral or bilateral representation. Brain (1941) has suggested, for example, that a conceptual and bilateral representation of both sides of the body might be stored in the left parietal lobe, whereas a strictly unilateral representation of the left half of the body could be stored in the right parietal lobe.

This model could explain why left parietal lesions provoke a bilateral disorder in body parts recognition (autotopoagnosia), whereas right parietal lesions give rise to a neglect for the left side of the body and of extrapersonal space. Much more recently, Heilman, Valenstein, and Watson (1985) have suggested that attentional cells of the left parietal lobe would attend only to the right half space, whereas the homologous cells of the right parietal lobe could have bilateral receptive fields. According to this model, left hemisphere lesions would not provoke unilateral neglect, since the intact right hemisphere could attend to both sides of space, whereas right hemisphere damage would provoke hemi-neglect, owing to the inability of the intact left hemisphere to attend to ipsilateral stimuli.

Although Heilman et al. (1985) have provided some empirical data in support of their theory, the weight of these data seem to us still insufficient to prove the existence of so strong qualitative differences between the attentional cells of the right and left parietal lobes.

In more recent years, an ingenious interpretation, aiming to explain the preferential involvement of the right hemisphere in unilateral neglect as a result of left hemisphere specialization, has been offered by Brown (1983a, 1983b). According to Brown, perception develops as an autonomous series of representations over levels in brain structure in a direction conforming to the evolution of the forebrain. This series of spatial representations is symmetrically organized until the end state, which has a unilateral left representation, being based on a feature analysis typical of this hemisphere. According to this model, the prevalence of neglect in right brain-damaged patients could result from the inability of the analytical mode of processing of the left hemisphere to access the preliminary holistic cognitive mode and hence to derive left visual field (right hemisphere) contents. This interpretation, although coherently inserted in an original theory on the microstructure of perception (see Brown, 1983a, 1983b) has, in our opinion, the disadvantage of being more speculative than operational and, hence of being difficult to submit to empirical testing.

Furthermore, it must also be acknowledged that the prevalence of neglect in right brain-damaged patients shows important variations from study to study, in that some authors have reported a striking prevalence of neglect among right brain-damaged patients (e.g., Faglioni, Scotti, & Spinnler, 1971; Gainotti, 1968; Hécaen & Angelergues, 1963) but others (e.g., Battersby et al., 1956; Costa et al., 1969; Ogden, 1985; Zarith & Kahn, 1974) have documented only a mild and sometimes nonsignificant difference between right and left brain-damaged patients.

The reason of this variability from study to study could be due to the fact that the task demands might differentially influence the tendency to neglect, according to the hemispheric side of lesion. If this were true, the existence of an interaction between hemisphere and type of task could have theoretical relevance. As a matter of fact, since neglect is a symptom characteristic of the right hemisphere lesions, its more typical manifestations should be more strongly lateralized to this hemisphere, whereas features of hemi-inattention due to less specific factors (such as the failure to compensate for visual field defects, owing, perhaps, to a widespread mental impairment) should be equally observed in right and left brain-damaged patients. An individualization of the patterns of neglect strongly lateralized to the right hemisphere should, therefore, allow to draw inferences about the mechanisms underlying the typical neglect syndrome. The guideline followed to search in the neuropsychological literature for possible interactions between hemisphere and type of task has been the distinction between two main components of visually guided behavior:

— the active movements of visual search (aiming to search and to detect in the environment new or relevant pieces of information)
— the eye fixation effects, allowing a detailed discriminative analysis of stimuli brought into foveal vision.

This choice was due to two reasons: (1) the fact that this distinction is widely accepted by students of vision; (2) the fact that the above mentioned sensorimotor, representational and attentional theories of hemi-neglect logically imply a prevalent disruption of one of these components of visually guided behavior. Different predictions about the component predominantly affected in right brain-damaged patients could, therefore, be advanced.

To be sure, theories assuming that unilateral spatial neglect is due to an oculomotor imbalance, deviating the gaze toward the side ispilateral to the lesion, should predict that the predominance of neglect in right brain-damaged patients should be greater on tasks emphasizing active movements of visual search than on tasks emphasizing information processing during the pauses of eye fixation. A similar prediction should be made by the representational theory viewing neglect as a consequence of a unilateral mutilation of the internal map, since exploratory movements should be almost absent in the external space corresponding to the mutilated part of the internal map.

By contrast, a greater prevalence of neglect in right brain-damaged patients during tasks emphasizing the eye fixation effects would be predicted by the sensory defect hypothesis and by the attentional defect hypothesis, if we assume that when the eye fixates on a stimulus to analyze it, attention too fixates on it.

Survey of the Available Neuropsychological Literature

Although no previous study had been undertaken to check the hypothesis that we have just advanced, some data relevant to the distinction between visual search and eye fixation effects could be found in the available neuropsychological literature.

Interestingly, all these data consistently suggested that the most significant differences between right and left brain-damaged patients are obtained on tasks emphasizing the eye fixation effects, and not on tasks requiring a voluntary exploration of the half space contralateral to the brain lesion. De Renzi et al. (1970), Chedru et al. (1973) and Chain et al. (1979) have compared, for example, the tendency to neglect in right and left brain-damaged patients, by means of visual searching tests based on the active exploration of the contralateral half space. Irrespective of the hemispheric side of lesion, a very similar pattern of visual search impairment, consisting in a prolongation of the searching time for items lying on the half space contralateral to the lesion, was observed. Furthermore, in studies conducted in right and left brain-damaged patients with different kinds of visual spatial tasks, the prevalence of neglect in right brain-damaged patients is usually greater on tasks emphasizing eye fixation effects than on those based on visual exploration movements. Gainotti, Messerli, and Tissot (1972) have noticed, for example, that on copying drawing tasks a very high proportion of right brain-damaged patients tend to leave unfinished the left part of simple figures (such as a cube or a house) that can be captured with one or with few eye fixations, whereas this pattern of error is exceptional in left brain-damaged patients. When, on the contrary, patients are requested to copy a complex model, consisting of many elements (a house, some trees and a wooden fence) ranging in a line from left to right, the omission of one of more elements on the side opposite to the hemispheric locus of lesion does not significantly distinguish right from left brain-damaged patients. Data consistent with the same point of view have been obtained by Colombo, De Renzi, and Faglioni (1976), who contrasted results obtained by right and left brain-damaged patients on drawing tasks, using small figures similar to those used by Gainotti et al. (1972) and on other tasks requiring the exploration of different portions of space. On the drawing task, right brain-damaged patients significantly neglected the sides of the models contralateral to the damaged hemisphere, whereas on a task requiring the exploration of a large part of extrapersonal space (the "ball and holes" test) no significant difference was observed between right and left brain-damaged patients. Both groups showed, in fact, a similar tendency to preferentially explore the hemi-field ipsilateral to the damaged hemisphere, at the expense of the contralateral half space.

However, since disorders at the level of eye fixation could be inferred in these studies only by results obtained on copying drawing tasks and since, in any case, none of these investigations had been devised to compare the influence of eye fixation and of visual search effects upon unilateral spatial neglect, we decided to take more directly into account this problem by means of an ad hoc designed experiment.

RESEARCH ON THE INFLUENCE OF VISUAL SEARCH AND EYE FIXATION DISORDERS ON UNILATERAL SPATIAL NEGLECT OF RIGHT AND LEFT BRAIN-DAMAGED PATIENTS

In this investigation, we contrasted results obtained by unselected groups of right and left brain-damaged patients on two visual recognition tasks devised to maximize respectively the following functions:

— attention focusing and drawing information from both sides of space during eye fixation;
— intentional search of visual stimuli by means of exploratory eye movements.

A test of overlapping figures was deemed as appropriate to study the capacity of brain-damaged patients to gather complex visual information from both sides of space during eye fixations, whereas a test of searching figures on a large board was considered as appropriate to thoroughly explore the half space contralateral to the damaged hemisphere by means of saccadic eye movements (Gainotti, D'Erme, Monteleone, & Silveri, 1986).

Testing Procedures

The test of visual recognition constructed to maximize neglect resulting from a poor exploration of the half space contralateral to the damaged hemisphere was a test of *Searching for Animals* on a large board. During this task, a large cardboard (75 × 50 cm) containing the black and white drawings of 20 animals, equally distributed on the right and left sides of the board (Figure 1) was put in front of the subject at a distance of about 60 cm, so that the cardboard subtended about 60° of the visual field of the subject. The figures of 40 different animals were then presented one at a time to the patient in a prearranged order: 20 of them were identical to those presented on the cardboard, whereas the other 20 were different. The patient was asked to look at each figure and to search for it on the board as quick as possible, pointing to the corresponding figure if he could find it, or saying "It is not here" if he did not find the animal on the display board.

FIGURE 1 Display board used in the Searching for Animals test. From Gainotti, D'Erme, Monteleone, and Silveri (1986). Mechanisms of unilateral spatial neglect in relation to laterality of cerebral lesions. *Brain*, 1986. Reprinted by permission of Oxford University Press.

The test of visual recognition devised to maximize neglect resulting from defective extraction of information from one side of space during eye fixation was a test of *Overlapping Figures*. Six cards (14 × 21 cm) bearing each 5 overlapping figures of common objects, drawn in black ink, were presented one at a time to the patients at a distance of about 40 cm, so that each visual pattern subtended less than 20° of the visual field of the subject. Each pattern was composed by two figures overlapping on the right, two overlapping on the left and a fifth figure, placed in the center of the card, which overlapped both the right-sided and the left-sided drawings. Patients were requested to recognize the figures of the composite diagram by pointing to identical figures drawn separately on a multiple-choice display, interspersed with other objects belonging to the same category, which were placed in vertical column just below the composite diagram. An item of the test of Overlapping Figures is reported in Figure 2.

The first item of the test was used as an introductory procedure during which attention was called to all the figures reproduced on the card. Then, the true testing sequence, consisting of 5 more overlapping figures was administered without further stimulating the patients.

Thus, in both tests patients had to recognize 20 stimuli equally distributed in the right and left parts of extrapersonal space, but in the Overlapping Figures test

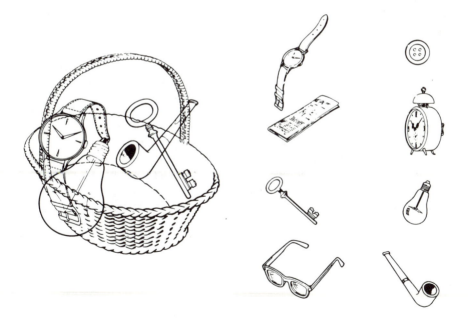

FIGURE 2 An item from the Overlapping Figures test. During the test, the display board, which is shown to the right of the composite diagram, was placed in a vertical column just below the stimulus pattern.

stimulus identification required the capacity to draw information from both sides of a pattern presented in central vision, whereas in the Searching for Animals task the patient was requested to actively search for the presented stimulus with a series of exploratory eye movements. Scoring systems and criteria followed to evaluate unilateral spatial neglect were identical on both tasks and consisted either in the presence of omissions only on the side contralateral to the damaged hemisphere or in a bilateral presence of omissions, but in number at least double on the contralateral than on the ipsilateral side. Furthermore, an algebraic sum of the number of omissions made on the right and left sides of space was used to obtain a more precise measure of unilateral spatial neglect.

Subjects. Thirty-eight normal controls, 90 right and 82 left brain-damaged patients were submitted to examination. The presence of visual field defects was documented in brain-damaged patients either by means of the Goldmann perimeter or by means of a confrontation test. Thirty-three right (37%) and 27 left (29%) brain-damaged patients were defined as hemianopic. This difference was not statistically significant.

Results. On the test of Searching for Animals no significant difference was observed between right and left brain-damaged patients, since 37 right out of 90 (41%) and 31 left out of 82 (37%) were considered as affected by unilateral spatial neglect.

By contrast, on the Overlapping Figures test a highly significant difference was put in evidence between patients with right-sided and left-sided lesions, since 32 right (36%), but only 9 left (11%) brain-damaged patients presented evidence of unilateral spatial neglect on this task ($X^2=12.95$; $p < .005$).

To obtain a more precise measure of the tendency to neglect one half of space, the algebraic sums of omissions made on the right and on the left sides of the tasks were computed in each individual patient, giving a positive score to left-sided errors and a negative score to right-sided errors. A significant interaction ($F = 3.12$; $p < .05$) between diagnostic group and type of tasks was again observed. On the Searching for Animals task, both right and left brain damaged patients obtained an algebraic sum of errors significantly different from normals (the number of omissions being in any case greater on the side of the board contralateral to the hemispheric side of lesion). On the contrary, on the Overlapping Figures task only right brain-damaged patients presented a distribution of errors significantly different from normals (omitting almost only figures lying on the left half of the pattern), whereas in left brain-damaged patients errors were distributed symmetrically on both sides of the pattern, so that their algebraic sums of errors did not differ from those obtained by the control group.

Thus the results of our research support the hypothesis that the kind of visual activity requested by the task has a differential influence on contralateral neglect resulting from right and left hemispheric lesions. In particular, our findings show that the prevalence of unilateral spatial neglect in right brain-damaged patients is greater on tasks maximizing the *eye fixation* effects than on tasks emphasizing the active movements of *visual search*. The main objection that could be raised to these conclusions concerns the fact that, since the Searching for Animals and the Overlapping Figures task differ not only along the dimension of extent of space to be explored (which had motivated their construction) but also along the dimension of perceptual complexity of the task, it was possible that the observed interaction between type of task and hemispheric side of lesion was due to the influence of the variable of *perceptual complexity* (Chain et al., 1979; Leicester et al., 1969) and not to the selective impairment of a mechanism acting during the pauses of eye fixation. To check this hypothesis, we controlled the number of errors made by right and left brain-damaged patients on the side of the Searching for Animals and of the Overlapping Figures tasks ipsilateral to the damaged hemisphere. We reasoned that, if the Overlapping Figures task is intrinsically more difficult for right brain-damaged patients, then they should score worse than left-sided patients also on the side of the test ipsilateral to the damaged hemisphere. Since in both the Overlapping Figures and the Searching for Animals task 10 figures were lying on the right and 10 on the left side of the display, the accuracy scores of right and left brain-damaged patients on the sides of the tests ipsilateral to the damaged hemisphere could easily be calculated. Results of this analysis showed that the perceptual complexity of the task cannot account for the selective contralateral neglect shown by right brain-damaged patients on the Overlapping Figures task. The mean number of errors obtained in this test on the half space ipsilateral to the damaged hemisphere was in fact slightly higher in left ($\bar{x} = .70$) than in right ($\bar{y} = .63$) brain-damaged patients with visual field defects, a finding that clearly contrasts with the striking prevalence of neglect shown by the same patients on the same task.

CLINICAL FINDINGS POINTING TO A SELECTIVE EYE FIXATION DISORDER IN UNILATERAL SPATIAL NEGLECT OF RIGHT BRAIN DAMAGED PATIENTS

Results of our research suggest that unilateral spatial neglect of right brain-damaged patients arises during the pauses of eye fixation on the relevant visual stimuli and does not primarily involve the movements of visual search. Obviously this interpretation must be considered with caution, as a recording of ocular movements, which could assist in elucidating this question was not available in our research.

However, the hypothesis that inability to extract visual information from both sides of stimuli during the pauses of eye fixation may be the most characteristic feature of contralateral neglect resulting from right hemisphere damage is supported by data reported by other authors and by clinical observations repeatedly made in patients studied in this investigation. Thus, Denny-Brown, Meyer, and Horenstein (1952) in their well-known single case study of a right brain-damaged patient presenting clear signs of unilateral neglect ("amor-phosynthesis") report that on the Poppelreuter's overlapping figures test their patient correctly named everything on the right side of the diagram, but failed completely to notice the figures lying on the left side of the picture.

However, the patient improved her performance when she was presented with a composite diagram of common fruits and vegetables, each barely sepa-rated from the others, and she obtained even better results when given a composite picture of objects more widely separated from each other.

As for our patients, they were usually given, as part of their routine neuropsychological examination, a copying drawing task similar to that original-ly proposed by Gainotti et al. (1972), consisting of many elements (a house and some trees) arrayed in a line from left to right. In this type of task some right (but no left) brain-damaged patients tended to leave unfinished the left side of various elements, reproducing, however, parts of the model placed even more laterally on the neglected half of space. Some examples of this pattern of behavior have been reported in Figure 3 since this kind of graphic activity provides, in our

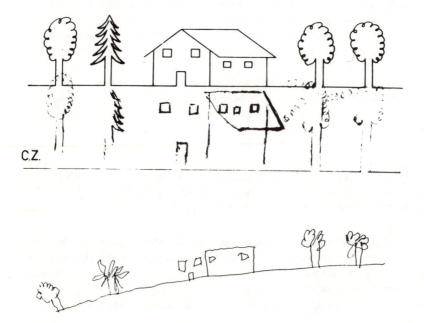

FIGURE 3   Examples of copies made by brain-damaged patients of the composite figure shown on the top. In each case patients left unfinished half of one or more elements, reproducing, however, parts of the model placed even more laterally on the neglected side of space.

opinion, a striking illustration of the features of neglect typical of right brain-damaged patients.

The patterns of behavior shown in Figure 3 clearly suggest that what is impaired in right brain-damaged patients with unilateral spatial neglect is not so much the active exploration of the left half of space as the extraction of information from the left half of stimuli during single eye fixations.

IMPLICATIONS OF THESE RESULTS FOR THEORIES OF HEMI-NEGLECT

If we come back now from the results of these clinical and experimental investigations to theories advanced to explain unilateral neglect phenomena, we see that our findings are clearly at variance with the defective exploration hypothesis and, to a lesser extent, with the representational theory, viewing neglect as a consequence of a mutilation of the internal map of the external world. The fact that the greater prevalence of hemi-neglect in right brain-damaged patients was observed in tasks emphasizing eye fixation effects is, on the other hand, consistent both with the sensory defect hypothesis and with the attentional theory, since it can be assumed that during tasks of visual analysis no distinction can be made between eye fixations and fixations of attention. There is, however, another finding in our research which argues against the sensory defect hypothesis (and hence in favor of the attentional theory): this finding shows that the incidence of visual field defects was not significantly different in our two groups of right and left brain-damaged patients. It is, therefore, very unlikely that the striking prevalence of neglect in right brain-damaged patients during the pauses of eye fixation was due to a purely perceptual disorder.

The inability shown by right brain-damaged patients to detect the images lying on the left side of the overlapping figures presents, in our opinion, a striking similarity with the extinction phenomenon, often observed during tasks of double stimulation of homologous regions of a sensory field and for which Poppelreuter (1917) coined first the term "Visual Inattention." In both cases there is, in fact, a competition between stimuli applied on both sides of the fixation point (the hands moving in the periphery of the visual fields during the visual field assessment with the confrontation technique and, respectively the figures overlapping on both sides of the composite pattern on the Overlapping Figures task) and in both cases the attention is attracted by the stimulus lying in the normal field at the expenses of that applied to the contralateral side.

A careful analysis of the components of visual attention that could be selectively impaired in these situations has been recently provided by Posner et al. According to these authors, who have analyzed in detail the act of orienting visual attention both in normal subjects and in various kinds of brain pathology (Posner, 1980; Posner et al., 1982, 1984; Posner & Cohen, 1984) attention may be oriented covertly to an internal representation of space, or overtly, by shifting the gaze. This orientation can occur automatically to visual stimuli or intentionally to their expected location and consists of three successive mental operations: (1) disengagement of attention from its previous focus; (2) movement of attention toward the target; and (3) engagement on the target. Posner et al. (1984) have claimed that parietal lobe damage produces a deficit in the automatic operation of disengaging attention from its current focus and have viewed the extinction phenomenon as a consequence of this inability to automatically disengage from the current focus of attention, orienting it to the contralateral half space.

Results of the present research, showing that right brain-damaged patients are selectively unable to draw visual information from the left half of stimuli which can be captured with single eye fixations, but are not particularly impaired in tasks of conscious exploration of the left half field, could perhaps be reconciled with Posner's views. As a matter of fact, the tasks used in our research differed along two of the dimensions stressed by Posner in his work:

— the automatic versus conscious orienting of attention;
— the kind of mental operation (disengaging, moving, engaging) involved in the act of shifting attention.

As for the first point, it can be admitted that on the Overlapping Figures task orientation of attention toward the figures lying on both sides of the fixation point occurs more automatically than consciously, whereas on the Searching for Animals task a conscious activity of exploration of the cardboard is explicitly requested of the patient.

As for the second point, it is possible to hypothesize that the main difficulty of right brain-damaged patients on the Overlapping Figures task perhaps consisted in the disengagement of attention from figures lying on the right side of the pattern (which were almost always perfectly recognized) whereas on the Searching for Animals task the operations of moving and of engaging attention to the targets seems more important than the disengagement of attention from its previous focus.

If this interpretation is correct, the dissociation noticed in the literature and confirmed in our research between tasks emphasizing eye fixation effects and tasks maximizing a visual search activity should be attributed to the different attentional demands of these tasks rather than to the raw extent of space to be explored. The lack of difference between right and left brain-damaged patients on visual searching tasks (using in general large boards) could be due to the fact that this type of task usually requires a conscious and deliberate displacement of attention (which is not particularly impaired in hemi-neglect). By contrast, the striking prevalence of neglect in right brain-damaged patients on tasks of copying or of pattern recognition using a restricted part of space could be due to the fact that in these types of tasks the eye fixation on the target is usually followed by more automatic small amplitude eye movements aiming to bring into central vision the parts of the pattern falling in the peripheral parts of the visual field. This automatic orienting of attention toward the part of the stimulus lying on the half space contralateral to the damaged hemisphere could be the component of visual attention selectively affected in unilateral spatial neglect.

REFERENCES

Albert, M. L. (1973). A simple test of visual neglect. *Neurology, 23,* 658–664.

Battersby, W. S., Bender, M. B., Pollack, M. & Kahn, R. L. (1956). Unilateral spatial agnosia (inattention) in patients with cerebral lesions. *Brain, 79,*68–93.

Bender, M. B., & Furlow, C. T. (1944). Phenomenon of visual extinction and binocular rivalry mechanism. *Transactions of the American Neurological Association, 70,* 87–93.

Bender, M. B., & Furlow, C. T. (1945). Phenomenon of visual extinction on homonymous fields and psychological principles involved. *Archives of Neurology and Psychiatry, 53,* 29–33.

Bisiach, E., Capitani, E., Luzzatti, C., & Perani, D. (1981). Brain and conscious representation of outside reality. *Neuropsychologia, 19,* 543–551.

Bisiach, E., & Luzzatti, C. (1978). Unilateral neglect of representational space. *Cortex, 14,* 29–133.

Bisiach, E., Luzzatti, C., & Perani, D. (1979). Unilateral neglect, representational schema and consciousness. *Brain, 102,* 609–618.

Brain, W. R. (1941). Visual disorientation with special reference to lesions of the right cerebral hemisphere. *Brain, 64,* 224–272.

Brown, J. W. (1983a). Rethinking the right hemisphere. In E. Perecman (Ed.), *Cognitive processing in the right hemisphere.* New York: Academic Press.

Brown, J. W. (1983b). The microstructure of perception: physiology and patterns of breakdown. *Cognition and Brain Theory, 6,* 145–184.

Caplan, B. (1985). Stimulus effect in unilateral neglect? *Cortex, 21,* 69–80.

Chain, F., Leblanc, M., Chedru, F., Lhermitte, F. (1979). Négligence visuelle dans les lésions postérieures de l'hémisphère gauche. *Revue Neurologique, 135,* 105–126.

Chedru, F., Leblanc, M., & Lhermitte, F. (1973). Visual searching in normal and brain damaged subjects (contribution to the study of unilateral inattention). *Cortex, 9,* 94–111.

Cohn, R. (1972). Eyeball movements in homonymous hemianopia following simultaneous bitemporal object presentation. *Neurology, 22,* 12–14.

Colombo, A., De Renzi, E., & Faglioni, P. (1976). The occurrence of visual neglect in patients with unilateral cerebral disease. *Cortex, 12,* 221–231.

Costa, L. D., Vaughan, H. G., Horowitz, M., & Ritter, W. (1969). Patterns of behavioral deficit associated with visual spatial neglect. *Cortex, 5,* 242–263.

Critchley, M. (1949). The phenomenon of tactile inattention with special reference to parietal lesions. *Brain, 72,* 538–561.

Critchley, M. (1953). *The parietal lobes.* New York: Hafner.

Denny-Brown, D., Meyer, J. S., & Horenstein, S. (1952). The significance of perceptual rivalry resulting from parietal lesions. *Brain, 75,* 433–471.

De Renzi, E. (1982). *Disorder of space perception and cognition.* New York: Wiley.

De Renzi, E., Colombo, A., Faglioni, P., & Gibertoni, M. (1982). Conjugate gaze paralysis in stroke patients with unilateral damage. *Archives of Neurology, 39,* 482–486.

De Renzi, E., Faglioni, P., & Scotti, G. (1970). Hemispheric contribution to the exploration of space through the visual and tactile modality. *Cortex, 6,* 191–203.

Faglioni, P., Scotti, G., & Spinnler, H. (1971). The performance of brain-damaged patients in spatial localization of visual and tactile stimuli. *Brain, 94,* 443–454.

Gainotti, G. (1968). Les manifestations de négligence et d'inattention pour l'hémispace. *Cortex, 4,* 64–91.

Gainotti, G., D'Erme, P., Monteleone, D., & Silveri, M. C. (1986). Mechanisms of unilateral spatial neglect in relation to laterality of cerebral lesions. *Brain, 109,* 599–612.

Gainotti, G., Messerli, P., & Tissot, R. (1972). Qualitative analysis of unilateral spatial neglect in relation to laterality of cerebral lesions. *Journal of Neurology, Neurosurgery and Psychiatry, 35,* 545–550.

Hecaen, H., Angelergues, R. (1963). La Cecitè Psychique. Paris: Masson

Heilman, K. M., Pandya, D. N., & Geschwind, N. (1970). Trimodal inattention following parietal lobe ablations. *Transactions of the American Neurological Association, 95,* 259–261.

Heilman, K. M., & Valenstein, E. (1972). Frontal lobe neglect in man. *Neurology, 22,* 660–664.

Heilman, K. M., Valenstein, E., & Watson, R. T. (1983). Localization of neglect. In A. Kertesz (Ed.), *Localization in neuropsychology* (pp. 371–392). New York: Academic Press.

Heilman, K. M., Valenstein, E., & Watson, R. T. (1985). The neglect syndrome. In P. J. Vinken, G. J. Bruyn, & H. L. Klawans (Eds.), *Handbook of clinical neurology. 45,* 152–183.

Kinsbourne, M. (1970). A model for the mechanism of unilateral neglect of space. *Transactions of the American Neurological Association, 95,* 143.

Kinsbourne, M. (1973). The control of attention by interaction between the cerebral hemispheres. In S. Kornblum (Ed.), *Attention and performance IV.* New York: Academic Press.

Kinsbourne, M. (1974). Direction of gaze and distribution of cerebral thought processes. *Neuropsychologia, 12,* 270–281.

Kinsbourne, M. (1977). Hemineglect and hemispheric rivalry. In E. A. Weinstein, & R. P. Friedland (Eds.), *Advances in neurology, Vol. 18.* New York: Raven Press.

Leicester, G., Sidman, M., Stoddard, L. T., & Mohr, J. P. (1969). Some determinants of visual neglect. *Journal of Neurology, Neurosurgery and Psychiatry, 32,* 580–587.

Marshal, C. R., & Maynard, R. M. (1983). Vestibular stimulation for supranuclear gaze palsy. *Archives of Physical Medicine and Rehabilitation, 64,* 134–146.

McFie, J., Piercy, M. F., & Zangwill, O. L. (1950). Visual spatial agnosia associated with lesions of the right hemisphere. *Brain, 73,* 167–190.

Meienberg, O., Harrer, M., & Wehren, C. (1986). Oculographic diagnosis of hemineglect in patients with homonymous hemianopia. *Journal of Neurology, 233,* 97–101.

Meienberg, O., Zangemeister, W. H., Rosenberg, M., Hoyt, F. T., & Stark, L. (1981). Saccadic eye movement strategies in patients with homonymous hemianopia. *Annals of Neurology, 9,* 537–544.

Mesulam, M.-M. (1981). A cortical network for directed attention and unilateral neglect. *Annals of Neurology, 10,* 309–325.

Ogden, J. (1985). Anterior-posterior interhemispheric differences in the loci of lesions producing visual hemineglect. *Brain and Cognition, 4,* 59–75.

Oxbury, J. M., Campbell, D. C., & Oxbury, S. M. (1974). Unilateral spatial neglect. *Brain, 97,* 551–564.

Piercy, M., Hécaen, H., & Ajuriaguerra, J. (1960). Constructional apraxia associated with unilateral cerebral lesions. Left and right cases compared. *Brain, 83,* 225–242.

Poppelreuter, W. L. (1917). *Die psychischen Schaedigungen durch Kopfschuss im Kriege 1914–1916. Die Stoerungen der niederen und hoheren Leistungen durch Verletzungen des Oksipitalhirns* (Vol. I). Leipzig: Leopold Voss. Referred to by Critchley, *Brain, 72,* 540.

Posner, M. I. (1980). Orienting of attention. The VIIth sir Frederic Bartlett Lecture. *Quarterly Journal of Experimental Psychology, 32,* 3–25.

Posner, M. I., & Cohen, Y. (1984). Components of visual orienting. In H. Bouma & D. Bowhuis (Eds.), *Attention and performance X* (pp. 531–556). Hillsdale, NJ: Lawrence Erlbaum Associates.

Posner, M. I., & Cohen, Y., & Rafal, R. D. (1982). Neural system control of spatial orienting. *Philosophical Transactions of the Royal Society of London, 298,* 187–198.

Posner, M. I., Walker, J., Friedrich, F. J., & Rafal, R. D. (1984). Effects of parietal injury on covert orienting of visual attention. *Journal of Neuroscience, 4,* 1863–1874.

Rubens, A. B. (1985). Caloric stimulation and unilateral visual neglect, *Neurology, 35,* 1019–1024.

Scheller, H., & Seideman, H. (1931). Zur Frage der Optischraumlichen Agnosie (zugleich ein Beitrag zur Dyslexie). *Monatschrift für Psychiatrie und Neurologie, 81,* 97–188. (Quoted by Critchley, M., 1953, The parietal lobes. Hafner, New York).

Schenkenberg, T., Bradford, D. C., & Ajax, E. T. (1980). Line bisection and unilateral visual neglect in patients with neurologic impairment. *Neurology, 30,* 509–517.

Schott, B., Jeannerod, M., & Zahin, M. A. (1966). L'agnosie spatiale unilatérale: perturbation en secteur des méchanismes d'exploration et de fixation du regard. *Journal de Medicine de Lyon, 47,* 169–195.

Silberpfennig, J. (1941). Contributions to the problem of eye movements. III Disturbances of ocular movements with pseudo-hemianopia in frontal tumors. *Confinia Neurologica, 4,* 1–13.

Sprague, J. M., Chambers, W. W., & Steller, E. (1961). Attentive, affective and adaptive behavior in the cat. *Science, 133,* 165–173.

Watson, R. T., Heilman, K. M., Cauthen, J. C., & King, F. A. (1973). Neglect after cingulectomy. *Neurology, 23,* 1003–1007.

Watson, R. T., Heilman, K. M., Miller, B. D., & King, F. A. (1974). Neglect after mesencephalic reticular formation lesions. *Neurology, 24,* 294–298.

Watson, R. T., Miller, B. D., & Heilman, K. M. (1978). Nonsensory neglect. *Annals of Neurology, 3,* 505–508.

Weinstein, E. A., & Friedland, R. P. (Eds.). (1977). *Hemi-inattention and hemispheric specialization. Advances in Neurology, 18.* New York: Raven Press.

Zarith, S. H., & Kahn, R. L. (1974). Impairment and adaptation in chronic disabilities: Spatial inattention. *Journal of Nervous and Mental Disease, 159,* 63–72.

7

Unilateral Misrepresentation of Distributed Information: Paradoxes and Puzzles

Edoardo Bisiach, M.D. and Anna Berti, M.D.

In contrast to many of my colleagues, I am not convinced that mere statements of fact or descriptions of experimental results suffice in the advancement of our science. We also need to reflect on the context of our work and permit ourselves some degree of speculation, if we are to make progress.

—R. Jung, 1952, p. 265

INTRODUCTION

As we move from the interface of nervous system and environment towards the interior, our insight of neural functions declines. Vast knowledge has accumulated concerning the way sensory input is initially processed to build up a lasting representation of the environment and aspects of the latter re-emerge in working memory and behavior. By contrast, very little is known about the structure and locus of acquired knowledge when it is not called on by ongoing surface activity. Although some brain lesions produce effects which seem to provide a clue to the understanding of deep representations, their symptoms are not without paradoxical aspects, some of which are considered in this chapter.

Our main purpose, here, is to expound three hypotheses about mental representation, which we formulated following observation of pathological behavior occurring in adults after focal brain damage. First, deep and surface representations are suggested to share a single basic code, which has analog properties. Second, stored information is multiplied and distributed over an extended neural net, so that a holographic model may capture some of its properties; its structure, however, departs from such a model in important respects. Third, the property usually referred to as "abstractedness," far from being a specific attribute of the deep code, is held to be a particular form of organization common to deep and surface representations.

145

NEUROPSYCHOLOGICAL EVIDENCE

Focal lesions of the right hemisphere resulting in hemi-neglect do not only impair perception and action in the left half of ego-centred space; they also affect mental representations such as visual imagery. Our patients were asked to imagine standing on one side of the main square in Milan, facing the cathedral, and to describe what they could see with their mind's eye (Figure 1, top). On this task, they reported a greater number of details to the right than to the left of the imaginary line of sight and often neglected very salient left-side particulars. When asked to do the same from the opposite vantage point (Figure 1, bottom), they could report previously neglected details from the right half of the second perspective, but ignored left-side items which they had reported a few moments

FIGURE 1 Facing the cathedral in Milan (top) and looking at the square from the cathedral's main door (bottom).

before (Bisiach & Luzzatti, 1978; Bisiach, Capitani, Luzzatti, and Perani, 1981). With one possible exception (see Case N. 77 of Bisiach et al., 1981), these patients were suffering from lesions involving the right temporo-parieto-occipital junction.

Barbut and Gazzaniga (1987) observed similar behavior in a patient with right parietal infarction. This patient was asked to imagine himself in New York, facing California, and to name the states which lay in front of him. Three days after the stroke he named 10, all on the right. On the 7th day he still ignored 6 states on the left but only 3 on the right.

Baxter and Warrington (1983) reported the case of a patient with left hemi-neglect who misspelled the left half of words (both forwards and backwards), as if he were reading, letter by letter, from words written on an imaginary board. The same phenomenon was observed by Barbut and Gazzaniga; in their patient, the disability also affected writing in a particular way: Errors in the left half of the words disappeared in mirror-reversed writing, as if he could properly represent the beginnings of words as soon as they were *artificially* transposed to the right.

These findings constitute a two-fold paradox. On the one hand, neglect patients seem to suffer impairment of the left half of their mental representations due to a lesion of the right half of their brain. This suggests the existence of a spatial isomorphism, at a cognitive level, between an object and its neural representation, parallel to the isomorphism present at more peripheral levels (e.g., in the calcarine cortex). However, the retained ability to adequately represent the impaired halves of *surface* representations in a different frame, shows that the stored information from which they originate is not lost after focal brain damage.

On the other hand, given that long-term information about the environment is still available after brain damage causing representational neglect, why are cognitive processes unable to retrieve it, or to monitor the failure of retrieval? Why are they unable to compensate for the representational scotoma, contrary to what happens with the perceptual scotoma in the case of pure hemianopia? This seems to be in striking contrast with the principle of massive connectivity characterizing the nervous processes at the highest levels of activity, a principle which is presupposed by claims of "isotropism" of cognitive processes (Fodor, 1983). The paradox is especially apparent in the failure to retain the representational content of consciousness at any given time as soon as the frame, but not the content, changes.

A parsimonious solution of the riddle may be attempted by making two basic assumptions. First, idle and working memory are implemented in the same mechanism, following common principles of neural organization. The content of working memory at a given time, however, is a subset of the potential activities which the mechanism may perform; a subset which is not only defined over the range of all possible mental representations, but has special constraints of its own, which will presently be discussed. Second, consciousness is identified with working memory and is therefore subject to the same constraints as the latter in accessing information laid down in the long-term store.

In what follows, we first address the issue of surface representations and then venture some speculation on the format of representations in idle memory.

A NEURAL MODEL OF A REPRESENTATIONAL SYSTEM

We have outlined elsewhere (Bisiach, Meregalli, & Berti, in press) a neural model of a representational system (Figure 2).

The model is an ego-centered spatial analog and its basic units are cell assemblies which can be recruited both by sensory input and input originating from within the nervous system. Sensory activation of the representational system is provided by the spatially isomorphic neural code generated on the sensory surface by an external stimulus (e.g., by an object MN horizontally elongated in a frontal plane) and transmitted by a transducer (layer I). Information carried by the latter does not immediately project to the working memory of the representational system (layers II and III). Before reaching this level, indeed, sensory information is assumed to undergo parallel processing of different features such as shape, color, location on the sensory surface and movement, by separate, dedicated components of the nervous system. Furthermore, and crucial to the purpose of this discussion, invariant spatial properties of the environment are assumed to be extracted, so that, for example, overwritten sensory messages resulting from different orientations of the receptor surface over a stationary array, or from objects in motion with respect to a stationary receptor surface, are

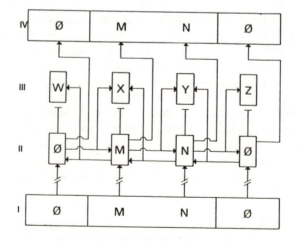

FIGURE 2   A neural model of a representational system.

disentangled and laid down on the ego-centered retinoid surface of the spatial analog, reinstating the spatial relationships among the corresponding objects in outer space (see Bisiach, Capitani, & Porta, 1985, for a discussion of the concept of ego-center). The surface of the representational analog is made up of cell assemblies (layer II) which accept orthogonal input from the sensory transducer and horizontal input from adjoining assemblies at the same functional level. Horizontal recruitment may account for inferential processes such as the perceptual completion corresponding to the projection of the retina's blind spot on single fixations, or the emergence of visual illusory contours, of which neural correlates have been found in area 18 of the monkey (von der Heydt, Peterhans, & Baumgartner, 1984).

Cell assemblies embedded in the representational analog may also accept endogenous input (top-down pathways are omitted in the diagram). Although artificially separated in the graph, sensory-driven and internally-driven cell assemblies (layers II and III, respectively) are assumed to share a common neural network. The activity of internally driven cell assemblies which do not match actual portions of the incoming message is damped down by spatially corresponding sensory driven ("veridical") assemblies. Thus, the output of the analog constitutes an adequate representation of current sensory stimulation, and, in normal waking conditions, no belief of reality is attached to endogenous mental images forming on the surface of the spatial analog, not even in the case of representations as vivid as hypnagogic images. According to the model, indeed, beliefs are fixed by default: If sensory driven cell assemblies are pathologically inactive, if they fail to signal the content (or the lack of content) of sensory transducers, then one can *see*—not just *imagine*—unicorns!

It must be noted that, for initial purposes, the model need not be identified with any definite anatomical structure. Indeed, it corresponds to a function which is unlikely to be implemented in a single mechanism, but might result from joint activities in the topologically structured areas which have been found to occupy most of what is still named "sensory association cortex," according to the traditional view, a revision of which has been advocated by Diamond (1979) (see also Merzenich & Kaas, 1980, and Cowey, 1985).

On the other hand it is worth specifying that by "cell assemblies" we explicitly refer to the classic Hebbian concept of more or less stable wiring patterns among subsets of neurons operating within a larger network, a concept updated by recent evidence and speculation concerning, among other things, the formation and the role of short-term neuronal groupings which instantly form and fade out depending on ongoing sensory and endogenous input (Crick, 1984; Goddard, 1980; von der Marlsburg, 1981). This specification is necessary to the introduction of a further basic property of our model, which radically qualifies that initially enunciated in the form of an analog device: namely, the capability of imposing structure upon the raw material delivered by sense organs. Indeed, the basic unit of the representational medium is not intrinsically meaningless pixels, but meaningful combinatorial activities of clusters of neurons. This endows the system with the ability to achieve different parsings of the same object and, conversely, to organize a given part into different hierarchies with varying degrees of complexity (see Hinton, 1979, for a discussion of such structures in mental imagery). It must also be added that, although in the diagram horizontal connections between cell assemblies forming the representational array are only shown for adjacent pairs, they are also held to link nonadjacent pairs, in order to ensure global, Gestalt-like interactions over the entire field.

The embodiment of a device capable of this kind of analysis and synthesis in the representational analog is the mandatory requirement for the latter to qualify as a cognitive system. There is some empirical support for the implementation of logical processes of this kind within the framework of an analog device. As noted by Pinker (1984, footnote on p. 22), a model embodying such parsing abilities predicts that, in hemi-neglect, meaningful fractions of complex objects are spared or misrepresented all of a piece, that is, not following haphazard contours, as would be predicted by models inspired uniquely by the laws of physical optics. This is indeed what is often seen when hemi-neglect patients draw or follow with their forefingers the contours of pictures. For example, although the clock-dial of Figure 3a is compatible with the idea of a literally picture-like representation, half-effaced as a consequence of the destruction of one half of the representational medium, that of Figure 3b shows how optical rules alone cannot wholly capture the essence of this medium. The inextricability of purely geomet-

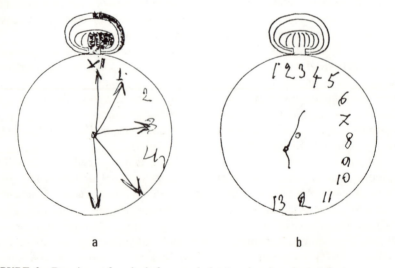

a   b

FIGURE 3   Drawings of a clock-face made by two hemi-neglect patients.

Reprinted with permission from Bisiach et al. (1981). Brain and conscious representation of outside reality. *Neuropsychologia, 19,* Copyright 1981, Pergamon Journals Ltd.

rical principles from other kinds of organizational rules is also demonstrated by the fact that the disorder of one half of the optical analog may even subvert nonspatial aspects of activities involving the unaffected half (Bisiach, Berti, & Vallar, 1985).

THE STRUCTURE OF REPRESENTATION IN LONG-TERM STORE

Up to this point, a possible representational mechanism has been hypothesized limited to working memory functions. What remains to be considered is the puzzle as to the format and locus of stored information when it does not surface in any ongoing activity. This subject, our ignorance of which is abysmal, is usually neglected in textbooks and cursorily dealt with even in more specific literature, which often fails to explicitly distinguish between idle and working aspects of representations.

Concerning the nature of the engram, however, there appear to be two basic options. Both start from the obvious truth that, near to the input and output interfaces, information about the environment can either be processed in a sensory-specific code or in the symbolic code provided by any natural language: *a rose is a rose* (a drawing) *is a rose* (a name). (For present purposes we regard working memory as constituting a relatively peripheral processing level, even when it is loaded with long-term memory, rather than with sensory information, and when its contents do not translate in overt behavior). According to one view, however, sensory and linguistic surface information converge towards a deep code; this is somewhat ambiguously termed "abstract," which may either mean neutral or imply distillation of some essential features of surface information. The second view is the well-known double-code thesis championed by Paivio, which stresses the distinction between sensory-specific and linguistic codes throughout the chain of vicissitudes undergone by information within the system. A further approach exists, which is considered to have originated from ideas exposed by Whorf in 1956; it maintains that language has a dominant role in shaping representations. Because this position is now only of historical interest, it is not further discussed here (short reviews can be found in Baddeley, 1976, p. 217, and in Paivio 1978, p. 377).

Our dissatisfaction with the first approach originates from several considerations.

This approach is typically embraced by adherents to uncompromising functionalism. Strongly influenced by computer science, this current has extended to nervous activity the duality of hard- and software, which naturally applies to man-made machines but acquires metaphysical overtones when forced upon the brain. In practice, this step leads to a dead end as far as the understanding of representations is concerned. In its extreme form, in fact, this doctrine denies any cognitive status to representational structures carrying the stigma of a sensory code (Pylyshyn, 1984). It postulates a semantic qualification which is not recognized *directly* in the net of interactions between ongoing and recorded sensory messages. The concept of "proposition," suggested for cognitive representations, although clear as far as its metaphorical reference to computer programmes is concerned, becomes fairly nebulous when applied to the brain. Whatever intuitions—including potentially very useful ones—may be conveyed by the term "proposition," the idea that sensory-specific information is (at a certain level) superseded would in our view be gratuitous and leave us with a vacuous system of free-floating referenceless symbols and symbolic operations. Similar criticism has been raised by Paivio (1977, pp. 56 ff.). We have developed our point in a recent discussion of the neural bases of visual imagery (Bisiach & Berti, forthcoming) and will not reiterate our arguments here.

As for the second approach, the same a priori argument directed against propositions would apply to the idea of an *autonomous* "second signalling system" running parallel to the sensory-specific flow of information. Such a system, indeed, would never be conceivable in isolation from its referential basis as long as it retained semantic competence, the criterion for which being satisfied by behavioral indications of a *coherent system of semantic relationships* joining words and object representations. This excludes pathological debris of merely verbal associations without a proper semantic basis, whereby, for example, a patient with disordered color gnosis may still assert that "snow is white." Granted that this does not seem to be the idea defended by the dual-code thesis, we fail to see any substantial difference between this approach and the view, favored e.g., by Hebb (1968), which posits the primary role of sensory-specific representations.

Although the assertion might at first sound outrageous, we should guard ourselves against exaggerate views of the role of language, both in phylogenesis and in ontogenesis. While acknowledging all merits of language as an advanced behavioral technology and as a vehicle of thought processes, we should keep in mind that at the input side verbal utterances belong to the same physical domain—and undergo the same neural processes—as the bell sounds employed by Pavlov to condition salivary responses. On the output side, they are enormously different in complexity, but not in principle, from the various shrieks which monkeys use to signal different emergency situations to the colony.

Far from constituting an "amodal" system, verbal representations undergo the same neurophysiological constraints as sensory-like representations, of which the previously mentioned observations by Baxter and Warrington and by Barbut and Gazzaniga provide clear evidence. It is worth adding that Barbut and Gazzaniga's patient not only beheaded words in reading and in writing, but also in spontaneous speech (for example, he said "bulance" for "ambulance"), which shows the pervasiveness of the spatial disorder which had befallen his verbal system.

Verbal representation of outside reality is of no avail to neglect patients unable to form adequate mental images in the left half of imaginary space; rather, it may aggravate the disorder by filling that space with uncontrolled, confabulated fantasies, which in their extreme form may give rise to "somatoparaphrenic" delusions (Gerstmann, 1942), i.e., to elaborate delusions about one half of the patient's body.

A possible objection maintaining that the above examples merely reveal a mirror-reversed Hoeffding step in the formation of mental representations in working memory and in their externalization as overt behavior, i.e., the top-down translation of amodal semantic content into cognitively impenetrable (i.e., physiologically constrained) structures, would be quite implausible. The absence of cognitive monitoring and compensation shows indeed that the mentioned disorders do not originate in peripheral structures, but proceed from the very core of the cognitive processes.

On the whole, the body of empirical evidence (as reviewed, e.g., by Paivio, 1978, and Paivio and te Linde, 1982) does not undermine Hebb's position which maintains that cognitive processes are basically nonverbal. In spite of differences in emphasis, there seems to be much agreement between this position and that transpiring from the cautious remark made by Paivio at the end of his 1978 chapter: "It remains to be determined just how much "cognitive work" can go on entirely within [the] verbal network, independently of its connections with perceptual representations." The final answer, in fact, might be: "nothing."

Assuming the nonsymbolic, sensory-derived character of the structures in which the basic representation of the environment is stored, we may attempt some conjecture about how a neural net preserves the traces of information conveyed by individual sensory channels. Given the architecture of the nervous system, we are apparently offered two options. Representational items should either be wholly couched in the memory of individual cells or in particular patterns of connectivity involving constellations of neurons.

One of the obvious advantages of the latter solution is that the combinatorial potential of the whole synaptic net involved in the task would grant the storage of an enormous amount of information in form of anagrams, in which any cell would be a member of more than one representational item. This could answer objections (e.g., Pylyshyn, 1973) relative to the prohibitive burden imposed on the nervous system by the storage of sensory-like representations (see Paivio, 1977, pp 57–58, for further arguments). Another advantage would lie in the fact that this solution is intuitively much more apt to explain generative processes such as the creation of unexperienced representations, of which hypnagogic images constitute a common and most impressive example. A third advantage would be that a common medium and a common format is offered to inactive and active phases of representation. Inactive phases of different working-memory representations (e.g., of the opposite views of the square of which our neglect patients were asked to form a mental image) would overlap, as it were, in the representational analog in which they are structured, as in Figure 4. They would be constituted by the pattern of connectivity which the experience of the environment has created in the neural net in which the representational system is implemented. Recruitment of particular cell assemblies on the basis of configurations already embedded in the framework of idle memory would give rise to surface representations.

Obviously, the idea conveyed by Figure 4, is a gross oversimplification of the spatial analog. As previously hinted, the neural architecture of the latter is conceivably distributed over a number of components, each responsible for the processing of individual characteristics of representations, such as shape, color, location in space, motion, etc. Moreover, it cannot be excluded that different processing levels might participate in its constitution. As suggested by Hebb (1968) and, more recently, by Shepard, the representational process might involve "resonances" (Shepard, 1984) which propagate in a direction contrary to that followed by perceptual information, thus explaining the variable degree of clarity in mental representation. The representational system, indeed, may globally be conceived as constituted by all sensory mechanisms which turn out to be susceptible to top-down activation.

Moreover, the pictorial characteristics suggested by Figure 4 should not be taken too literally. They do correspond to the pictoriality of the subjective experience we have when we form a visual image. They are also in accordance with the firm indications of spatial isomorphism between represented objects and representing neural activities drawn from the behavior of neglect patients, which offer a tangible confirmation of the analog theory of mental representation in

FIGURE 4 Overlap of the two perspectives shown in Figure 1.

working memory developed by Shepard, by Kosslyn and by their associates (see Shepard, 1975, and Kosslyn, 1980, for reviews; see also Bisiach & Berti, in press, for neuropsychological arguments). However, they are likely to be very far from portraying the neural organization of long-term sensory-specific memory in all its complexity.

For example, if we assume a common substrate for active and idle representation, the fact that the imaginary sensory field experienced in mental representations overlies the perceptual field in an ego-centered space and that ego-centered structures in working memory may be inferred from neuropsychological findings seems to contrast with the ability of visual cells in area IT of the monkey to respond in a highly specific way to particular patterns, independent of their location and orientation (Desimone, Albright, Gross, & Bruce, 1984). This might suggest the existence of a representational system storing shapes in terms of object-centered coordinates (see Marr & Nishihara, 1978), separate from the system which represents the same shapes in working memory in terms of ego-centered coordinates.

The contrast, as it will presently be argued, may only be apparent, and does not undermine the hypothesis of a unitary representational system for long-term and working memory.

In the nervous system there must obviously be mechanisms which extract, store, and reactivate information about objects and classes of objects, and which generalize over the variety of spatial locations, orientations, sizes, etc. (see Weiskrantz & Saunders, 1984, and Desimone et al., 1984), corresponding to Hebb's concept of higher-order cell assemblies. These mechanisms are likely to be multiplied for single representational items over the expanse of the synaptic net of the system to ensure the degree of equipotentiality required to account for the relative resistance of their functions to brain damage. Lashley's claim (1960) was to a large extent right, and Pribram has reiterated it by suggesting the holographic metaphor of brain activity (Pribram, 1971, 1977; Pribram, Nuwer, & Baron, 1974). The holographic hypothesis is appealing since it carries the idea of an imaginal character of long-term representations (to the extent to which a hologram may be considered an image); it must however be complemented in order to provide a long-term basis for the realization of the cognitive structures which have previously been considered at the level of working memory representation.

A device exclusively subjected to the laws of physical optics, such as the hologram, is an unintelligent device which does not fully qualify as a metaphor for the representational system of the brain, unless further principles of organization are posited which exploit its resources. If we want to avoid merely functional concepts such as *propositions,* which downgrade sensory-specific representation to the role of raw material, perpetuate the unnatural dissociation between hard- and software aspects of nervous activity, and may lead one astray by suggesting improper attributions to inner language, we must resort to some known or conceivable properties of the nervous system. At present, the concept of cell assembly may be deemed too sketchy and versatile to serve the purposes of any cognitive theory. Yet it seems to be the best we have to start with.

Cell assemblies may have componential properties apt to encode as unitary engrams stimuli as complex as faces, a fact, however, which might perhaps be accounted for by a hierarchy of simple to hypercomplex neurons, as suggested by Desimone et al. (1984). They may "abstract," in the sense of extracting, e.g., the "concepts" of *roundness* from a circle and a hexagon, of *angularity* from a hexagon and a square, and of *regular geometrical figure* from the three of them by discriminating what the cell assemblies relative to each figure have in common; a task, presumably, which might also be accomplished by a hierarchy of detectors. They constitute, however, the ideal medium in which various kinds of manipulations of mental representation such as rotation, translation, etc. can be modeled (see Trehub, 1977), and in which could presumably be modeled the emergence of unforeseen Gestalten, e.g., when the image of a wire-frame cube is rotated in space so that two opposite corners lie on a vertical line (Hinton, 1979). It must be noted that although Gestalten such as the upright and inverted "tripods" formed by the edges converging onto the upper and lower corners of the rotated cube are easily nameable, and supplying their verbal labels can prompt their individuation by people to whom it has not spontaneously occurred, such Gestalten must initially emerge at a perceptual, not at a linguistic level. This is true of any ambiguous pattern such as the well-known "wife-mother in law" figure.

Furthermore, cell assemblies, whatever their actual structure in the neural net, are articulated patterns. This means that they can have (and in fact *must* have) handles, as it were, so that the representations implemented in them could be referred to an ego-centered representational frame when activated in working memory, which, as previously argued, regularly happens.

In other words, cell assemblies must both be object- and viewer-centered. Whereas the object-centered organization is intrinsic in a cell assembly (wherever this is located—for example in area IT), the spatial indexing system providing an ego-centered frame of reference for that assembly might be located elsewhere: it is likely to be implemented in the neural structures where lesion entails hemi-neglect. In man at least, a crucial locus is to be found near the temporo-parieto-occipital junction (see, however, Heilman, Watson, & Valenstein, 1985, and Vallar & Perani, 1987). The ego-centered spatial indexing system is called in whenever an idle representation is activated in working memory. The representation is thus constrained into one out of a multitude of ego-centered perspectives. The portion of it which, according to the selected perspective, corresponds to a local failure of the indexing system cannot surface into active memory. In spite of its integrity in the long-term store, that portion does not emerge into the subject's consciousness.

CONCLUSIONS AND PROSPECTS

In arguing for the three hypotheses stated in the introduction, we have suggested a representational mechanism which may apply to any sensory analyzer. (It has not been considered to what extent parts of this mechanism are shared by different sensory modalities). An oversimplified model of this mechanism has been described, the actual implementation of which in the nervous system is admittedly quite problematic. The major value of this mechanism would be that of providing a coherent means of tying together surface aspects of sensory representation (in which analog properties can easily be recognized) and deep aspects of the same (in which analog properties are not clearly discernible) in a single functional complex which could account for cognitive processes, no matter how sophisticated, without resorting to language or to explanatory principles which deliberately abstain from making reference to the nervous system. This mechanism is held to be unitary but not monolytic; the problem of its parsing has already been attacked by Kosslyn and associates in split-brain patients (Kosslyn, Holtzmann, Farah, & Gazzaniga, 1985) and by Farah in patients with focal brain damage (Farah, 1984; Levine, Warach, & Farah, 1985) with intriguing results (see Kosslyn, 1987, for a review).

Partial failures of the mechanism at issue correspond to clinical disorders such as hemi-neglect, anosognosia, and related disorders.

According to our model, a complete circumscribed impairment of the ego-centered indexing system entails the inability to activate cell assemblies which should project information into the corresponding sector of the spatial analog for working memory, whereas the same assemblies may be activated if recruited outside the representational scotoma, as in the previously mentioned instances of representational neglect. Damage limited to the interface between spatial analog and sensory transducer, by preventing a normal activation of sensory-driven cell assemblies (layer II), leaves room for "confabulatory" firing of cell assemblies unrelated to current sensory stimulation, resulting in phenomena of pathological completion, or delusory beliefs related to one side of egocentric space *(somatoparaphrenia)*. In the latter condition, the patient may deny the ownership of a limb on one side of his body, or recognize it as his own though denying its being paralyzed *(anosognosia)*. In some instances the patients acknowledge the impossibility of moving a limb but misinterpret it as being due, for example, to rheumatism; this constitutes particularly striking evidence for a high-level cognitive dysfunction, since it shows that what is lacking in these cases is the capability to realize the loss of willed control over one part of the body.

By merging hemi-neglect and phenomena such as somato-paraphrenia and anosognosia in a unitary syndrome, different aspects of which would appear as consequences of different dysfunctions of the same mechanism—and for which we revived the term "dyschiria," adopted by Zingerle in 1913—, we were fully aware of the implications of our analog model for a theory of consciousness. According to this model, in fact, anosognosia and related misbeliefs cannot be explained away as being a psychodynamic reaction to the catastrophe engendered by the illness (see also Bisiach et al., 1986, for further arguments), but must be interpreted as a *local* disorder of consciousness. This is tantamount to saying that intentional aspects of the mind do not proceed from a unitary entity at the summit of the cognitive processes, free from the topological constraints which characterize sensory and motor activities, but are themselves structured in an analog format.

It was not without concern that we set out to test the model's most momentous prediction. According to it, the severe disorder of consciousness resulting in anosognosia, although cognitively impenetrable (in the sense which Pylyshyn gives to these terms), that is unmodifiable by the complex of knowledge implicit in the patient's mind or made explicit to him by the examiner, should yield to noncognitive manoeuvres which have been proven to influence hemi-neglect. By recovering a forgotten, though very important observation by Silberpfennig (1941), Rubens (1985) and Jason Brown (personal communication) have shown that caloric vestibular stimulation ipsilateral to the brain lesion transitorily removes visual hemi-neglect. The effect is unlikely to depend on contralateral eye deviation due to unilateral stimulation of the vestibular system. Indeed, we have obtained the same result in an eye-closed condition in which patients had to reach with the unaffected right hand for a target (their contralateral hand) located in the neglected hemispace (Cappa, Sterzi, Vallar, & Bisiach, 1987). The four cases of hemi-neglect in whom we investigated the effects of ipsilesional caloric stimulation (or contralateral inhibition) to test our model, had left hemiplegia and were severely anosognosic. They persisted in denying their motor defect even after the examiner had demonstrated its presence with routine neurological procedures. Although hemi-neglect was transitorily removed or markedly attenuated in all four patients during vestibular stimulation—thus confirming Rubens' results as well as those of Jason Brown—anosognosia remained unchanged in two. The other two, however, showed a regression of the symptom, mild in one but clearcut in the other. These results, if confirmed, would lend strong empirical support to the model we have suggested. In particular, they would buttress our contention that the most critical aspect of cognitive activities, consciousness, is intimately tied to the texture of sensory representation and shows the same analog properties which are shown by the latter.

ACKNOWLEDGMENTS

The preparation of this chapter was in part supported by grants from CNR and MPI to the first author. We would like to express our appreciation to Allan Paivio for his helpful comments on our first draft.

REFERENCES

Baddeley, A. D. (1976). *The psychology of memory*. New York: Basic Books.

Barbut, D., & Gazzaniga, M. S. (1987). Disturbances in conceptual space involving language and speech. *Brain, 110,* 1487–1496.

Baxter, D. M., & Warrington, E. K. (1983). Neglect dysgraphia. *Journal of Neurology, Neurosurgery and Psychiatry, 46,* 1073–1078.

Bisiach, E., & Berti, A. (in press). Waking images and neural activity. In A. Sheikh & R. G. Kunzendorf (Eds.), *Psychophysiology of mental imagery: Theory, research, and application*. Baywood Publishing Co.

Bisiach, E., Berti, A., & Vallar, G. (1985). Analogical and logical disorders underlying unilateral neglect of space. In M. I. Posner & O. S. M. Marin (Eds.), *Attention and performance XI,* 239–246. Hillsdale, NJ: Lawrence Erlbaum Associates.

Bisiach, E., Capitani, E., Luzzatti, C., & Perani, D. (1981). Brain and conscious representation of outside reality. *Neuropsychologia, 19,* 543–551.

Bisiach, E., Capitani, E., & Porta, E. (1985). Two basic properties of space representation in the brain. *Journal of Neurology, Neurosurgery and Psychiatry, 48,* 141–144.

Bisiach, E., & Luzzatti, C. (1978). Unilateral neglect of representational space. *Cortex, 14,* 129–133.

Bisiach, E., Meregalli, S., & Berti, A. (in press). Mechanisms of production-control and belief-fixation in human visuospatial processing: Clinical evidence from hemispatial neglect. In M. L. Commons, S. M. Kosslyn, & R. J. Herrnstein (Eds.), *Pattern recognition and concepts in animals, people, and machines*. Hillsdale, NJ: Lawrence Erlbaum Associates.

Bisiach, E., Vallar, G., Perani, D., Papagno, C., & Berti, A. (1986). Unawareness of disease following lesions of the right hemisphere: Anosognosia for hemiplegia and anosognosia for hemianopia. *Neuropsychologia, 24,* 471–482.

Cappa, S., Sterzi, R., Vallar, G., & Bisiach, E. (1987). Remission of hemineglect during vestibular stimulation. *Neuropsychologia, 25,* 775–782.

Cowey, A. (1985). Aspects of cortical organization related to selective attention and selective impairments of visual perception: A tutorial review. In M. I. Posner, & O. S. M. Marin (Eds.), *Attention and performance XI,* 41–62. Hillsdale, NJ: Lawrence Erlbaum Associates.

Crick, F. (1984). Function of the thalamic reticular complex: The searchlight hypothesis. *Proceedings of the National Academy of Sciences, 81,* 4585–4590.

Desimone, R., Albright, T. D., Gross, C. G., & Bruce C. (1984). Stimulus-selective properties of inferior temporal neurons in the macaque. *Journal of Neuroscience, 4,* 2051–2062.

Diamond, I. T. (1979). The subdivisions of neocortex: A proposal to revise the traditional view of sensory, motor, and association areas. *Progress in Psychobiology and Physiological Psychology, 8,* 1–43.

Farah, M. J. (1984). The neural basis of mental imagery: A componential analysis. *Cognition, 18,* 245–272.

Fodor, J. (1983). *The modularity of mind.* Cambridge, MA: MIT Press.

Gerstmann, J. (1942). Problem of imperception of disease and of impaired body territories with organic lesions. Relation to body scheme and its disorders. *Archives of Neurology and Psychiatry, 48,* 890–913.

Goddard, G. V. (1980). Component properties of the memory machine: Hebb revisited. In P. W. Jusczyk, & R. M. Klein (Eds.), *The nature of thought. Essays in honor of D. O. Hebb* (pp. 231–247). Hillsdale, NJ: Lawrence Erlbaum Associates.

Hebb, D. O. (1968). Concerning imagery. *Psychological Review, 75,* 466–472.

Heilman, K. M., Watson, R. T., & Valenstein, E. (1985). Neglect and related disorders. In K. M. Heilman, & E. Valenstein (Eds.), *Clinical neuropsychology* (pp. 243–293). New York: Oxford University Press.

Hinton, G. (1979). Some demonstrations of the effects of structural descriptions in mental imagery. *Cognitive Science, 3,* 231–250.

Jung, R. (1962). Summary of the conference. In V. B. Mountcastle (Ed.), *Interhemispheric relations and cerebral dominance* (pp. 264–277). Baltimore: The Johns Hopkins Press.

Kosslyn, S. M. (1980). *Image and mind.* Cambridge, MA: Harvard University Press.

Kosslyn, S. M. (1987). Seeing and imagining in the cerebral hemispheres: A computational approach. *Psychological Review, 94,* 148–175.

Kosslyn, S. M., Holtzmann, J. D., Farah, M. J., & Gazzaniga, M. S. (1985). A computational analysis of mental image generation: Evidence from functional dissociations in split-brain patients. *Journal of Experimental Psychology: General, 114,* 311–341.

Lashley, K. S. (1960). Persistent problems in the evaluation of mind. In F. A. Beach, H. W. Nissen, & E. G. Boring (Eds.), *The neuropsychology of Lashley* (pp. 455–477). New York: McGraw-Hill.

Levine, D. N., Warach, J., & Farah, M. (1985). Two visual systems in mental imagery: Dissociation of "what" and "where" in imagery disorders due to bilateral posterior cerebral lesions. *Neurology, 35,* 1010–1018.

Marr, D., & Nishihara, H. K. (1978). Representation and recognition of the spatial organization of three-dimensional shapes. *Proceedings of the Royal Society, London. B 207,* 187–217.

Merzenich M. M., & Kaas, J. H. (1980). Principles of organization of sensory-perceptual systems in mammals. *Progress in Psychobiology and Physiological Psychology, 9,* 1–41.

Paivio, A. (1977). Images, propositions and knowledge. In J. M. Nicholas (Ed.), *Images, perception, and knowledge* (pp. 47–71). Dordrecht, Holland: Reidel.

Paivio, A. (1978). The relationship between verbal and perceptual codes. In C. Carterette & M. P. Friedman (Eds.), *Handbook of Perception, Vol. VIII* (pp. 375–397).

Paivio, A., & te Linde, J. (1982). Imagery, memory, and the brain, *Canadian Journal of Psychology, 36,* 243–272.

Pinker, S. (1984). Visual cognition: An introduction. *Cognition, 18,* 1–63.

Pribram, K. H. (1971). *Languages of the brain.* Englewood Cliffs, NJ: Prentice-Hall.

Pribram. K. H. (1977). Holonomy and structure in the organization of perception. In J.
    M. Nicholas (Ed.), *Images, perception, and knowledge* (pp. 155–185).
Pribram, K. H., Nuwer, M., & Baron, R. (1974). The holographic hypothesis of memory
    structure in brain function and perception. In R. C. Atkinson, D. H. Krantz, R. C.
    Luce, & P. Suppes (Eds.), *Contemporary developments in mathematical psycholo-
    gy, Vol II* (pp. 416–457). San Francisco: Freeman.
Pylyshyn, Z. W. (1973). What the mind's eye tells the mind's brain: A critique of mental
    imagery. *Psychological Bulletin, 80,* 1–24.
Pylyshyn, Z. W. (1984). *Computation and cognition.* Cambridge, MA: MIT Press.
Rubens, A. B. (1985). Caloric stimulation and unilateral visual neglect. *Neurology, 35,*
    1019–1024.
Shepard, R. N. (1975). Form, formation and transformation of internal representations. In
    R. L. Solso (Ed.), *Information processing and cognition: The Loyola symposium*
    (pp. 87–122). Hillsdale, NJ: Lawrence Erlbaum Associates.
Shepard, R. N. (1984). Ecological constraints on internal representations. Resonant
    kinematics of perceiving, imagining, thinking and dreaming. *Psychological Review,
    91,* 417–477.
Silberpfennig, J. (1941). Contributions to the problem of eye movements. III. Dis-
    turbances of ocular movements with pseudo hemianopsia in frontal tumors. *Confinia
    Neurologica, 4,* 1–13.
Trehub, A. (1977). Neuronal models for cognitive processes: Networks for learning,
    perception and imagination. *Journal of Theoretical Biology, 65,* 141–169.
Vallar, G., & Perani, D. (1987). The anatomy of spatial neglect in humans. In M.
    Jeannerod (Ed.), *Neurophysiological and neuropsychological aspects of spatial
    neglect* (pp. 235–258). Amsterdam: North-Holland.
von der Heydt, R., Peterhans, E. & Baumgartner, G. (1984). Illusory contours and
    cortical neuron responses. *Science, 224,* 1260–1262.
von der Malsburg, C. (1981). *The correlation theory of brain function.* Internal Report
    81-2, Department of Neurobiology, Max-Planck-Institute for Biophysical chemistry,
    D-3400 Goettingen, West-Germany.
Weiskrantz, L., & Saunders, R. C. (1984). Impairments of visual object transforms in
    monkeys. *Brain, 107,* 1033–1072.
Wharf, B. L. (1956). *Language, thought and reality.* Cambridge, England: Technology
    Press.
Zingerle, H. (1913). Ueber Stoerungen der Wahrnehmung des eigenen Koerpers bei
    organischen Gehirnerkrankungen. *Monatschrift für Psychiatrie und Neurologie, 34,*
    13–36.

IV
Disorders of Visual Imagery

8

Comments on Some Positive Visual Phenomena Caused by Diseases of the Brain

Lawrence Jacobs, M.D.

INTRODUCTION

Unusual sensory experiences are sometimes spontaneously reported by patients with neurologic disorders and "subjective visual sensations" (Gowers, 1895) continue to receive considerable attention from clinicians. Increasing awareness by clinicians of various unusual aberrations of vision has led to more frequent recognition of them during neurologic examination and phenomena previously thought of as being extremely rare have been discovered to occur more commonly when sought for by careful history taking. In this chapter I review several positive visual phenomena that may occur spontaneously in disease states of the brain. It is likely that cerebral irritation due to partial deafferentation is at the basis of each type of aberration. Palinopsia is considered first and in greatest detail because it often seems to be an integral component of the other visual illusory phenomena. Related positive phenomena in the acoustic realm are also briefly described.

PALINOPSIA

Palinopsia is an illusion of persistence or recurrence of a visual percept after the real, external stimulus is no longer in view (Bender, Feldman, & Sobin, 1968). The phenomenon is not hallucinatory because the persisting or recurring image is of an object that was actually seen by the patient (usually in the relatively immediate past) and is recognized as such. In some cases of palinopsia there is only unusual persistence of an image; in others, the persistent image fades only to recur after an illusion-free interval of variable length; in still others, the palinoptic image only recurs after an illusion-free interval after viewing the real external stimulus. In the strict sense of the word palinopsia applies to illusions that recur after illusion-free intervals (palin-again, Gr) and visual perseveration applies to the persistence of visual images (seconds to minutes) immediately following stimulus removal. However, there is no critical image duration which distinguishes palinopsia from extended normal after-images and there have been many patients who experienced palinopsia both as a perseveration immediately following stimulus removal and as an illusion that recurred after an illusion-free interval. A variation of palinopsia consists of an illusory extension of the visual perception over an area greater than that which the stimulus object would be expected to excite. This illustory visual spread is clearly different from palinopsia because the illusion only occurs so long as the actual visual stimulus remains in view and disappears as soon as it is removed.

These phenomena, previously described under the general category of hallucinations or "visual attacks" by previous authors (see Horrax, 1923; Robinson & Watt, 1947), were first clearly defined as distinct types of visual perseveration in time ("paliopsia") and space ("illusory visual spread") by Critchley (1949). Subsequent reports and excellent reviews of this topic have been published by Critchley (1951), Bekeny and Peter (1961), Kinsbourne and Warrington (1963), and Bender et al. (1968). Table 1 summarizes the pertinent clinical features of nine new patients (Cases 2–10) with palinopsia examined at the Dent Neurologic Institute during the past 6 years and one patient (Case 1) who was previously repoted (see Bender et al., 1968; Jacobs, Feldman, & Bender, 1972).

CHARACTERISTICS OF PALINOPSIA; CLINICAL CIRCUMSTANCES IN WHICH IT OCCURS

Typically palinopsia occurs in patients with posteriorly located cerebral lesions which produce cerebral irritation and homonymous visual field defects. Most of the lesions causing palinopsia have been in the parieto-occipital region (mostly neoplastic or vascular in nature) and the illusory image was projected into the contralateral defective field of vision. The phenomenon is integrally related to visual perceptual impairment and careful serial visual field examinations of such patients over time have demonstrated that palinopsia occurs during the evolution of or resolution from complete homonymous field defects. Typically the palinoptic image consists of only a part of the whole previously viewed scene. The illusory image is often a literal or near perfect replica of the original.

Case 1 (See Table 1), a 67-year-old male with a right parieto-occipital glioma and left homonymous field defect (reported by Bender et al., 1968 and Jacobs et al., 1972) demonstrated some of the foregoing points. He had a grand mal convulsion followed, in 4 days time, by episodes of palinopsia. On one occasion he initially saw his eyeglasses placed horizontally before him on a desk.

TABLE 1
Pertinent Clinical Data on Ten Patients Who Experienced Palinopsia

Case	Perseveration	Type	Visual Field Defect	EEG	Lesion Site	Lesion Nature	Clinical Seizures	Distortions	Persev. Locat.
1-67 yo M	Eyeglasses; Performer's hands; Zebra stripes; Traffic light Duration–to 1 hour Frequency–5 times in 3 wks	Palinopsia	L. Homon. Incomplete	NT	R. Par-Occ	Glioma	Yes (Generalized)	Some exact replicas, others not.	LVF
2-36 yo F	Childs toy lawn-mower Duration–30 min Frequency–Once.	Palinopsia	None Demonstrated	Nl	None Demonst.	Epilepsy	Yes (Focal R.)	Small, oscillating, color changes	RVF
3-14 yo F	Bottle; Hat; Starfish; Top half of a person; Other small people. Duration–5 min Frequency–variable	Palinopsia	R. Homon. at Sz onset	Sz Focus L. Par-Occip.	Corpus collosum agenesis	De-velopmental	Yes (Focal R & Generalized)	Small, sometimes in black and white.	RVF
4-40 yo M	Children TV Actor Face Duration–3–4 min Frequency—3 times in 1 month. Then once 2 years later.	Palinopsia	L. Homon. Incomplete	Sz Focus R Temp-Par-Occip.	R. Post Temp- Par.	Ischemia & Infarct	Yes	None "Frames" on one occasion.	LVF

167

TABLE 1 (Continued)

Case	Perseveration	Type	Visual Field Defect	EEG	Lesion Site	Lesion Nature	Clinical Seizures	Distortions	Persev. Locat.
5–74 yo M	Cats; People; "Others" Frequency– "Almost constant." Duration–48 hours	Palinopsia & simple unformed visual halluc.	R. Homon. Incomplete	Delta-theta; L. Post Temp-Par.	L. Temp & Par. Occ	Metastasis	No	Small; Black and white	RVF
6–44 yo F	Pieces of furniture. Frequency–once Duration–10 min	Palinopsia	None Demonstrated	Nl	Unknown	Epilepsy	Yes (Generalized)	None	Unknown
7–66 yo F	Small people, "prettily dressed-moving fast." "Magicians bouquet." Numerous objects just seen. Frequency–6-7 times Duration–min	Palinopsia & simple unformed visual halluc.	L. Homon. Incomplete	Sz Focus & Delta-Theta. R Pos Temp Par	R. Temp - Par	Ischemia & Infarct	No	Small; moving "gliding"	LVF
8–64 yo M	"Gray automobile" "Green tool boxes" Frequency–Twice Duration–Several hours	Palinopsia & Un-formed vis. halluc.	L. Homon. Incomplete	Theta, R. Post Temp Occip	R. Post Temp and Par-Occip Metastasis		No	None	LVF

TABLE 1 (*Continued*)

Case	Perseveration	Type	Visual Field Defect	EEG	Lesion Site	Lesion Nature	Clinical Seizures	Distortions	Persev. Locat.
9–74 yo F	"Cups, brooms, numerous other objects" she had seen. Frequency–daily for 3 weeks Duration–min	Palinopsia & simple unformed vis. halluc.	R. Homon. Incomplete	Nl	L. Par-Occip	Ischemia & Infarct	No	None	RVF
10–31 yo F	Adults, a child, cushion, refrigerator, lamp, elevator door, sidewalk Frequency–Daily to every 6 months during 7 years Duration–3–15 min	Palinopsia & Visual Allesthesia	L. Homon Incomplete	Sz Focus R. Temp Par-Occip	R. Par-Occip.	Arteriovenous Malformation	Yes	-Allesthetic, -oscillating, -homonymous diplopia, -small	LVF

Note. Homon = homonymous, NT = not tested, Temp = temporal, Par = parietal, Occip = occipital, Sz = seizure, L, R = left, right, VF = Visual Field, Persev = perseveration

Seconds later, after turning away, the eyeglasses were no longer in view, but he continued to see an image of them off to his left on the floor (Figure 1). The illusory eyeglasses appeared so realistic that he reached out attempting to pick them up from the floor before he realized that they were still there on the desk in front of him. He continued to see an image of the eyeglasses in his left visual field wherever he looked for the next 5 minutes. On another occasion he saw a television performer's pair of hands rubbing her face. When he turned away and looked at his wife (seated to his left), he saw a pair of hands on her face and asked "Why are you rubbing your face?" before he saw that her hands were actually on her lap. During the 3-week period when palinoptic episodes occurred, the only abnormality demonstrated on serial examinations was rapid adaptation and extinction of perception of colored targets in the left homonymous visual field (perception of objects and motion preserved). He later developed progressive hemimotor-hemisensory deficits and complete homonymous hemianopsia on the left and then palinopsia ceased.

The literature contains descriptions of a wide variety of parts of people, objects, faces, letters or unnoticed details that were perseverated in a similar fashion to the case described (Brown, 1985). Table 1 lists the objects perseverated by the 10 patients in the current study. Sometimes the perseverations were integrated, at least partially, into ongoing visual reality. Thus, on one

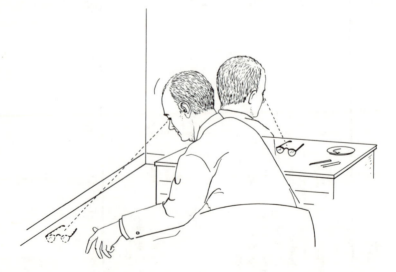

FIGURE 1 Case 1. Palinopsia. Patient initially viewed his eye glasses placed horizontally on a desk in front of him. Seconds later he looked away, but continued to see an image of the eyeglasses off to his left on the floor. He reached out to pick them up from the floor before he realized that they were still on the desk in front of him. From Jacobs (1980).

occasion, the patient described above saw the image of his wife rubbing her face immediately after seeing an actress rubbing her face on television (Bender et al., 1968). Potzl (1954) described a case in which a hat, initially seen on one person, recurred in proper position on other people. On another occasion, after looking at a bald-headed doctor, this patient saw all people with bald spots for a few minutes. Michel and Troost's (1980) case 1 initially looked at herself in a mirror and then later thought that everyone around her was wearing the same (i.e., her) dress. Frequently the perseverations were distorted appearing larger or smaller than real; the palinoptic images of cases 2 and 10 of Bender et al. (1968) appeared larger when viewed against a distant background. A patient of Le Beau and Wolinetz (1958) saw the illusory images as larger when they were regarded as being closer. In five of our cases the palinoptic image appeared smaller than real (Table 1). Sometimes the perseverated image appeared to be oscillating or flipping in the vertical plane in four cases in current series (See Table). Though palinoptic images were often in the true colors of the original, there have been instances in which the illusory colors were distorted or the illusion was achromatic (Bender et al., 1968, Bodis-Wollner, Bender, & Diamond, 1984; Brown, 1985). Perceived movement of the illusory object (as with case 1 above—"hands rubbing face" and Case 7, See Table) is distinctly unusual. Palinoptic images of moving objects may appear as a series of static objects causing the illusion of polyopia (see below). Palinoptic images may appear to move with eye movement, but that movement is not purposeful. Palinopsia and simple unformed elementary hallucinations may occur together; occasionally one type of visual aberration may evolve into the other. Thus, a patient of Bodis-Wollner et al. (1984) saw "flashing rings" in the left visual field; then the face of his examining physician (which he had seen moments before) appeared in the center of one of the rings.

There is considerable evidence indicating that palinopsia is a manifestation of cerebral irritation and seizures. The illusory episode may be followed after a brief interval by a focal or major convulsion in which the sensory event may appear to be a precipitating factor or the illusory experience may be viewed as an aura of the seizure. There have been numerous cases demonstrating this relationship in the literature extending from the early to the most current studies of visual aberrations caused by brain lesions. Harris (1897) reported a patient with partial right homonymous hemianopsia who had frequent visual illusions of previously seen faces of his children, pet dog, or running school children in his right visual field. They were often experienced without subsequent convulsion, but they sometimes occurred immediately before the commencement of fits, many of which were right sided Jacksonian attacks. Harris considered the sensory experiences as visual hallucinations in a hemianoptic field but they were clearly palinoptic by modern definition. The lateralized nature of the illusions and the subsequent seizure indicated that both originated from the same focus of irritated cerebral parenchyma.

There have been several subsequent reports of focal cerebral irritation producing palinopsia and seizures lateralized to the same side (Bender et al., 1968; Robinson & Watt, 1947). Two cases in our most recently compiled series demonstrated this relationship (See Table). Case 2, a 36-year-old man, initially saw his daughter playing with her toy lawnmower on a patio before him. When he looked away he continued to see an image of the lawnmower off to his right (Figure 2). The illusory lawnmower was smaller than real, appeared to be "oscillating," "flipping" vertically and was in color. He confirmed by monocular testing that the illusion was present only in the right homonymous field. The illusion persisted for 30 minutes until he had a right-sided focal seizure with adversive components followed by a Todd's paralysis on the right. He was treated with phenytoin and there has been no recurrence of seizures or palinopsia during the ensuing 4 years. Case 3, a 14-year-old female had frequent adversive fits in which her eyes and head would turn to the right. Simultaneously she would see an illusion of a "coke bottle, hat, starfish" or "top half of a man" all of which she had actually previously seen at a swimming pool or a beach. The adversive

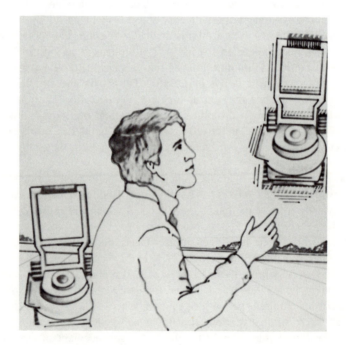

FIGURE 2   Case 2. Palinopsia preceeding focal convulsion. Patient initially saw a toy lawnmower on a patio before him. When he looked away he continued to see an image of the lawnmower off to his right. The illusion was smaller than real and seemed to be oscillating. It persisted in his right visual field for 30 minutes and then he had a right-sided convulsion.

deviation of head and eyes and the palinopsia typically lasted 5 minutes and then either relented (without alteration in consciousness) or was followed by right sided or generalized convulsions (with loss of consciousness). The electroencephalogram demonstrated left parieto-occipital seizure activity. Examination during the onset of a seizure revealed a right homonymous hemiachromatopsia. Seizures and palinopsia relented on anticonvulsant medications, but recurred periodically during the ensuing 6 years when she neglected to take her medications.

Cases such as these illustrate an obvious integral relationship between palinopsia and seizures. However, it is more typical for palinoptic episodes to occur without overt disturbances of consciousness and not as an integral part of a major seizure. In most cases the relationship to overt seizures is more remote and only obtained by careful history or suggested by the paroxysmal nature of the visual illusory phenomena. In many cases it seems that the perseverations may be abortive seizures or isolated sensory seizures with the patient remaining alert throughout the entire episode (Bender et al., 1968; Jacobs et al., 1972). Electroencephalography must be relied upon to establish the relationship in most cases. This has been overlooked by some investigators reporting palinopsia in the absence of seizures simply because their patients did not have overt convulsions, but electroencephalography was not done (Michel & Troost, 1980). Analysis of the pertinent literature indicates that palinopsia and seizures are strongly correlated as shown by the general failure of the illusory phenomena to occur when seizures (clinical and/or electrical) have not developed or are controlled by anticonvulsant medications. High incidences (70–75%) of clinical and/or electrical seizures were found in the palinoptic patients reported by Bender et al. (1968) and Jacobs et al (1972). Seven patients in the current series had seizures and 6 had overt clinical convulsions as well as electroencephalographic evidence of epilepsy (See Table).

Foerster (1931) found that electric stimulation of cortical areas 17 and 18 caused patients to see simple, unformed hallucinations of light flashes and color. More rostral stimulation of area 19 elicited the appearance of more organized images. Penfield and Perot (1963) found that electric stimulation of the posterior temporal cortex near the visual sensory area of the occipital lobe induced a "re-experiencing" of past visual percepts in 19 patients. The illusory images were readily recognized by the patients as scenes they had actually visualized in the past. Thus, it seems that either electric stimulation of the cortex of conscious humans through implanted electrodes, or spontaneous irritation of the cortex due to pathology producing seizures may induce a repetition or "replay" of visual percepts which then appear as reality. However, electric stimulation generally induced visual percepts from the patients' remote past whereas the persistent or recurring scenes of palinopsia occurring spontaneously in disease states are usually of the much more recent past (seconds to days) (Bender et al., 1968; Jacobs et al., 1973). The basis of simple hallucinations and formed visual illusions of palinopsia that occur spontaneously in disease states may be partial deafferentation of visual cortex (primary, association) which causes spontaneous discharges and apparitions within specific visual field defects (Lance, 1976). Such cortical irritation may produce overt seizures in some patients but not others in whom there may not even be a discernable electroencephalographic abnormality. In those instances the epileptic nature of the visual disturbance is indicated by its paroxysmal nature and responsiveness to anticonvulsants.

In some ways palinopsia seems to be an extension of normal after-images. The two phenomena are similar in some ways and different in others; these were reviewed by Kinsbourne and Warrington (1963), Bender, et al. (1968) and Brown (1985) and are listed below.

1. The intensity and duration of the initial visual stimulus determines the intensity and duration of after-images, but this has usually not been the case in patients with palinopsia. Brightness, illumination or color-figures background usually does not determine which objects will persist or recur as palinoptic images. There have however, been rare exceptions in which the prominence and duration of palinoptic images were dependent on the intensity and duration of the initial stimulus.

2. After-images appear larger when visualized against a far surface compared with a near surface, but palinoptic images only rarely show this characteristic. Two of the cases reported by Bender, et al. (1968) experienced enlargement of the palinoptic image at a distance. The image appeared larger when regarded as near by a patient of Le Beau and Wolinetz (1958). However, usually the palinoptic image shows no change in size wherever it is viewed. Indeed, often it appears micropsic against near and far surfaces as was seen in 5 of the cases in the current series (See Table).

3. After-images appear in complementary (negative) colors when viewed against a light background. Palinoptic images may appear in the same colors as the original or as black and white under these circumstances. There have been rare exceptions; the reports of Kinsbourne and Warrington (1963) and Bekény and Péter (1961) each contained one patient who saw palinoptic images in complementary colors compared with the original.

4. After-images are prolonged or reappear after a blink, wave of the hand before the eyes or stroboscopic flashes, but these procedures usually have no influence on palinoptic images. Kinsbourne and Warrington's (1963) cases were exceptional in this regard and experienced revival and prolongation of palinoptic images following these procedures.

5. After-images may form in both the central and peripheral portion of the visual field. Palinoptic images usually appear in a fixed portion of a defective visual field (Bender et al., 1968; Bodis-Wollner et al., 1984).

6. After-images of a stimulus applied to one eye are perceived binocularly. When this was tested for in patients with palinopsia, the perseverated images elicited on monocular viewing were also seen binocularly.

7. Both after-images and palinoptic images move in the direction of active eye movement and may move in an opposite direction of passive displacement of the eyeball.

POLYOPIA AND MONOCULAR DIPLOPIA

Polyopia—The illusion of seeing multiple images on viewing one object and monocular diplopia—the illusion of seeing two images with one eye are rare clinical phenomenon. These visual distortions may occur in hysteria, diseases of the ocular media, strabismus, cerebellar and vestibular disorders with associated nystagmus in which the polyopia may be horizontal or vertical (depending on the vector of the nystagmus) (Bender, 1945). Polyopia and monocular diplopia may also occur in association with lesions of the central visual pathways. Indeed the phenomenon of polyopia was first described in cases of occipital trauma (Mingazzini, 1908). Subsequent experience demonstrated that these illusions can be caused by parieto-occipital lesions and are often integrally related to palinopsia. Bekény and Péter (1961) considered polyopia as a form of visual perseveration in space and palinopsia as visual perseveration in time. However, it is clear that the development of palinoptic images can produce both the spatial and temporal perseveratory phenomenon. Jacob's (1980) case with a right parieto-occipital lesion and left homonymous hemiachromatopsia viewed a cushion in her right visual field which then also appeared as a palinoptic image in her left visual field resulting in diplopia so long as the real cushion remained in view. Bodis-Wollner et al. (1984) reported similar phenomenon in a patient who, while watching a basketball game on television, simultaneously saw a black and white replica of the action on television in his defective left homonymous field as a palinoptic image. In these instances diplopia was caused by the simultaneous viewing of a real object and its palinoptic image and persisted only so long as the real object was viewed. Some patients develop double or even multiple images of the palinoptic image and in these instances the diplopia or polyopia is typically restricted to the defective homonymous field of vision, is present after the real object is removed and persist on monocular viewing (because it is a homonymous illusion). The polyopia can be induced by sequential presentations of an object in the defective field of vision after a palinoptic image of the object has developed. A patient described by Bender et al. (1968) could be induced to see two to several palinoptic images of a pencil in her defective left visual field by sequential representations of the pencil in that field. The polyoptic palinoptic images persisted for 1 minute after the pencil was removed.

Movement of the target in the defective visual field can also produce polyopia because palinoptic images of moving targets are usually perceived as a series of static images over the range of motion (stroboscopic effect). Thus a patient with a left visual field defect reported seeing a series of disks appearing along the path of the real disk (single) being moved from right to left before her (Bender, Rudolph, & Stacy, 1985). The multiple images were perceived to her left; the disk appeared single when it was moved into her right visual field. Another patient (examined by the author and M. B. Bender, but not published), a 30-year-old male with a right parieto-occipital vascular ischemic lesion and an incomplete left homonymous field defect, experienced numerous episodes of palinopsia in his left visual field. On two occasions the development of palinoptic images of moving objects caused left homonymous polyopia. While driving along a highway at night, he saw the headlights of an approaching vehicle which appeared to double, triple, and quadruple until there was a series of stationary headlights located anteroposteriorly in the left visual field corresponding to his visualization of the real vehicle in that field as it approached and then passed him on his left. The illusory row of headlights persisted to his left for the next 5 minutes. On another occasion he watched an airplane taking off. It remained single while it was off to his right, but then appeared to multiply into a series of "still frames" located along the trajectory of the real plane as it passed across his left visual field. Multiple palinoptic images of the airplane then persisted in his left homonymous field for the next few minutes. In these instances the polyopia resulted from visualization of a real object moving across a defective (but not blind) visual field that was retained perceptually as a series of palinoptic "stills."

Eye motion can also induce polyopia in patients experiencing palinopsia. One of the patients described by Bender et al. (1968, 1985) saw multiple images of a previously viewed bunch of carnations. The palinoptic carnations appeared as single flowers that multiplied in a vertical row projected on drapes across the room as she moved her eyes upward. The polyopia occurred in her defective right visual field. In the great majority of instances the polyopia experienced by patients with palinopsia is restricted to the defective visual field. However, there have been rare exceptions; a patient with a left homonymous field defect described by Michel and Troost (1980) saw multiple illusory images of a previously viewed banana throughout both of her visual fields.

The physiologic basis for the diplopia and polyopia of cerebral origin is unknown, but clearly involves the development of palinoptic images in many instances. The partially deafferented visual cortex tends to retain visual percepts viewed in a defective but not blind visual field (Jacobs et al., 1972; Lance, 1976; Jacobs, 1980). The resulting palinoptic image may be tied to the retinal coordinates so that it appears in extrafoveal space at the same time the real object is being visualized by the fovea (resulting in diplopia so long as the real object remains in view (See Bodis-Wollner et al., 1984). Polyopia developing during eye movement has been explained on the basis of an imbalance during the act of fixation between intact and damaged occipital regions (Bender, 1945; Teuber & Bender, 1949). The multiple images may result from conflict between the true fovea and a false (pseudo) fovea. The pathologic conditions producing palinopsia also seem to cause a defect in the cortex's capacity to perceive motion and visualization of a moving object in the defective field results in multiple central perceptions ("deposits") which are retained as a series of still replicas of the moving original.

VISUAL ALLESTHESIA

Visual allesthesia, in which visual images are transposed from one homonymous half-field of vision to another is extremely rare and its pathophysiology is not understood. The case reported by Jacobs (1980) demonstrated that the conditions leading to palinopsia can, in some instances, also produce visual allesthesia. The patient, a 24-year-old woman, with a right parieto-occipital arteriovenous malformation and left homonymous hemiachromatopsia experienced paroxysmal illusory left homonymous transpositions of objects viewed in the right homonymous field (Table, Case 10). Objects viewed in the right homonymous visual field suddenly appeared in the left (defective) homonymous field as well, resulting in diplopia as long as the actual object remained in view (Figure 3). The diplopia disappeared as soon as she turned her gaze away from the real object but the illusory object persisted in view off to her left as a palinoptic image for up to 15 minutes. A variety of animate and inanimate objects (adults, a child, a cushion, a refrigerator, a lamp, an elevator door, a sidewalk) were so transposed and perseverated. The transpositions were always of an object she was looking at on her right, occurred suddenly, persisted for 3–15 minutes as an illusory image off to her left, and then ceased abruptly ("switched off"). The palinoptic images were smaller than real, appeared to be "flipping" vertically or "oscillating" and appeared unusually bright. Otherwise they were exact replicas of what she had just seen off to her right. Episodes of visual allesthesia were accompanied by other manifestations of seizures (queasiness, pallor, automatic behavior, face and arm twitching, and amnesia for the terminal portions of some of the spells). Serial electroencephalograms revealed a right parieto-occipital epileptogenic focus; administration of anticonvulsant medication resulted in cessation of electroencephalographic epileptogenic activity and disappearance of all clinical manifestations of seizures including visual allesthesia.

This case demonstrated that cerebral irritation and seizures, a defective but not blind half-field of vision and the development of palinoptic images are essential components of at least some cases of visual allesthesia. In classical palinopsia the real object is initially viewed in the defective field and then perseverated in that field. However, in the case of visual allesthesia presented, the perseverations in the defective field were of objects initially visualized in the normal homonymous field. The physiologic basis for the transposition of images from a normal to a defective field of vision may involve interhemispheric transfer of a visual percept from a normal to an irritated parieto-occipital lobe which then

178

L. Jacobs

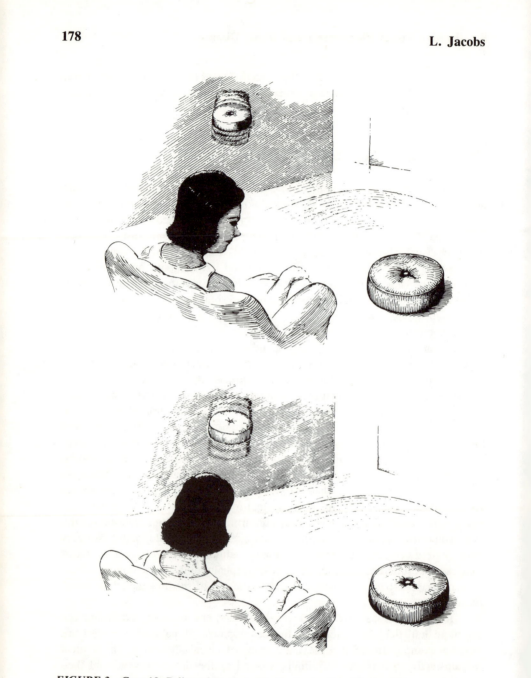

FIGURE 3 Case 10. Palinopsia and visual allesthesia. Top; The cushion viewed in the right homonymous visual field suddenly appears in the left (defective) homonymous field as well, resulting in diplopia as long as the actual object remains in view. Bottom; Illusory image was palinoptic, persisting 15 minutes after she turned to the left and the real cushion was no longer in view. The illusory image was smaller than real and appeared to be oscillating. Otherwise it was an exact replica of the original. From Jacobs (1980).

retains it as a palinoptic image (Jacobs, 1980). Previously visual allesthesia was only rarely discussed in detail and sometimes ascribed to hysteria or schizophrenia (see Critchley, 1949; Bender et al., 1985; Magin, 1888; Hermann, 1923; Hermann & Potzel, 1928; Bender, Wortis, & Cramer, 1948; Bender, 1970; Duke-Elder & Scott, 1971). When associated with organic diseases, it usually occurred in patients with gross visual field defects (near blind or blind) who also had defects in hearing, somatic sensibility, and organic mental syndrome; the visual phenomenon seemed to be part of hemispatial neglect, and the allesthesia was from the defective to the normal visual field (Hermann, 1923; Hermann & Potzel, 1928; Bender, 1970). However, Critchley (1949) reported one case with a left temporoparietal neoplasm and right-sided visual field defect who experienced four episodes of visual allesthesia in which the allesthetic images were palinoptic and the transpositions were from the normal to the defective visual field (similar to Jacobs' (1980) case).

RELATED PHENOMENA

Palinacousis.   A disorder similar to palinopsia has been described by Jacobs et al. (1971, 1972, 1973) in the acoustic sphere and is termed palinacousis. This phenomenon is encountered more rarely than palinopsia. Voices or sounds from the past are heard again either immediately or up to 24 hours following the initial acoustic stimulus. The persistent or recurring auditory sensations are extremely realistic and compelling. One patient returned to answer the door several times because she heard an illusory ringing several times during a 30 minute period after the doorbell had actually rung. Another patient turned around looking for the source of the illusory "Hi Charlie" which she heard repetitively in her left ear for 5 minutes after a man on her left had actually greeted his friend. The acoustic perseverations of voices were usually fragmented; but those of other sounds (e.g., "buzzer," "wheels grinding") were not. Palinacoustic phenomena were associated with demonstrable temporal lobe lesions and seizures in 85% of the cases and the illusory acoustic sensations were projected into the auditory space contralateral to the responsible temporal lesion (Jacobs et al., 1971, 1973). Palinacoustic phenomena were similar to the auditory experiences elicited on electric stimulation of the temporal region of conscious humans at surgery, (but the content of spontaneous palinacousis was usually of much more recent hearing experiences than those elicited at surgery) (Penfield & Perot, 1963; Penfield & Rasmussen, 1950; Mahl, Rothenberg, Delgado, & Hamlin, 1964). It is likely that irritation of the temporal cortex due to partial deafferentation is the cause of palinacousis, just as irritation of the parieto-occipital region is the cause of palinopsia. Indeed, 2 of the 7 patients in the initial report had palinopsia as well as palinacousis at different stages in the evolution of their disease processes (Jacobs et al., 1972, 1973). Another patient experienced simple unformed visual hallucinations as well as palinacousis. Cases have been described in which the acoustic and visual illusions occurred together on organic bases (Critchley, 1951), but such simultaneous illusions are usually caused by psychiatric disease.

Auditory–Visual Synesthesia.   The inherent potential of the normal brain for "cross-talk" between the auditory and visual senses is demonstrated by normal visual after-images sometimes being elicited as conditioned responses to acoustic stimuli (Lessell, 1975) and rare healthy individuals who sometimes see lights and colors when they hear certain sounds (Colman, 1898; Ortman, 1933; Critchley, 1977). It is likely that these phenomena are generated at the cortical level. Such auditory-visual synesthesias may also occur in disease states affecting the anterior portions of the visual apparatus which cause partial deafferentation of lower, more elemental nuclei of the visual pathway. Jacobs, Karpick, Bozian, and Gothgen (1981) described nine patients with visual loss due to lesions of the optic nerve or chiasm who experienced photisms induced by sound. These varied from simple flashes of white light to complicated colorful hallucinations likened to a flame, a petal of oscillating lines, a kaleidoscope, or an ameba. The photisms always appeared within a defective portion of the visual field as demonstrated by perimetry. The provoking sounds were usually those of normal daily life and always seemed to be heard by the ear ipsilateral to the eye in which the photism was seen. The phenomena occurred under circumstances that would promote a startle reaction to sound, and each patient was startled when the photism occurred. Visual evoked responses demonstrated partial deafferentation of the eye in which the photisms occurred. The phenomenon is probably due to a sound-startle effect on the partially deafferent anterior visual pathway. The likely origin of the photism is the lateral geniculate nucleus which is known to be responsive to sounds as well as visual stimuli under normal physiologic conditions Jacobs et al. (1981). This form of auditory-visual synesthesia is relatively rare, but could probably be discovered more often by careful questioning of patients with optic nerve and chiasm disorders. A series of patients with optic nerve lesions who experienced this phenomenon was also reported by Lessell and Cohen (1979).

ACKNOWLEDGMENT

Supported in part by grants from the Baird Foundation and Delaware North Companies, Buffalo, New York.

REFERENCES

Bekény, G., & Péter, A. (1961). Uber polyopie und palinopsie. *Psychiatria et Neurologia, 142,* 154–175.
Bender, M. B. (1945). Polyopia and monocular diplopia of cerebral origin. *Archives of Neurology and Psychiatry, 54,* 323–338.

Bender, M. B. (1970). Perceptual interactions. In D. Williams (Ed.), *Modern trends in neurology* (pp. 1–28). London: Butterworth.

Bender, M. D., Feldman, M., & Sobin, A. J. (1968). Palinopsia. *Brain, 91*(III), 321–338.

Bender, M. B., Rudolph, S. H., & Stacy, C. B. (1985). The neurology of the visual and oculomotor systems. In A. B. Baker & R. J. Joynt (Eds.), *Clinical neurology* (pp. 40–59). Philadelphia: Harper & Row.

Bender, M. B., Wortis, S. B., & Cramer, J. (1948). Organic mental syndrome with phenomena of extinction and allesthesia. *Archives of Neurology and Psychiatry, 59,* 273–279.

Bodis-Wollner, I. Bender, M. B., & Diamond, S. P. (1984). Clinical observations of palinopsia: Anomalous mapping from retinal to non-retinal coordinates of vision. In L. Spillman & T. B. Wooten (Eds.), *Sensory experience adaptation and perception* (pp. 659–676). Hilldale, NJ: Lawrence Erlbaum Associates.

Brown, J. W. (1985). Hallucinations, imagery and the microstructure of perception. In P. J. Vinken, G. W. Bruyn, & H. L. Klawans (Eds.), *Handbook of clinical neurology* (Vol. *1*(45), pp. 351–372).

Brown, J. W. (1985). Imagery and the microstructure of perception. *Journal of Neurolinguistics, 1,* 89–141.

Colman, W. L. (1898). Further remarks on 'colour hearing. *Lancet, 1,* 22–24.

Critchley, M. (1949). Metamorphopsia of central origin. *Transactions of the Ophthalmologic Society of the United Kingdom, 69,* 111–121.

Critchley, M. (1951). Types of visual perseveration: "Paliopsia" and "illusory visual spread." *Brain, 74,* 267–299.

Critchley, M. (1977). Ecstatic and synaesthetic experiences during musical perception In M. Critchley & R. A. Henson (Eds.), *Music and the brain* (pp. 217–232). Springfield IL: Charles C. Thomas.

Duke-Elder, S., & Scott, G. I. (1971). *System of ophthalmology* (Vol. 12, p. 521). St. Louis: C. V. Mosby.

Foerster, O. (1931). The cerebral cortex in man. *Lancet, II,* 309–312.

Gowers, W. R. (1895). The Bowman lecture on subjective visual sensations. *The Lancet, I,* 1564–1625.

Harris, W. (1897). Hemianopia with especial reference to its transient varieties. *Brain, 20,* 308–364.

Hermann, G. (1923). Uber eine eigenartige propektionsstorung bei doppelseitiger grobhirnlasion. *Monatsschrift fur Psychiatrie und Neurologie, 55,* 99–104.

Hermann, G., & Pötzl, O. (1928). *Die optische alloasthesia: Studien zur psychopathologie der raumbildung.* Berlin: Karger.

Horrax, G. (1923). Visual hallucinations as a cerebral localizing phenomenon with especial reference to their occurrence in tumors of the temporal lobes. *Archives of Neurology and Psychiatry, 10,* 532–547.

Jacobs, L. (1980). Visual allesthesia. *Neurology, 30,* 1059–1063.

Jacobs, L., Feldman, M., & Bender, M. B. (1971). Palinacousis or persistent auditory sensations. *Transactions of the American Neurological Association, 96,* 123–126.

Jacobs, L., Feldman, M., & Bender, M. B. (1972). The persistence of visual or auditory percepts as symptoms of irritative lesions of the cerebrum of man. *Zeitschrift fur Neurologie. Brl.*, *203*, 211–218.

Jacobs, L., Feldman, M., Diamond, S. P., & Bender, M. B. (1973). Palinacousis: Persistent or recurring auditory sensations. *Cortex, IX*, 275–287.

Jacobs, L., Karpick, A., Bozian, D., & Gothgen, S. (1981). Auditory-visual synesthesia: Sound-induced photisms. *Archives of Neurology, 38*, 211–216.

Kinsbourne, M., & Warrington, E. K. (1963). A study of visual perseveration. *Journal of Neurology, Neurosurgery and Psychiatry, 26*, 468–475.

Lance, J. W. (1976). Simple formed hallucinations confined to the area of a specific visual field defect. *Brain, 99*, 719–734.

Le Beau, J., & Wolinetz, E. (1958). Le phenomene de perseveration visuelle. *Revue Neurologique, 99*, 524–534.

Lessell, S. (1975). Higher disorders of visual function: Positive phenomena. In J. S. Glaser & J. L Smith (Eds.), *Neuro-ophthalmology* (Vol. 8, pp. 27–44). St. Louis: C. V. Mosby.

Lessell, S., & Cohen, M. M. (1979). Phosphenes induced by sound. *Neurology 29*, 1524–1527.

Magin, P. (1888). Allochirie visuelle chez une hysterique hypnotisee. *Compt Rewd Soc Biol* (Paris), *40*, 57–58.

Mahl, C. F., Rothenberg, A., Delgado, J.N.R., & Hamlin, H. (1964). Psychologic response in the human to intracerebral electrical stimulation. *Psychosomatic Medicine, 26*, 337–368.

Michel, E. M., & Troost, B. T. (1980). Palinopsia: Cerebral localization with computed tomography. *Neurology 30*, 887–889.

Mingazzini, G. (1908). Uber symptome infolge von verletzungen des occipitallapens dureh Geschosse. *Neurologisches Zentralblatt, 27*, 1112.

Ortman, O. (1933). Theories of synesthesia in the light of a case of color-hearing. *Human Biology, 5*, 155–211.

Penfield, W., & Perot, P. (1963). The brain's record of auditory and visual experience. *Brain, 86*, 595–696.

Penfield, W., & Rasmussen, T. (1950). Hearing and equillibrium. In *The cerebral cortex of man*. New York: Macmillan.

Pötzl, O. (1954). Uber palinopsia. *Wien Z Nerv Heiln, 8*, 161–186.

Robinson, P. K., & Watt, A. C. (1947). Hallucinations of remembered scenes as an epileptic aura. *Brain, 70*, 440–448.

Teuber, H.-L., & Bender, M. (1949). Alterations in pattern vision following lesions of occipital lobes in man. *Journal of General Psychology, 40*, 37–57.

9

The Neuropsychology of Mental Imagery

Martha J. Farah

INTRODUCTION

Imagine standing in your living room. Now, mentally rearrange the furniture so that the sofa is facing the opposite wall. How does this new arrangement look? For present purposes, the aesthetic results of this exercise are less important than the cognitive process it illustrates, namely, mental imagery. Imagery has long been associated with creative thought in the arts and sciences (Shepard, 1978), as well as with more mundane but nevertheless essential acts of nonverbal problem solving such as planning routes through the environment (Benton, 1969) or understanding and using mechanical devices (McKim, 1980). The scientific study of mental imagery is a recent development in psychology, even by the standards of the relatively young field of cognitive psychology. One of the most recent developments of all in this field is the study of the neural basis of mental imagery. This chapter reviews current research on this subject.

What are the main research issues in the neuropsychology of mental imagery? First, there has been considerable interest recently in the localization of imagery in the brain. Is mental imagery ability lateralized? Is it localizable intrahemispherically? Does it involve the same parts of the brain that subserve like-modality perception (e.g., vision in the case of visual imagery)? A second set of issues concerns the *functional* architecture of imagery ability, as opposed to the questions of physical or neural architecture posed above. Here, psychologists have used patterns of association and dissociation among abilities after brain damage to determine whether imagery shares components with, or is independent of, perceptual ability, language, nonvisual memory ability, etc. In addition, the same type of analysis carried out in a more fine-grained manner involves testing hypotheses about the internal structure of the imagery system by asking whether a particular pattern of breakdown could be produced by a particular componential model of imagery being damaged.

The organization of this review makes use of a very general distinction between representations and processes in mental imagery. The first section focuses on the representations used in imagery, and addresses the question of whether they are some of the same representations used in perception. The second section focuses on the generation of mental images from memory, and addresses questions of the lateralization and functional architecture of this process.

REPRESENTATION IN MENTAL IMAGERY

Probably the oldest hypothesis about the nature of mental images is that images are faint reactivations of perceptual representations (e.g., Hume, 1739/ 1969). This intuitively appealing idea has been recast as an hypothesis about the neural substrate of imagery, according to which mental images are efferent activations in the neural structures that subserve perception (e.g., Brain, 1950; Hebb, 1968). In the vivid terms of Brain (1950), the idea is that "the image (might be), as it were, displayed upon the visual cortex" (p. 470). Data from a variety of sources has been interpreted as supporting this hypothesis. Before discussing these data, it is useful to make a distinction between two types of perceptual representations that could be activated during mental imagery.

Sensory representations occur relatively earlier in perceptual processing than *nonsensory* representations, and represent stimuli in terms of relatively simple categories such as local intensity, contour, color, spatial frequency, and direction of motion. They are often topographically mapped, that is, they preserve the spatial relations of the scene or object represented. In contrast, nonsensory representations occur later in perceptual processing and represent stimuli in terms of relatively abstract categories such as such as object identity (e.g., "face") or absolute location (e.g., with respect to a world-centered reference frame).

In the context of this distinction, there are two ways in which the proposition that imagery and perception share neural representations could be true: First, they could share sensory representations, such that one or more regions of the occipital lobes entertain patterns of activation from both afferent sources, in the case of perception, and efferent sources, in the case of mental imagery. Second, it is possible that nonsensory representations of appearances and locations are shared by the imagery and perceptual systems, such that some of the same representations participate in the recognition and localization of afferent patterns of activation delivered by sensory systems, and the generation of efferent patterns of activation during imagery. Let us now examine the evidence that one or both of these hypotheses is true.

Nonsensory Visual Representations. If the idea of imagery as the efferent activation of perceptual structures is a common and intuitively appealing one, then certainly the most widely held version of this general idea is that imagery activates relatively late, nonsensory representations. In fact, there is a fair amount of evidence that this is true. The two main sources of evidence are studies of brain-damaged patients with selective visual disorders, and the relatively recent "brain imaging" techniques, some of which have been used to investigate regional brain activity during mental imagery.

The finding that brain-damaged patients with nonsensory visual deficits have parallel deficits in their imagery ability suggests that the defective aspect of visual processing is shared by both imagery and perception. The best known and most thoroughly studied of these imagery-perception parallels involves the phenomenon of visual neglect. Patients with visual neglect fail to detect stimuli presented in the half of space opposite their lesion despite adequate elementary sensory processes. For example, right parietal-damaged patients, the patient group most likely to display neglect, may bump into people and things on their left, leave food on the left side of their plate when they are still hungry, and so on, even though they are capable of seeing objects on the left side of space if their attention can be drawn there. Neglect for mental images appears to accompany visual neglect (Bisiach, Capitani, Luzzatti, & Perani, 1981; Bisiach & Luzzatti, 1978; Bisiach, Luzzatti, & Perani, 1979; Ogden, 1985). In Bisiach and Luzzatti's initial report, two right hemisphere-damaged patients, who displayed considerable neglect of the left half of visual space in perceptual tasks, also neglected the left halves of imagined scenes. Both patients were familiar with the Piazza del Duomo, a famous square in Milan, and when asked to imagine standing at a certain vantage point and describe the view, these patients failed to mention the buildings that would have appeared on the left side of that scene. However, when asked to imagine the scene again from a vantage point on the opposite side of the square, they then named the buildings that they had previously omitted and omitted those they had previously named, that is, they again named just the buildings on the right side of the imagined scene.

Bisiach, Luzzatti, and Perani followed up these case studies with a group study of neglect. Right hemisphere-damaged patients with left-sided visual neglect and a normal control group of patients were shown cloud-like shapes passing behind a screen with a narrow vertical slit. Because all of the stimulus input is presented centrally in the visual field, any effect of left-sided neglect in this task cannot be attributed to inadequate perception of the stimuli. After viewing pairs of such shapes, the patients were to decide whether the two members of the pair were identical or different. This requires mentally reconstructing the appearance of the stimuli from the successive narrow vertical views. Bisiach and his colleagues considered this constructed representation a mental image. (Although this seems a reasonable enough assumption, it should be noted that the term "mental image" usually refers to representations constructed from memory rather than from fractionated immediate visual input, and it is an open empirical question whether the resulting short-term visual memory representation is of the same type in both cases.) Bisiach et al. found that the patients who neglected the left half of the visual stimuli also neglected the left half of mentally reconstructed stimuli, as evidenced by the greater number of errors when pairs of shapes differed on their left sides than when they differed on their right sides in this task.

Bisiach's work on neglect for mental images constitutes a strong demonstration that common mechanisms underlie imagery and perception. It is difficult, however, to be precise about what component of imagery and perception is shared. Although Bisiach interprets his findings in terms of the loss of half of a spatially mapped "representational schema" it is also possible that the locus of the common imaginal and perceptual deficit in this task is not impaired representational structures but rather impaired attentional processes, which would normally "read off" the left halves of both images and percepts. In fact, to the extent that it is possible to tease apart this issue of structure versus process (see Anderson, 1978), some more recent evidence gathered by Ogden (1985) is somewhat more compatible with a process interpretation. Ogden tested a variety of unilaterally brain-damaged patients on a version of the Bisiach et al. (1979) task, including left hemisphere-damaged patients, anteriorly damaged patients, and right and left hemisphere-damaged patients who showed no neglect in visual perception. She found that all patients neglected the contralesional side of their images, regardless of whether they showed neglect in perception, and regardless of the location of their lesion. If we interpret "representational schema" as a relatively localized representational structure, then Ogden's finding of imagery neglect following a damage to a wide range of cortical loci is not compatible with the idea that neglect for images consists of a loss of one half of the schema on which they are normally constructed. On the other hand, the idea of independent and opposed hemispheric orienting tendencies, which could conceivably be reduced by damage located over a range of intrahemispheric loci, has some independent validity (Kinsbourne, 1977).

Levine, Warach, and Farah (1985) attempted to study the imagery correlates of two distinct forms of nonsensory visual representation, associated with what Ungeleider and Mishkin have called the "what" and "where" cortical visual systems (Ungeleider & Mishkin, 1982). Our subjects were two patients who presented a double dissociation between object recognition ("what") and object localization ("where") in visual perception. Case 1 was a young man who sustained rather extensive brain damage in an automobile accident, including bilateral temporal lobe damage. At the time he was studied, several years after the accident, his only remaining abnormalities were in the visual domain, consisting primarily of bilateral visual field defects, acquired color blindness, mild difficulty recognizing drawings of common objects, i.e., mild object agnosia, and a pronounced inability to recognize live or photographed faces (i.e., severe face agnosia, also called prosopagnosia). In contrast to his difficulties with visual recognition, he was able to demonstrate an accurate sense of the spatial location of objects, by pointing, reaching, or verbal description.

Case 2 was a middle-aged man who had suffered bilateral parieto-occipital damage following multiple strokes. His perceptual abilities were the mirror image of Case 1: He was able to recognize objects, drawings, and faces with little difficulty, but could not point to them, reach for them, or describe their positions in space. We studied the imagery abilities of these two patients with special attention to the distinction between spatial *location* information and single object *appearance* information in visual images. We found that the preserved and impaired aspects of vision in each patient were similarly preserved or impaired in imagery. The patient with object identification difficulties was unable to draw or describe the appearances of familiar objects, animals, and faces from memory, despite being able to draw and describe in great detail the relative locations of cities and states on a map, furniture in his house, and landmarks in his city. The patient with object localization difficulties was unable to describe the relative locations of landmarks in his neighborhood, cities in the United States, or when blindfolded, to point to furniture in his hospital room. He was, however, able to give detailed descriptions of the appearance of a variety of objects, animals, and faces. In a review of the literature for similar cases, we found that for a majority of the published cases of selective visual "what" or "where" deficit, when the appropriate imagery abilities were tested they showed parallel patterns of imagery deficit, and in no case was there a well-documented violation of this parallelism.

A source of potentially more fine-grained information about the relation between representations of object appearance (i.e., "what" system representations) in perception and imagery may be obtained by comparing the recognition of, and imagery for, particular classes of stimuli in agnosic patients. Within a group of agnosic patients reported in published case reports to have accompanying imagery deficits, Farah (1984) found that the particular stimulus categories that were difficult for patients to recognize were also more likely to be difficult to image. Of the four cases in the literature in which imagery ability was tested for both the impaired and relatively spared categories of stimuli, the patients demonstrated or reported better imagery ability for the better-recognized stimuli. For example, Shuttleworth, Syring, and Allen's (1982, Case 2) patient had a selective face recognition deficit, and was also reported to "have no voluntary visual recall (revisualization) of faces but was able to revisualize more general items such as buildings and places." Again, this implies that the nonsensory visual structures that normally subserve object recognition are also involved in object imagery.

Sensory Representations. A more radical version of the hypothesis that imagery and perception share representations is that imagery activates sensory as well as nonsensory perceptual representations. The earliest suggestion of this came from case reports of cortically blind patients who appeared to be unable to use mental imagery (for a review of cases of cortical blindness, some of which include imagery deficits, see Symonds and MacKenzie, 1957). Cortical blindness refers to blindness caused by bilateral destruction of the primary visual cortex. Although the assessment of imagery capabilities in patients with symmetrical destruction of sensory visual areas could, in principle, yield information about the neural basis of shared representational structures for mental imagery and perception, in practice this approach has not been successful, nor is it likely to be. The reason for this is that in addition to their sensory deficits, cortically blind patients generally have other serious deficits, including attentional and memory disorders, disorientation, and delusions (Gassel, 1969; Hécean & Albert, 1978; Symonds & MacKenzie, 1957). Evidently, the events that cause bilateral destruction of the primary visual cortex and neighboring visual areas do not stop there, but also routinely affect both cortical and subcortical structures necessary for personal orientation, memory, higher visual processes, and attention. Therefore, the finding that a cortically blind patient fails an imagery task is uninformative unless it can be demonstrated that the same patient performs normally on a variety of control tasks matched for difficulty with the imagery task. None of the cases of cortically blind patients in the literature provide such data from control tasks, and it is unlikely that cortically blind patients could be found who could in fact perform normally on cognitive tests during the early phases of recovery when blindness is complete.

Another source of information about the neural structures that subserve imagery representation is the use of brain imaging techniques with normal subjects. Using a variety of indices of regional cerebral activity, such as electrical activity, metabolic activity or blood flow, these techniques offer far greater spatial precision than the effects of naturally-occurring brain damage for the functional isolation and anatomical localization of cognitive systems. Five recent studies using brain imaging techniques have revealed activation during mental imagery in sensory regions of the visual system.

Roland and Friberg (1985) measured regional cerebral blood flow during three types of cognitive processes: verbal rehearsal of a familiar jingle, mental arithmetic (subtracting threes starting with 50), and a visual imagery task involving a "mental walk" through the subject's neighborhood, making alternately left and right turns. Each of the three types of cognitive task produced different patterns of regional cerebral blood flow, which were reliable across subjects. The pattern of regional blood flow for the imagery task differed from those of the other tasks by being greatest in the posterior regions of the cortex, the occipital and posterior parietal, and temporal lobes; in other words, both sensory and nonsensory visual areas were engaged by the mental imagery task.

Another study of imagery using cerebral blood flow was reported by Goldenberg, Podreka, Steiner, and Willmes (1987). They gave normal subjects the task of learning auditorily-presented lists of concrete words, and varied the instructional conditions: one group was told to just listen to the words and try to remember them, while the other group was told to use imagery, and visualize the referents of the words as a mnemonic strategy. The patterns of blood flow in the two groups of subjects differed by two distinct measures. First, there was relatively more blood flow to the occipital lobes in the imagery condition than in the nonimagery condition in which the identical stimulus words were being memorized. Second, the pattern of covariation of blood flow among brain areas (calculated by a Smallest Space Analysis, Lingoes, 1979), which provides another index of regional brain activity, was also greater in the occipital and posterior temporal areas of the brain in the imagery condition compared to the nonimagery condition.

In a second experiment, Goldenberg et al. (in press) have also studied the blood flow correlates of spontaneously-evoked imagery, rather than imagery use evoked by instructions to image. They compared the patterns of regional blood flow while subjects tried to answer two types of questions: Questions that require visual imagery to answer (e.g., "Is the green of pine trees darker than the green of grass?") and questions that do not require imagery to answer (e.g., "Is the categorial imperative an ancient grammatical form?"). Despite the superficial similarity of the two types of task, the patterns of regional cerebral blood flow differed significantly: the imagery questions caused greater occipital blood flow than the nonimagery questions. The results of the Smallest Space Analysis again implicated occipital activity in the imagery condition, as well as revealing activity in the posterior temporal and parietal visual processing areas. In contrast, the nonimagery condition did not reveal visual area activation.

Evidence that mental imagery evokes visual sensory activity in normal subjects also comes from electrophysiological techniques: EEG (electroenceph-alography) and ERP (event-related potentials). In EEG techniques, supression of alpha rhythm (EEG activity in a certain range of frequencies) is associated with increased brain activity. It has long been noted that visual imagery is accom-panied by alpha rhythm attenuation over the visual areas of the brain (Barratt, 1956; Brown, 1966; Davidson & Schwartz, 1977; Golla, Hutton, Walter & Grey, 1943; Short, 1953; Slatter, 1960). In Davidson and Schwartz's (1977) study, EEG alpha rhythm was measured simultaneously over the visual (occipi-tal) and tactile (parietal) areas of the brain under three conditions: during visual imagery (imagining a flashing light), tactile imagery (imagining one's forearm being tapped) and during combined visual and tactile imagery (imagining the flashes and taps together). Whereas there was no difference in total alpha attentuation between the visual and tactile imagery conditions (i.e. the overall effects of tactile and visual imagery on general effort and arousal were the same), the site of maximum alpha attenuation in the visual imagery condition was over the visual areas and the site of maximum alpha attenuation in the tactile imagery condition was over the tactile areas. Alpha attenuation in the combined visual ant tactile imagery condition showed an intermediate balanced pattern of distribution across both visual and tactile areas.

More recently, event-related potential techniques have been used to examine regional brain activity during imagery. ERPs measure just the electrical activity of the brain that is synchronized with (and thus presumably "related" to) the processing of a stimulus. Farah, Peronnet, and Weisberg (1987) recorded ERPs during mental imagery by presenting printed words to subjects under two differ-ent instructional conditions: In the "reading only" condition, subjects were told to simply read the words. In the "imagery" condition, subjects were told to read the words and image their referents (e.g., if the word is "cat," image a cat). ERPs were recorded from sixteen standard sites on the scalp including occipital, parietal, temporal and frontal locations. The first 450 msec of the ERPs in both conditions were indistinguishable, reflecting their common visual and lexical processing stages. However, later components of the two conditions differed from one another: In the imagery condition there was a highly localized increase in positivity of the ERP, relative to the "reading only" condition, at the occipital electrodes, implicating occipital activity during the process of imaging.

Farah, Peronnet, Gonon, and Giard (in press) examined the effects of imagery on the ERP to visual stimuli, reasoning that the location of the interaction between imagery and visual stimulus processing would index the location of the shared neural substrates for imagery and vision. Subjects imaged stimuli while viewing real stimuli, so that the effect of imagery on the ERP to stimuli could be observed. If imagery has a systematic effect on the ERP to stimuli, then there must be some common brain locus at which imagery and perceptual processing interact. More importantly, if the interaction between imagery and perception is content-specific—that is, for example, if imaging an H affects the ERP to H's more than the ERP to T's, and imaging a T affects the ERP to T's more than the ERP to H's—then that interaction must be taking place at some brain location where information about the differences between H's and T's is preserved, that is, at a representational locus. In this experiment, subjects imaged H's and T's, while performing a detection task in which an H, a T, or no stimulus was presented on each trial. The image that the subject was instructed to form on a given trial was nonpredictive of the upcoming stimulus. The ERPs to H's and T's while subjects were imaged the same letter were compared to the ERPs to H's and T's while subjects imaged the other letter. In this way, the content-specific effect of imagery on the visual ERP could be observed, while holding constant the actual stimuli to which the ERPs were recorded (equal numbers of H's and T's in both conditions) and the effort of forming and holding an image (equal numbers of H and T images in each condition). Assuming that there is a content-specific effect of imagery on the visual ERP, its scalp location will put constraints on the brain location of representations accessed by both imagery and perception. Imagery had a content-specific effect on the first negative component of the visual evoked potential and this effect was maximal at the occipital recording sites, suggesting that imagery and perception share representations in the occipital lobe.

In summary, measures of regional cerebral blood flow and electrical activity have demonstrated visual cortical involvement in imagery, including the involvement of regions classically considered to be sensory processing areas. Other evidence, from studies of focally brain-damaged patients, highlight some of the nonsensory components of vision that are shared with mental imagery. On the one hand, these results support the old and intuitively appealing idea, first expressed by Hume, that mental images are reactivations of perceptual experiences. On the other hand, they count as strong disconfirming evidence against the current view of some cognitive psychologists that mental images are abstract, propositional memory representations unrelated to perception (e.g., Chambers & Reisberg, 1985; Phillips & Christie, 1977; Pylyshyn, 1981).

MENTAL IMAGE GENERATION

The results summarized above raise another set of questions concerning *how* perceptual representations are activated during imagination. Whereas perception is primarily stimulus-driven (i.e., initiated by the peripheral nervous events triggered by the stimulus), the ability to generate mental images requires additional components of processing outside of the perceptual system proper. In this section, recent studies of the localization and functional architecture of image generation are presented. These studies have focused on two main issues, namely the localization of image generation, and the relation between image generation and other, nonvisual forms of memory recall.

In an initial review of the neurological literature on loss of imagery ability following brain damage, Farah (1984) identified a subset of cases of loss of imagery in which the impaired component of imagery processing was the image generation component. These patients had imagery deficits by one or more of the following criteria: They could not draw from memory but could draw objects shown to them; they could not describe the appearance of objects from memory but were neither aphasic nor did they have a visual-verbal disconnection syndrome; they reported that they could no longer visualize objects from memory, but maintained that their vision was unchanged. In each case, they were unable to perform an imagery task but were able to perform the corresponding task without imagery.

Eight of the patients with imagery deficits were able to recognize visually presented objects. For these patients, the underlying deficit was inferred to be in the image generation process by the following logic. To explain the imagery deficit in perceptually intact patients we must postulate damage to some component of the imagery system that is not shared with visual perception; that is, if visual recognition is intact, then both the nonsensory and sensory representation normally involved in visual perception are presumably intact. By a process of elimination, this implies that the image generation process, which activates efferently the visual representations normally activated during perception, is the impaired component of imagery ability.

What can we learn about the functional architecture of mental imagery from these patients? First, they present us with a dissociation between the recall of visual appearance memory for other, nonvisual material, because they did not have difficulty recalling other, nonvisual information. This dissociation speaks to the relation between imagery and other forms of memory representation. In particular, it is difficult to account for in terms of "single code" theories of mental representation, according to which the recall of visual information, even when accompanied by the phenomenology of a "picture-in-the-head," is carried out by the same processes used for the recall of nonvisual material such as lists or descriptions (Pylyshyn, 1981). The status of mental imagery as a separate memory system is also strengthened by the existence of the opposite dissociation, namely patients who are amnesic but can generate images. Studies of imagery mnemonics in amnesic patients have confirmed that amnesic patients are capable of forming images from memory. The juxtaposition of intact imagery ability with a profound amnesia is illustrated in a striking way by patient H.M., amnesic for 3 decades, who when asked to draw objects such as a radio or an alarm clock from memory, drew accurate, detailed pictures of 1950s-style objects (Milner, 1984).

These cases also suggest that image generation is a localizable process. In these eight patients the predominant site of damage was the posterior left hemisphere. Since this original case review was written, three other cases of loss of imagery with intact object recognition, i.e., image generation deficit, have been presented (Farah, Levine, & Calvanio, in press; Grossi, Orsini, Modafferi, & Liotti, in press; Pena-Casanova, Roig-Rovira, Bermudez, & Tolosa-Sarro, 1985). In each case, the lesion was in the distribution of the left posterior cerebral artery, and affected mainly the occipito-temporal regions of the left hemisphere.

Whatever the precise intrahemispheric localization of image generation, one of the most interesting aspects of the results reviewed above is that they seem to suggest that image generation is a lateralized function of the brain. Furthermore, these results contradict the widely held assumption, first explicitly noted by Ehrlichman and Barrett (1983), that imagery processes are carried out in the right hemisphere. Ehrlichman and Barrett's review of the neuropsychology literature found little evidence supporting this assumption. We can now ask the alternative question, is there other evidence in favor of the left hemisphere localization for image generation? The studies reviewed below are relevant to this question.

Further Studies on the Laterality of Image Generation.   Farah (1986) attempted to test the hypothesis of left hemisphere specialization for image generation using a lateralized tachistoscopic paradigm. The basic idea of the experiment was to use the *facilitating* effect of imagery in visual discrimination tasks as a measure of the presence or quality of images. The logic of the experiment was that, if image generation is a lateralized function of one hemisphere, then images should be directly available for further processing in that hemisphere, but only indirectly available (by means of callosal transmission) in the other hemisphere.

The experimental paradigm was a lateralized visual discrimination task, in which the subject is to decide whether a stimulus, presented briefly and to one side of a fixation point, is or is not a predesignated "target." The two targets were a plus sign and a rectangular-shaped capital "O" character. Nontargets were characters selected for being visually similar to either the plus of the "O." The work of Cooper and Shepard (1973), Posner, Boies, Eichelman, and Taylor (1969), and others has shown that a visual image of the target can be used as a template to facilitate discriminations between target and nontarget stimuli. In the present experiment, subjects performed two versions of the lateralized discrimination task. In the "Baseline" condition, they are precued with the information about the side on which the stimulus will occur before the stimulus presentation. Their task was to respond "target" to either of the targets and "nontarget" to any of the nontargets. In the "Imagery" condition, they were precued as before with the side on which the stimulus would occur, and they were also shown one of the two targets (in central vision), which they were instructed to image in the position of the upcoming stimulus. The image should facilitate the visual discrimination between targets and nontargets, particularly when the image and stimulus are visually similar. Thus, there were two, independent measures of the effectiveness of imagery in the present experiment: the degree of facilitation with an image, relative to performance in the same visual discrimination task without an image, and the degree of facilitation with an image that is visually similar to the stimulus being presented, relative to performance in the same visual discrimination task with an image that is visually different from the stimulus being presented. If the left hemisphere is specialized for image generation, then these measures of image-mediated facilitation should be greatest when the image-stimulus overlap occurs in the right hemifield-left hemisphere, where the image was generated.

Performance in the baseline condition did not depend on which hemisphere initially received the stimulus: mean response times for the left and right hemispheres were 836 msec and 842 msec respectively. The corresponding error rates were 24.2% and 24.1%. That is, there is no detectable difference between the abilities of the two hemispheres to perform the basic visual discrimination task of the baseline condition. In contrast, when the same task was performed using an image as a template, there was an overall left hemisphere superiority: The mean response times for the right and left hemispheres were 784 msec and 757 msec, respectively. The corresponding error rates were 24.6% and 22.9%.

The left hemisphere advantage in the imagery condition was greater when the images and stimuli were similar than when they were different: Mean response times for the left and right hemispheres were 718 msec and 756 msec respectively with a similar image (with error rates of 21.1% and 25.0%, respectively) and were 795 msec and 812 msec respectively with a different image (with error rates of 24.6% and 24.2% respectively). Both of these predicted interactions were statistically significant.

To summarize, the effect of image generation on visual discrimination performance in normal subjects is asymmetrical in a direction consistent with a left hemisphere basis for image generation.

The results of the lateralized tachachistoscopic experiment with normal subjects add support to the hypothesis that the left hemisphere is *relatively* more adept at image generation than the right, but do not directly confirm the stronger hypothesis suggested by the focally brain-damaged patients, namely that only the left hemisphere is able to generate mental images. However, a recent study of a split-brain patient speaks to this issue.

In this initial study (Farah, Gazzaniga, Holtzman, & Kosslyn, 1985), my collaborators and I adapted a simple imagery task from one already used in imagery studies for use with split-brain patient J. W. The task was a letter classification task used by Weber and others (Weber & Castleman, 1970; Weber & Malmstrom, 1979). In the orignal version, subjects went through the alphabet from memory classifying the lower case forms of each letter from a to z as "ascending" (e.g., "d"), "descending" (e.g., "g"), or neither (e.g., "a"). In the version we adapted for use with the split-brain patient, a particular letter was cued by the presentation of its upper case form. So, for example, if the stimulus was "P," the correct response was "descending." In order to cue just one hemisphere at a time with the letter to be imaged and classified, we presented the upper case forms at 1 ½° to the left or to the right of the patient's fixation. This results in only the contralateral hemisphere receiving the visual input, and thus only that hemisphere is in a position to respond to the stimulus. An additional minor change in the present task is that the ascending and descending response categories were collapsed, resulting in "medium" (e.g., "a") and "not medium" (e.g., "f," "g") response categories.

In order to infer that a failure in this task reflects a hemispheric image generation deficit per se, additional control tasks were developed to assess each hemisphere's ability to perform all other components of the imagery task. A task analysis of the imagery task suggests that the following processing steps are required: (1) The recognition of the upper case letter (i.e., matching the visual input with long-term visual memory), (2) the retrieval of the associated lower case form with the upper case stimulus, (3) the generation of an image of the lower case letter, (4) the classification of the lower case letter into the appropriate response category, and (5) the execution of a response (in this case pressing one of the two buttons). The following two control tasks together require all of the above processes except for image generation. In the *letter association* task, upper case letters were presented to a single hemisphere (1 ½° out from fixation) and the patient's task was to select the corresponding lower case form from a nonalphabetically arranged array of letters in free vision. Successful performance of this task shows that the hemisphere receiving the upper case letter is capable of recognizing the upper and lower case letters and associating them correctly. In the *perceptual classification* task, lower case letters were presented to a single hemisphere and the patient's task was to classify the letter into the appropriate response category (medium or not medium) and respond. Unlike the imagery task, this task simply requires the patient to classify what he can actually see. Successful performance on this task shows that the hemisphere receiving the letter is capable of performing the letter height discrimination and responding. It follows that if a hemisphere can perform both control tasks, a failure in the imagery task cannot be attributed to a difficulty in perceptual encoding, letter recognition and association, height discrimination, or response production.

Both hemispheres were able to perform the control tasks. The right hemisphere made one error out of 26 trials in the *letter association* task and the left hemisphere performed errorlessly in the same number of trials. In the *perceptual classification* task, the right hemisphere was able to correctly classify 90% of the lower letters presented to it as "medium" or "not medium," and the left hemisphere correctly classified all of the lower case letters presented to it. In contrast to the control tasks, the performance of the two hemispheres diverged sharply on the imagery task: The right hemisphere performed at chance level, 43% correct, whereas the left hemisphere continued to perform essentially perfectly, 97% correct. These results suggest that the left hemisphere has an *absolute* rather than a relative, specialization for image generation.

Many other neuropsychological studies have found evidence of left hemisphere involvement in image generation, although in most cases these studies were not undertaken with this hypothesis in mind. In many cases, results of these studies were discounted by the original investigators as representing the involvement of (or contamination by) language or "analytic" strategies in their imagery tasks. However, there appears to be no strong reason to interpret these findings thus, except for the a priori belief that imagery is not a left hemisphere function (cf. Ehrlichman & Barrett, 1983) and the knowledge that language is.

Read (1978) compared the performance of right and left temporal lobectomy patients and normal control subjects in the use of mental imagery for solving three-term series problems (e.g., "A is fatter than B and B is fatter than C, who is fattest?"). Contrary to his stated expectations of a right temporal deficit in this task, the worst performance was associated with left temporal lobectomy patients, who were as a group significantly worse than the right temporal lobectomy patients and controls, whereas the performance of the right temporal lobectomy patients was not significantly worse than that of the controls. The inference that the left temporal lobectomy patients were displaying a deficit in image generation *per se,* as opposed to deficits in other cognitive processes required by this task, is supported by the normal performance of these patients on the Token Test and IQ tests, as well as by their post-experimental reports that they were unable to solve the problems because they could not form images. Read cautiously interpreted the result as a deficit in image creation, making the important point that "it is naive to suppose that the cognitive activity of the left hemisphere is solely involved with language processing" (p. 125), but also suggested the need for a distinction between different kinds of images, concluding that the left hemisphere mediates the creation of images based on "verbal symbolic information."

Gutbrod, Mager, Meier, and Cohen (1985) compared the performance of aphasic left hemisphere-damaged patients and right hemisphere-damaged patients in a reaction time task which required verifying whether a set of features (size, shape, and color) correctly describes a particular visual stimulus. In one condition the features preceded the stimulus. Based on work by Clark and Chase (1972) with normal subjects, Gutbrod et al. expected subjects to form an image of the stimulus described by these features for use in a template match with the stimulus. In the other condition, the stimulus preceded the features, and the expected strategy as a serial verification of each feature. In both conditions, the features were sometimes given verbally (as lists of words, similar to the Token Test) and sometimes given pictorially (using large and small bars to represent size, outline forms to represent shape, and irregularly shaped color patches to represent color). The greatest impairment in this task was seen with the left hemisphere-damaged patients in the first condition, in which subjects were expected to form mental images. This impairment was present with both verbally and pictorially represented features. This led Gutbrod et al. to the conclusion that their left hemisphere-damaged subjects had "a deficit in organizing the verbally as well as the pictorially presented information into a visual image." They also note DeRenzi, Faglioni, and Previdi's (1978) earlier speculation that the aphasic deficit on the Token Test can be at least partly explicable in terms of an impairment in mental image generation.

An imagery task that has been frequently studied in the neuropsychology literature is the color-figure matching task, in which a subject is shown a black and white line drawing of an object that normally possesses a characteristic color, such as a carrot, and is asked to select the crayon or color patch that matches the depicted object's color (Basso, Faglioni, & Spinnler, 1976; Cohen & Kelter, 1979; DeRenzi & Spinnler, 1967; DeRenzi, Faglioni, Scotti, & Spinnler, 1972; Kinsbourne & Warrington, 1964). Generally, the objects used in these studies are not verbally associated with colors (e.g., as "sky" is associated with "blue"). Most people have the introspection that in performing this task, the depicted object is imaged, and its color "inspected" by the mind's eye; indeed, the task is often called a mental imagery task by its investigators (e.g, DeRenzi & Spinnler, 1967). Left hemisphere-damaged patients, particularly aphasics, have the most trouble with this task. However, the deficit has been observed in a severe form in the absence of aphasia (Varney & Digre, 1983), and extends to tasks involving the matching of figures with achromatic intensities (Cohen & Kelter, 1979). Thus, it is not strictly speaking an aspect of aphasia, nor is it a problem with colors per se. At present the most straightforward interpretation is that left hemisphere-damaged patients have difficulty generating mental images.

Cohen (1975) investigated hemispheric differences in the utilization of precues in a lateralized visual discrimination task in which subjects discriminated between normal and mirror-reversed characters (letters and numbers) presented at different orientations. Subjects were sometimes given advance information about the identity of a target, and were told to image the predicted target in preparation for seeing it. The design of Cohen's experiment is thus very similar to the lateralized tachistoscopic experiment presented earlier, particularly if one considers only those trials in which no mental rotation was required. For this subset of trials, the remaining differences are the nature of the stimulus materials, the nature of the visual discrimination, and the cue-validity of the image cues (i.e., Cohen's cues were completely predictive of the stimulus, the cues in the other experiment were completely nonpredictive). Cohen found a left hemisphere superiority in the use of images in her task when mental rotation was not required. This finding was interpreted in terms of hemispheric differences in the use of advance information, and the author discussed the possible weighting of the hemispheric advantage towards the left by the use of alphanumeric stimuli.

Lempert (1987) reported two experiments in which the hemispheric locus of image generation was assessed by measuring its interference with left and right-sided motor activity. Subjects listened to sentences while tapping as quickly as possible with either the right or the left hand. In one experiment, the use of imagery was manipulated by the presence or absence of overt instructions to image the sentence, and in another by the nature of the sentences themselves (e.g., "The giant chased the jogger," which evokes spontaneous image generation, versus "The mood suited the moment," which does not). Imagery use was validated by better recall for imaged than nonimaged sentences. With the exception of the male subjects, who did not show a recall advantage with imagery, the imagery conditions were associated with greater tapping decrement on the right side (controlled by the left hemisphere), than on the left side.

Mazziotta, Phelps, Carson, and Kuhl (1982) obtained information about regional cerebral metabolic activity associated with imagery, in the context of a PET study of short-term memory retention of auditorally-presented tone sequences. They presented normal subjects with the Seashore tonal memory task, in which a short sequence of tones is presented, followed by an interval of silence, followed by a second sequence of tones. The object of the task is to decide whether the second tone sequence is the same as or different from the second tone sequence, and thus successful performance demands the retention of the first tone sequence in memory during the silent interval. When the patterns of regional cerebral metabolic activity during the retention interval were examined in 12 normal subjects, two distinct patterns were observed. Three subjects showed focal left posterior metabolic activity (mainly in the posterior temporal lobe), and nine subjects showed diffuse right hemisphere greater than left hemisphere metabolic activity. As the stimuli and responses for the two types of subjects were identical, Mazziota et al. reasoned that the difference must lie in the cognitive strategy adopted by the subjects during the retention interval, and accordingly devised a postexperiment questionnaire about cognitive strategies for retention of the tone sequences. The questionnaire revealed that all and only the three subjects who showed evidence of focal left posterior activity reported a visual imagery strategy. Although the most straightforward interpretation of this result is that the focal left posterior activity indexed the use of visual imagery, a somewhat less straightforward interpretation was offered by the authors, viz., that the three subjects with left posterior activity (only one of whom visualized musical notation) had adopted a more analytic approach to the retention of the tones.

Some of the studies described earlier in the section on *Sensory Representations* in mental imagery are also relevant to the issue of the laterality of mental image generation. The highest mean increases in blood flow in Roland and Friberg's (1985) imagery experiment were in the left hemisphere, particularly the inferior posterior temporal cortex and the posterior superior parietal cortex. Goldenberg et al. (1987) found that blood flow was greater in the left hemisphere during memorization using imagery mnemonics (which requires mental image generation) than during the other conditions of their experiment. A salient focus of blood flow was observed in the left inferior occipital-temporal region. Goldenberg et al. (in press) found the same left occipital-temporal maximum when image generation was manipulated during question-answering by the nature of the question. Similarly, Farah et al.'s (1987) ERP study of image generation revealed a significant asymmetry at the temporo-occipital electrodes, greater on the left side.

CONCLUSIONS

Compared to the study of the neural bases of language and verbal memory, the neuropsychology of mental imagery is a very recent development. A glance at the references cited confirms that much of our current understanding of mental imagery and the brain is only a few years old. This is perhaps not surprising, given the relative recency with which mental imagery joined language and verbal memory as bona fide subjects of scientific study in cognitive psychology, and the hysteresis which seems to operate between developments in cognitive psychology and developments in cognitive neuropsychology. Yet, even in the relatively short history of the neuropsychology of mental imagery, it is clear that both subdisciplines of cognitive psychology and neuropsychology have benefited: Long-standing controversies in the cognitive study of imagery, such as the relation between imagery and perception, and the modularity of image generation with respect to other memory recall processes, have found a new source of evidence, strongly favoring the view that images are perceptual representations efferently activated by a special-purpose recall process. Similarly, at least a bit of light has been shed on the long-standing problem in neuropsychology of systematizing and explaining the variety of visual/spatial disorders that have been observed in brain-damaged patients: By using the theoretical concepts and experimental paradigms developed in the cognitive study of mental imagery, a set of visual/spatial disorders has been explained in terms of the dysfunction of one or another component of the mental imagery system.

REFERENCES

Anderson, J. R. (1978). Arguments concerning representation for mental imagery. *Psychological Review, 85,* 249–277.

Basso, A., Faglioni, P. & Spinnler, H. (1976). Non-verbal colour impairment in aphasics. *Neuropsychologia, 14,* 183–192.

Benton, A. L. (1969). Disorders of spatial orientation. In P. J. Vinken & G. W. Bruyn (Eds.), *Handbook of clinical neurology (Vol. 3, Disorders of higher nervous activity).* New York: Wiley.

Bisiach, E., Capitani, E., Luzzatti, C., & Perani, D. (1981). Brain and conscious representation of outside reality. *Neuropsychologia, 19,* 543–551.

Bisiach, E., & Luzzatti, C. (1978). Unilateral neglect of representational space. *Cortex, 14,* 129–133.

Bisiach, E., Luzzatti, C., & Perani, D. (1979). Unilateral neglect, representational schema and consciousness. *Brain, 102,* 609–618.

Brain, W. R. (1950). The cerebral basis of consciousness. *Brain, 465–479.*

Chambers, D., & Reisberg, D. (1985). Can mental images be ambiguous? *Journal of Experimental Psychology: Human Perception and Performance, 11,* 317–328.

Clark, H. H., & Chase, W. G. (1972). On the process of comparing sentences against pictures. *Cognitive Psychology, 3,* 472–517.

Cohen, G. (1975). Hemispheric differences in the utilization of advance information. In P. M. A. Rabbit & S. Dornic (Eds.), *Attention and performance, Vol. 5.* New York: Academic Press.

Cohen, R., & Kelter, S. (1979). Cognitive impairment of aphasics in a colour-to-picture matching task. *Cortex, 15,* 235–245.

Cooper, L. A., & Shepard, R. N. (1973). Chronometric studies of the rotation of mental images. In W. G. Chase (Ed.), *Visual information processing.* New York: Academic Press.

DeRenzi, E., Faglioni, P., Scotti, G., & Spinnler, H. (1972). Impairment in associating color with form concomitant with aphasia. *Brain, 95,* 293–304.

DeRenzi, E., Faglioni, P., & Previdi, A. (1978). Increased susceptibility of aphasics to a distractor task. *Brain and Language, 6,* 42–49.

DeRenzi, E., & Spinnler, H. (1967). Impaired performance on color tasks in patients with hemispheric lesions. *Cortex, 3,* 194–217.

Ehrlichman, H., & Barrett, J. (1983). Right hemisphere specialization for mental imagery: A review of the evidence. *Brain and Cognition, 2,* 39–52.

Farah, M. J. (1984). The neurological basis of mental imagery: A componential analysis. *Cognition, 18,* 245–272.

Farah, M. J. (1985). Psychophysical evidence for a shared representational medium for visual images and percepts. *Journal of Experimental Psychology: General, 114,* 93–105.

Farah, M. J. (1986). The laterality of mental image generation: A test with normal subjects. *Neuropsychologia, 24,* 541–551.

Farah, M. J., Gazzaniga, M. S., Holtzman, J. D., & Kosslyn, S. M. (1985). A left hemisphere basis for visual mental imagery? *Neuropsychologia, 23,* 115–118.

Farah, M. J., Levine, D. N., & Calvanio, R. (in press). A case study of mental imagery deficit. *Brain and Cognition,* .

Farah, M. J., Peronnet, F., & Weisberg, L. (1987). *Brain activity underlying mental imagery: An ERP study*. Paper presented at the 28th Annual Meeting of the Psychonomic Society, Seattle.

Gassel, M. M. (1969). Occipital lobe syndromes (excluding hemiznopia). In P. J. Vinken & G. W. Bruyn (Eds.), *Handbook of clinical neurology* (vol. 4). Amsterdam: North Holland.

Goldenberg, G., Podreka, I., Steiner, M., & Willmes, K. (1987). Patterns of regional cerebral blood flow related to memorizing of high and low imagery words. An emission computer tomography study. *Neuropsychologia, 25,* 473–486.

Goldenberg, G., Podreka, I., Steiner, M., Suess, E., Deeke, L., & Willmes, K. (in press). Regional cerebral blood flow patterns in imagery tasks—Results of single photon emission computer tomography. In M. Denis, J. Englekamp, & J. T. E. Richardson (Eds.), *Cognitive and neuropsychological approaches to mental imagery*. Dordrecht, The Netherlands: Martinus Nijhoff.

Grossi, D., Orsini, A., Modafferi, A., & Liotti. M. (in press). Visual imaginal constructional apraxia: On a case of selective deficit of imagery. *Brain and Cognition, 5,* 255–267.

Gutbrod, K., Mager, B., Meier, E., & Cohen, R. (1985). Cognitive processing of tokens and their description in aphasia. *Brain and Language, 25,* 37–51.

Hebb, D. O. (1968). Concerning imagery. *Psychological Review, 75,* 466–479.

Hécaen, H., & Albert, M. L. (1978). *Human neuropsychology*. New York: Wiley.

Hume, D. (1969). *A treatise in human nature*. Baltimore: Pelican Books. (Originally published, 1739)

Kinsbourne, M. (1977). Hemi-neglect and hemispheric rivalry. In E. A. Weinstein & R. P. Friedland (Eds.), *Advances in neurology*. New York: Raven Press.

Kinsbourne, M., & Warrington, E. K. (1964). Observations on color agnosia. *Journal of Neurology, Neurosurgery, and Psychiatry, 27,* 296–299.

Lempert, H. (1987). Effect of imaging on concurrent unimanual performance. *Neuropsychologia, 25,* 835–839.

Levine, D. N., Warach, J., & Farah, M. J. (1985). Two visual systems in mental imagery: Dissociation of 'What' and 'Where' in imagery disorders due to bilateral posterior cerebral lesions. *Neurology, 35,* 1010–1018.

Mazziotta, J. C., Phelps, M. E., Carson, R. E. & Kuhl, D. E. (1982). Tomographic mapping of human cerebral metabolism: Auditory stimulation. *Neurology, 32,* 921–.

McKim, R. H. (1980). *Experiences in visual thinking*. Monterey, CA: Brooks/Cole.

Milner, B. (1984). *Temporal lobes and memory disorders*. Paper presented at the American Psychological Association Convention, Toronto, Canada.

Ogden, J. A. (1985). Contralesional neglect of constructed visual images in right and left brain-damaged patients. *Neuropsychologia, 23,* 273–277.

Pena-Casanova, J., Roig-Rovira, T., Bermudez, A., & Tolosa-Sarro, E. (1985). Optic aphasia, optic apraxia, and loss of dreaming. *Brain and Language, 26,* 63–71.

Phillips, W. A., & Christie, D. F. M. (1977). Interference with visualization. *Quarterly Journal of Experimental Psychology, 29,* 637–650.

Posner, M. I., Boies, S. J., Eichelman, W. H., & Taylor, R. L. (1969). Retention of visual and name codes of single letters. *Journal of Experimental Psychology Monograph, 79.*

Pylyshyn, Z. W. (1981). The imagery debate: Analogue media versus tacit knowledge. *Psychological Review, 88,* 16–45.

Read, D. E. (1981). Solving deductive-reasoning problems after unilateral temporal lobectomy. *Brain and Language, 12,* 116–127.

Roland, P. E., & Friberg, L. (1985). Localization of cortical areas activated by thinking. *Journal of Neurophysiology, 53,* 1219–1243.

Shepard, R. N. (1978). The mental image. *American Psychologist, 33,* 125–137.

Shuttleworth, E. C., Syring, V., & Allen, N. (1982). Further observations on the nature of prosopagnosia. *Brain and Cognition, 1,* 302–332.

Symonds, C., & MacKenzie, I. (1957). Bilateral loss of vision from cerebral infarction. *Brain, 80,* 28–448.

Ungeleider, L. G., & Mishkin, M. (1982). Two cortical visual systems. In D. J. Ingle, M. A. Goodale, & R. J. W. Mansfield (Eds.), *Analysis of visual behavior.* Cambridge, MA: MIT Press.

Varney, N. R., & Digre, K. (1983). Color amnesia without aphasia. *Cortex, 19,* 551–555.

Weber, R. J., & Castleman, J. (1970). The time it takes to imagine. *Perception and Psychophysics, 8,* 165–168.

Weber, R. J., & Malmstrom, F. V. (1979). Measuring the size of mental images. *Journal of Experimental Psychology: Human Perception and Performance, 5,* 1–12.

10

A Dual Coding Perspective on Imagery and the Brain

Allan Paivio

This chapter reviews neuropsychological data on imagery from the viewpoint of a general theory of cognition that has guided my research for more than 20 years. The findings are interesting to me particularly because they bear directly on the assumptions of the theory. The relation is reciprocal, however, in that a well-founded theory can also guide research directed specifically at understanding the cognitive functions of the brain. Such theoretical guidance is especially important in the case of imagery, which is psychologically complex and is bound to be neurologically complex as well.

The complexity of the problem is evident in the diversity of views concerning the cerebral localization of imagery. The most common and longstanding view, supported by considerable evidence (see Ley, 1983), is that imagery is predominantly a right hemisphere function. Recently, however, Martha Farah and her colleagues (e.g., Farah, 1984, Kosslyn, Holtzman, Farah, & Gazzaniga, 1985) have proposed that the left hemisphere predominates in image generation, though not necessarily in other imagery functions. Farah's own research, summarized in this volume (chapter 9), is providing increasing evidence for that hypothesis. Yet another interpretation is that both hemispheres "contain" the information and mechanisms required for experiencing and using imagery. That view, too, has been empirically supported, specifically by Bisiach and his colleagues (e.g., Bisiach, Capitani, Luzzatti, & Perani, 1981), although the research on hemifield neglect in imagery that Bisiach and Berti describe in chapter 7 of this volume suggests the right posterior cortical structures are especially crucial to conscious visual imagery.

My own reviews of the evidence (Paivio, 1986; Paivio & te Linde, 1982) have persuaded me that all of the above conclusions are partly correct: Neural structures in both hemispheres must have the representational information and processing capabilities associated with imagery phenomena, but they participate differentially in different functions of imagery. I will review some of the crucial findings and show how they can be organized and interpreted within the empirical and conceptual framework of dual coding theory.

THE EMPIRICAL APPROACH: CONVERGENT OPERATIONS

Our empirical approach to the study of imagery relies on multiple procedures that are assumed to converge on the probability that imagery of a
particular kind will be used in a given task and will have effects predicted from
the guiding theory. These procedures include (a) variation in relevant item
attributes, such as the concreteness or image-evoking value of stimulus words,
(b) experimental manipulations such as instructions to image, and (c) individual
differences in imagery abilities and preferences. We also use verbal reports of
imagery as additional validation that our procedures converged on imagery
processes. This convergent operational approach differs in emphasis from the
traditional one in the neurological literature, in which imagery is inferred primarily from verbal reports of patients with neurological pathologies of one kind
or another (e.g., see the recent reviews of that literature by Farah, 1984, and
Brown, 1985), although relevant performance tests have also been used, especially by neuropsychologists.

THEORETICAL ASSUMPTIONS AND EVIDENCE

The main assumptions of dual coding theory concern a) independence and
partial interconnectedness of verbal and nonverbal representational systems, (b)
a conceptual distinction between symbolic and sensorimotor representational
systems, (c) types of structural interconnections and processing levels, (d)
organizational and transformational properties of the two systems, and (e) general adaptive functions they serve. These assumptions, as defined and elaborated
on below, were based originally on behavioral data independent of neuropsychological considerations. The behavioral evidence has been comprehensively reviewed elsewhere (e.g., Paivio, 1971, 1986) and is not discussed here. The
review concentrates instead on neuropsychological findings relevant to each of
the assumptions, with special emphasis on imagery. Some untested implications
of the theory are also mentioned.

Verbal and Nonverbal Representational Systems

At the top of the list is the verbal-nonverbal symbolic distinction, which is
the most general defining feature of the theory. Figure 1 schematizes that
distinction along with information related to specific structural assumptions.
Cognition is assumed to be served by two functionally independent but partially
interconnected symbolic systems, a verbal system that is specialized for dealing
with linguistic stimuli and generating speech, and a nonverbal system specialized
for dealing with nonverbal objects and events behaviorally as well as through the
medium of imagery. The systems are independent in the sense that either system

can be active without the other or both can be active concurrently. Partial interconnectedness implies that one system can activate the other through associative connections between specific verbal and nonverbal representational units. The nature of the interconnections and related processes are discussed in a subsequent section. Here we deal only with the evidence for independent systems.

There is general agreement that verbal and nonverbal stimuli or processing modes are dependent on different parts of the brain. For most people, the left hemisphere controls speech and is more efficient than the right hemisphere in a variety of tasks with verbal material, including perceptual recognition, episodic memory, and comprehension. Conversely, the right hemisphere has the advantage in such nonverbal tasks as face identification and discrimination, recognition of nonverbal sounds, memory for faces and spatial patterns, and so on. From the dual coding perspective, it is important that the generalization holds for different sensory modalities, justifying the conclusion that the distinction is a verbal-nonverbal *symbolic* one that cuts across sensory modalities, and that the two symbolic systems are functionally independent.

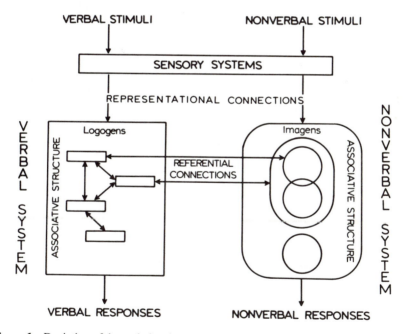

Figure 1 Depiction of the verbal and nonverbal symbolic systems of dual coding theory, showing the representational units and their referential (between system) and associative (within system) interconnections as well as connections to input and output systems. Reprinted from A. Paivio (1986). *Mental representations: A dual coding approach.* New York: Oxford University Press.

Symbolic Versus Sensorimotor Systems

The distinction between symbolic and sensorimotor modalities is illustrated in Table 1, which shows the orthogonal relation between the two dimensions: Verbal and nonverbal information alike come in different modalities—visual objects versus written language, environmental sounds versus speech, and the haptic feel of familiar objects versus writing as a motor pattern. The orthogonal system is incomplete because some sensory systems (e.g., taste and smell) are not used to construct linguistic symbols. The general point, however, is that both nonverbal and verbal systems must be capable of using different kinds of sensorimotor information symbolically, as in memory. More accurately stated, both symbolic systems are composed of modality specific sensorimotor representational units and processes that operate on them.

The orthogonality assumption implies that symbolic and sensory modalities are functionally independent. Neurological data showing functional dissociation of the two dimensions are consistent with the assumption. For example, whereas printed names are usually recognized better when presented to the left hemisphere, pictures of familiar objects are recognized equally easily when presented to either hemisphere. Thus, the pattern of asymmetries varies with the verbal-nonverbal symbolic distinction when the sensory input modality is constant, i.e.,

TABLE 1

Orthogonal conceptual relation between symbolic systems and sensorimotor systems with examples of types of modality-specific information represented in each subsystem.

Sensor-imotor	Symbolic Systems	
	Verbal	Nonverbal
Visual	Visual words	Visual objects
Auditory	Auditory words	Environmental sounds
Haptic	Writing patterns	"Feel" of objects
Taste		Taste memories
Smell		Olfactory memories

visual in both cases. Comparison of the picture results with those for nonverbal sounds yields a contrasting pattern: Whereas pictures show hemispheric symmetry, such environmental sounds as a car starting are recognized better by the left ear, hence the right hemisphere, in dichotic listening tasks (Curry, 1976). In this contrast, therefore, the pattern of hemispheric asymmetries varies with sensory modality (auditory *versus* visual) when the symbolic modality of the material is nonverbal in each case. Selective deficits resulting from brain damage provide further evidence of such dissociations. A familiar example is pure alexia, where damage to posterior regions of the left hemisphere results in an inability to process visual language while speech recognition remains intact. Thus, the functional deficit is again related to sensory modality when symbolic modality remains constant, in this case on the verbal side. Other supportive patterns can be found in the neuropsychological literature, but the above examples suffice to illustrate the neuropsychological reality of the distinction between symbolic and sensorimotor modalities.

Interconnections and Processing Levels

The next set of assumptions pertains to the processes involved in activating representational units by relevant stimuli and through structural interconnections. The structural model (Figure 1) shows the units and interconnections. The term, logogen, borrowed from John Morton (1969, 1979), refers to the verbal representational units in long term memory; the parallel term, imagen, refers to the representations that correspond to objects or their parts and presumably are the basis of consciously experienced images.

The theory distinguishes between representational, referential, and associative connections, and the different levels of processing activity associated with those interconnecting pathways. Representational processing refers to relatively direct activation of logogens and imagens by familiar verbal or nonverbal stimuli and accounts for our ability to recognize objects through a matching process of some kind. The referential level refers to cross-system activation via the interconnections between verbal and nonverbal representations, which accounts for such phenomena as our ability to name objects or their properties and image to words. Finally, the associative level refers to associative interconnections among representational units within each system. Processing at this level entails spreading activation among representations within each system, as illustrated by word associations and by experiences in which objects or their images arouse images of associated objects or scenes. Complex tasks may require all three levels of processing, perhaps iteratively. The assumption that verbal and nonverbal representations can be activated in different ways helps to make sense out of some of the complexities in the neuropsychological literature.

Representational processing   We begin with representational level processing and its implications for imagery. Carole Ernest and I (Paivio & Ernest, 1971)
reported a perceptual recognition experiment in which letters, familiar pictures,
or geometric forms were flashed tachistoscopically to right or left visual fields at
brief durations. The novel aspect of the study was that our subjects were divided
into high and low visual imagery ability groups on the basis of their combined
scores on two spatial manipulation tests, the Minnesota Paper Form Board and
Space Relations, and a questionnaire dealing with imaginal and verbal modes of
thinking. The crucial results are shown in Figure 2.

Note that high ability subjects were far superior to low ability subjects in
recognition of pictures presented to either field. Field had no effect and the
apparent interaction trend was not significant. These data suggest, first, that
representations necessary for recognition of visual objects are equally available
in both hemispheres; and second, that they are more available or accessible for
subjects who are high rather than low in visual imagery ability. Thus, we can
deduce that both hemispheres have the representations and processing skills
necessary for generating mental images of familiar objects. The hemispheric
symmetry is especially significant because it occurred despite the fact that the
subjects indicated their recognition by naming the pictures, which is a verbal
referential task that would be expected to favor the left hemisphere. Since this
did not happen, it must mean that recognition performance was dependent
mainly on the availability of nonverbal representations rather than on the verbal
indicator of recognition. In support of that inference, Carole Ernest (1983)
subsequently replicated the picture results using a recognition test that did not

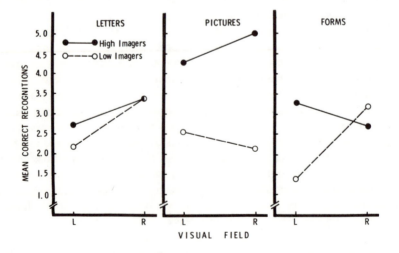

Figure 2   Recognition accuracy scores as a function of imagery ability, stimulus attribute, and visual field. From Paivio and Ernest (1971).

require naming. Other data in the literature (e.g., St. John, 1981), including those obtained with split-brain patients, also support the generalization that object representations are available in both hemispheres.

The results were quite different for letters and forms. Letters were recognized better in the right field than in the left by both groups of subjects, who did not differ in recognition performance. The field effect is consistent with the general literature in showing left hemisphere superiority in recognition of verbal stimuli, even letters. The absence of an imagery ability effect shows that superiority of high imagery subjects in picture recognition was not due to a general superiority in dealing with spatial patterns. The same conclusion emerges from the results for geometric forms, with a further qualifying interaction which indicates that high imagery subjects were far superior to low imagers in right hemisphere recognition of forms, whereas the difference reversed slightly in the case of the left hemisphere. The interaction also shows a strong left hemisphere advantage for low imagers, as though they relied on a verbal strategy to recognize forms.

Referential processes   We have not similarly compared high and low imagery subjects in tasks that are more dependent on referential interconnections and processes, but the neuropsychological literature is rich in information that implicates this level of processing. The anomias generally provide clear evidence that damage to the left hemisphere can result in naming difficulties without accompanying difficulties in recognizing the visual objects themselves or in producing the names to printed words or verbal contextual cues. Thus, the anomias indicate that nonverbal-to-verbal referential interconnections or processing skills have been impaired while verbal representational and associative connections or processes remain intact.

Other studies similarly implicate specific referential imagery pathways. Luria (1973) described cases of patients with lesions in the posterior regions of the left-temporal lobe who were unable to draw named objects while retaining the ability to copy pictured objects. Such syndromes are clear evidence of disrupted referential interconnections implicating imagery. Similar image generation difficulties also result from lesions in occipital or parieto-occipital regions of the left hemisphere, as shown by research by Bisiach et al. (1981), and other studies reviewed by Farah and by Benson in their chapters in this volume. Such problems could indicate damage either to the nonverbal representational systems that are necessary for image generation or to the referential connections between language and image systems, inasmuch as the imagery deficits are inferred from the inability to generate images to verbal cues.

It is theoretically important to show that such deficits are specific to between-system referential connections that can be functionally distinguished from associative connections within either the verbal system or the nonverbal imagery system. Beauvois (1982), and Beauvois and Saillant (1985) described a case of visual anomia or optic aphasia for colors that provides the necessary evidence. The syndrome resulted from a left hemisphere lesion that extended from the occipital lobe to the inferior temporal lobe, but spared the hippocampus (Beauvois & Saillant, 1985). The color aphasia was inferred from a series of carefully constructed tests, some of which could be answered entirely on the basis of verbal knowledge or on the basis of nonverbal visual information, whereas others required a crossover from verbal to nonverbal information or vice versa. Thus, the patient could point to correctly colored pictures of such objects as traffic signs, indicating that nonverbal associations were preserved. She also gave the appropriate verbal responses to such questions as, "What color name is usually associated with envy?", indicating that verbal associations were intact. Her performance was drastically impaired, however, when she was required to switch symbolic modes by naming presented colors, or pointing to a color when asked to do so. For example, she could not respond correctly to the request, "Show me what color a cherry is." The referential processing impairment was also revealed by purely verbal tests in which the response depended on imagery. For example, after being instructed to "imagine a beautiful snowy landscape" she was unable to answer the question, "Tell me what color snow is," although she was able to do so when asked "What do people say when they are asked what color snow is?"

The evidence from such studies permits us to conclude that the left hemisphere dominates in tasks that require referential processing, including ones in which mental images must be generated to words or, conversely, described verbally. The lateralization of such referential processing may be a neuroanatomical consequence of the left hemisphere representation of the language systems used in image generation or description.

The data and the interpretation are also generally consistent with Kosslyn's and Farah's findings and their theory of left hemisphere image generation. However, the left hemisphere hypothesis of Kosslyn et al. (1985) is restricted to multipart images rather than global shapes of objects and I'm not sure that the available evidence justifies that conclusion, particularly since most of their experimental tests with split brain patients involved generation of images of letters, for which left hemisphere superiority would be expected anyway. One of their experiments did compare global and multipart image generation using animal names as stimuli, but the tasks differed in factors other than the global-multipart distinction. The global image task required the subject to decide which was larger, "goat" or "other," where "other" referred to a different animal name presented just before comparison cues appeared. Thus, the task involved generation of images of pairs of animals and verbal cues for the comparison. The multipart image task, however, involved names of single animals and a decision about whether the animal's ears pointed up or flopped down, with stylized drawings of heads and ears as the decision cues. Until the global-multipart comparison is replicated with all extraneous variables controlled, it remains possible that the left hemisphere superiority in nonverbal image generation tasks occurs whenever referential processing is the main requirement in the task, regardless of whether it involves global or multipart images. At the same time, we know that receptive language functions have been demonstrated for the right hemisphere, and so some degree of language-evoked imagery should also be possible in that hemisphere.

Associative processing   From the dual coding perspective, image generation should also be possible via associative processing entirely within the nonverbal system. An example would be when an environmental sound, such as the ring of a telephone, arouses a visual image of the object, in this case a telephone. Curry's (1976) finding that certain environmental sounds, such as a car starting, are better recognized by the left ear than by the right suggests that the right hemisphere might predominate in such processing. Other evidence, however, seems to favor the left hemisphere, at least when the components to be associated are both visual. Thus, Farah (chapter 9, this volume) describes a patient with damage to the posterior left hemisphere who had difficulty associating line drawings of objects with their appropriate colors and completing drawings of complex objects from partial cues. Beauvois and Saillant (1985) also reported evidence that form-color associative processing can be selectively impaired by left hemisphere damage that does not disrupt color-name referential processing. Thus, we have neuropsychological evidence supporting the distinction between referential and associative level processing involving the nonverbal image system, but uncertainty remains concerning hemispheric dominance in "pure" associative imagery tasks.

Organization and Transformation of Information

The next processing category in the list concerns organizational and transformational properties of verbal and nonverbal systems. The generalization here is that organization and transformation are constrained and determined by the structure of representations in the two systems. Verbal units are organized sequentially into higher order structures, and processing is constrained by that structure, so that any organizational or transformational activity involving language occurs on a sequential frame. For example, we can change word order or substitute new words for others in the sequence (sensory transformations can also occur, as in changing the pitch of auditorily imaged speech, but we will not be concerned with such paralinguistic phenomena here). Conversely, nonverbal visual representations in particular are organized hierarchically into larger spatial units, such as the human face, in which the components are synchronously or simultaneously available for processing. The processing constraints are spatial and sensory in this case, so that transformations entail changes on such spatial dimensions as size, shape, and orientation, or changes in sensory modality of represented information. For example, spatial manipulation tests require the subject to recognize or produce spatial transformations or reorganize spatial components in some way. Let us now consider relevant neuropsychological evidence.

I am unaware of any neuropsychological information on mental transformations along sensory dimensions, such as the ability to imagine objects in different colors. We have clear evidence that the right hemisphere dominates in tasks that require mental organization and transformation of complex spatial patterns. Examples include perceptual closure (e.g., Mooney faces), mental rotation, and spatial transformational ability tests (Space Relations). Performance on such tasks is particularly disrupted by lesions to the parietal or tempero-occipital regions of the right hemisphere.

Sequential processing tasks show a different pattern. Studies of patients with brain damage (e.g., Efron, 1963) as well as dichotic listening studies with normal subjects (e.g., Mills & Rollman, 1979) indicate that the left hemisphere dominates in tasks that require discrimination of temporal order, even when the tasks do not involve speech. Moreover, the focal lesion studies indicate that the left temporal lobe is particularly important in such tasks, as it is in tasks that require sequential organization of speech (Kimura, 1982). Such observations suggest that the sequential processing skills of the verbal system derive from a more general temporal processing capacity involving both motor and acoustic systems, for which the left hemisphere has somehow become specialized.

BASIC ADAPTIVE FUNCTIONS

The last set of dual coding distinctions concern the general adaptive functions that are served by the two representational systems in complex tasks in which the individual must solve a problem or achieve some behavioral goal. The evaluative function refers to the determination of absolute and relative values of representational information before or after it has been operated on by transformational or other processes. For example, mental comparisons of objects on perceptual properties (e.g., Which is bigger, a cat or a toaster?) requires an evaluative decision that could be based on imagery. The motivational-emotional function refers to the role of verbal processes and imagery in mediating goal oriented activity and affective arousal. In dual coding terms, affect is a nonverbal reaction that is associated with objects and situations and thus becomes associated with imagery. Affect could also be evoked directly by words, constituting a kind of diffuse referential reaction. The mnemonic function refers to the use of imagery or verbal processes in memory tasks, where they have been extensively studied.

I will comment mainly on brain areas that seem to be especially implicated in motivational-emotional and mnemonic functions, with only an incidental mention of evaluative functions.

Bryden and Ley (1983) reviewed various kinds of evidence suggesting that the right hemisphere is particularly involved in the perception and expression of emotion (see also Tucker, 1981). The most relevant finding in the present context was that requiring subjects to memorize a list of high imagery words that were also high in affective value apparently primed the right hemisphere so that the subjects showed a relative improvement in left-visual field recognition of emotional facial expressions and in left-ear recognition of dichotically presented emotional words. Bryden and Ley (1983) interpreted their results partly in terms of dual coding theory, concluding that "Study of a high-imagery list of emotional words leads to a representation of the word list that includes not only verbal coding mechanisms that presumably are represented in the left hemisphere, but also image-based and affective components that are localized in the right hemisphere" (p. 38). I would qualify this conclusion only by the reminder that other evidence suggests that imagery can occur in either hemisphere, and that the Bryden and Ley results should be interpreted to mean that affective imagery in particular may be a right hemisphere function. In dual coding terms, the effect can be viewed as a special case of nonverbal associative level processing involving visual images of objects and associated affective reactions.

I have left memory functions to the last because this is the domain in which we have the largest amount of systematic neuropsychological information (for a more comprehensive review, see Paivio & te Linde, 1982). Much of the work has been done or inspired by Brenda Milner and her colleagues. The general picture is that the temporal lobe, and in particular its hippocampal structure, is crucial to performance in a wide range of episodic memory tasks. More important for dual coding theory, the left and right temporal lobes are functionally distinguished on the verbal-nonverbal symbolic dimension. Thus, removal of the left temporal lobe selectively impairs memory for verbal material ranging from word lists to sentences, whether heard or read, whereas comparable damage on the right side results in no such loss. Conversely, removal of the right temporal lobe selectively impairs memory for nonverbal material, such as faces, melodies, nonsense patterns, and spatial locations. This double dissociation between material-specific memory functions of the two hemispheres is especially strong evidence for the functional independence of verbal and nonverbal systems, as postulated in dual coding theory.

The pattern of effects suggests that the memory functions of imagery might be localized in the right temporal lobe, or at least that it plays a crucial role in such functions. Despite the obvious nature and popularity of this hypothesis, direct supporting evidence has been difficult to obtain and it is still sparse. As an example of the difficulties, Marilyn Jones (1974) tested patients with right or left temporal lobe removals in memory tasks using concrete and abstract word pairs that were learned with or without the aid of imagery instructions. She found that recall was generally poorer among the left temporal than among the right temporal subjects, but that both groups benefited equally from imagery mnemonics, and both remembered proportionately more concrete than abstract pairs. Thus, the imagery effects were unqualified by the locus of damage.

In a subsequent experiment, Jones-Gotman and Milner (1978) did demonstrate a specific imagery memory deficit among right temporal lobectomy patients using two paired-associate learning tasks. One involved a long list of concrete pairs learned under instructions to use visual imagery, and the other, a shorter list of abstract pairs learned under instructions to link the pairs by putting them in sentences. The patient group performed more poorly than a matched normal control group with the imagery-linked concrete pairs, but the two groups performed equally well with the sentence-linked abstract pairs. This finding and a few others in the literature suggest that the right temporal lobe may be especially important for episodic memory functions of imagery, especially interactive imagery that involves associations between imaged objects.

Note that the generalization applies specifically to *episodic* memory and not semantic memory tasks. For example, Wilkins and Moscovitch (1978) found that patients who had their left or right temporal lobes removed were unimpaired relative to normals in a task in which they classified named or drawn objects as larger or smaller than a chair. This is a comparative evaluation task in which performance presumably depends on analogue representations in the nonverbal system and on which subjects typically report using imagery. Thus, a semantic memory task that implicates imagery is not differentially dependent on either temporal lobe (recall that the split brain subject tested by Kosslyn et al., 1985, also could perform such a task using either hemisphere), whereas imagery-based episodic memory appears to be especially dependent on an intact right temporal lobe.

GENERAL CONCLUSIONS

I conclude from my review that imagery is multifaceted and not localized in any specific brain area. Different regions in both cerebral hemispheres and perhaps subcortical regions as well are responsible for different imagery functions. Posterior regions of both hemispheres appear to contain the representational information necessary for the activation or generation of images of objects and both may be equally efficient in such semantic memory tasks as symbolic size comparisons of objects. The left hemisphere may dominate when the task simply requires referential imagery, that is, generation of unitary images to verbal cues, or when images must be described. The left hemisphere might not be as uniformly favored if images are generated associatively to nonverbal cues, although some current evidence implicates the left hemisphere even in that case. Posterior regions of the right hemisphere appear to be crucial in nonverbal spatial organizational and transformational functions involving imagery, at least as inferred from performance on tests usually thought to implicate visual imagery. The right hemisphere might also dominate in emotional and memory functions of imagery, perhaps because both require associative processing or integrative (spatial) organization of nonverbal information. More specifically, the right temporal lobe may be the focal region for storage or retrieval of episodic memory images, or a crucial mediator of such functions in other areas. These observations on the neuropsychology of imagery and the complementary functional and task distinctions that implicate verbal representations generally correspond to the structural and processing distinctions of dual coding theory.

REFERENCES

Beauvois, M. F. (1982). Optic aphasia: A process of interaction between vision and language. *Philosophical Transactions of the Royal Society of London.*, *298*, 35–47.

Beauvois, M., & Saillant, B. (1985). Optic aphasia for colours and colour agnosia: A distinction between visual and visuo-verbal impairments in the processing of colours. *Cognitive Neuropsychology*, *2*, 1–48.

Bisiach, E., Capitani, E., Luzzatti, C., & Perani, D. (1981). Brain and conscious representation of outside reality. *Neuropsychologia*, *19*, 543–551.

Brown, J. W. (1985). Imagery and the microstructure of perception. *Journal of Neurolinguistics*, *1*, 89–141.

Bryden, M. P., & Ley, R. G. (1983). Right-hemispheric involvement in the perception and expression of emotion in normal humans. In K. M. Heilman & P. Staz (Eds.), *Neuropsychology of human emotion*. New York: Guilford.

Curry, F. K. W. (1976). A comparison of left-handed and right-handed subjects on verbal and non-verbal dichotic listening tasks. *Cortex*, *3*, 343–352.

Efron, R. (1963). Temporal perception, aphasia and déja vu. *Brain*, *86*, 403–44.

Ernest, C. (1983). Spatial-imagery ability, sex differences, and hemispheric functioning. In J. C. Yuille (Ed.), *Imagery memory and cognition: Essays in honor of Allan Paivio*. Hillsdale, NJ: Lawrence Erlbaum Associates.

Farah, M. J. (1984). The neurological basis of mental imagery: A componential analysis. *Cognition*, *18*, 245–272.

Jones, M. K. (1974). Imagery as a mnemonic aid after left temporal lobectomy: Contrast between material-specific and generalized memory disorders. *Neuropsychologia*, *12*, 21–30.

Jones-Gotman, M., & Milner, B. (1978). Right temporal lobe contribution to image-mediated memory. *Neuropsychologia*, *16*, 61–71.

Kimura, D. (1982). Left-hemisphere control of oral and brachial movements and their relation to communication. *Philosophical Transactions of the Royal Society of London, 298,* 135–149.

Kosslyn, S. M., Holtzman, J. D., Farah, M. J., & Gazzaniga, M. S. (1985). A computational analysis of mental image generation: Evidence from functional dissociations in splitbrain patients. *Journal of Experimental Psychology: General, 114,* 311–341.

Ley, R. G. (1983). Cerebral laterality and imagery. In A. A. Sheikh (Ed.), *Imagery: Current theory, research, and application.* New York: Wiley.

Luria, A. R. (1973). *The working brain: An introduction to neuropsychology.* New York: Penguin.

Mills, L., & Rollman, G. B. (1979). Left hemisphere selectivity for processing duration in normal subjects. *Brain and Language, 7,* 320–335.

Morton, J. (1969). Interaction of information in word recognition. *Psychological Review, 76,* 165–178.

Morton, J. (1979). Facilitation in word recognition: Experiments causing change in the logogen model. In P. A. Kolers, M. Wrolstead, & H. Bouma (Eds.), *Processing of visible language* (Vol. I, pp. 259–268). New York: Plenum.

Paivio, A. (1971). *Imagery and verbal processes.* New York: Holt, Rinehart, & Winston. (Reprinted 1979, Hillsdale, NJ: Lawrence Erlbaum Associates)

Paivio, A. (1986) *Mental representations: A dual-coding approach.* New York: Oxford University Press.

Paivio, A., & Ernest, C. (1971). Imagery ability and visual perception of verbal and nonverbal stimuli. *Perception & Psychophysics, 10,* 429–432.

Paivio, A., & te Linde, J. (1982). Imagery, memory, and the brain. *Canadian Journal of Psychology, 36,* 243–272.

St. John, R. C. (1981). Lateral asymmetry in face perception. *Canadian Journal of Psychology, 35,* 213–223.

Tucker, D. M. (1981). Lateral brain function, emotion, and conceptualization. *Psychological Bulletin, 89,* 19–46.

Wilkins, A., & Moscovitch, M. (1978). Selective impairment of semantic memory after temporal lobectomy. *Neuropsychologia, 16,* 73–79.

V

Theoretical Issues

11

Taxonomy of the Subjective: An Evolutionary Perspective

Ernst Pöppel

Local injuries of the brain may lead to specific losses of visual functions, like color vision, movement perception, or face recognition. This kind of specificity is also true for the auditory or somatosensory modality. I use these observations as building-blocks for a general classification of subjective phenomena. This classification—or taxonomy—will provide a more precise description of neuropsychological and psychopathological phenomena.

The basic hypothesis underlying this taxonomy is that psychological functions are based on neuronal programs that have developed during evolution and that psychological functions are necessarily dependent on the integrity of neuronal structures or neuronal algorithms. I am not the sole proponent of this thesis. At the end of his famous work "The origin of species" (1962/1859), Darwin proposed the following view of the subjective: "In the future I see open fields for far more important research. Psychology will be securely based on the foundation already well laid by Mr. Herbert Spencer, that of the necessary acquirement of each mental power and capacity by gradation. Much light will be thrown on the origin of man and his history." Popper recently (1982) presented a similar opinion: "It seems reasonable to assume, in spite of the metaphysical character of the assumption, that the human mind evolves, that it can be regarded as a product of evolution—of an evolution in which the emerging mind plays a very active part."

Mental activity as mentioned here by Popper is a particular feature of the subjective. Pointing out that psychological functions depend on sensory processes does not imply that organisms are passively exposed to their environment. In evolutionary theory, the term "Baldwin-Effect" applies, which was characterized by Popper (1982) in the following way: "With the emergence of exploratory behavior, of tentative behavior, and of trial and error behavior, mindlike behavior plays an increasingly active part in evolution. This does not mean that Darwinian selection is transcended, but it means that active Darwinism, the

219

search for a friendly environment, the selection of a habitat by the organism, becomes important."

The thesis expressed here refers to one basic feature of the subjective that has recently been stressed by Searle (1983)—intentionality. Intentionality describes the fact that our mental states are directed at something, or about something, or that they refer to something, e.g., "I see *something;* I believe in *something;* I expect *something;* I am afraid of *something*." However, not all mental states appear to be intentional. Examples for nonintentional subjective states are, "I am nervous; I am tired; I am depressed." In this case, the subjective state is not related to a particular object or state, it just describes as general state of being.

In order to visualize the phenomenon of intentionality, I want to use a simple example (Figure 1). Everybody probably sees a square here although no contour of a square is given. The particular stimulus configuration of the contours suggests to the perceptual apparatus that something like a square should be present. An intentional relationship is built up between the active mind of the observer and the stimulus configuration. This intentional relationship from subject to object becomes more apparent because of this special stimulus configuration.

The example of a pattern formation on the basis of virtual contours also permits the formulation of a law which is true in general for all perceptual processes—not only for visual perception: "Perception is the verification or falsification of a hypothesis which at a given moment an observer has about the state of the world, the behavior of others." This law of perception implies that the classical stimulus response model of perception is obviously incorrect. In the tradition of Descartes (1955/1644), psychologists believed—and many do so even today—that a particular stimulus unequivocally determines a response. This Cartesian concept, which can also be called "bottom-up" (Figure 2) in the theory of perception, contradicts our experience (as we have seen in Figure 1). Mental

FIGURE 1   Virtual contours

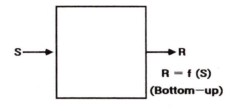

Cartesian Concept

FIGURE 2   Scheme of the classic (or Cartesian) concept of the stimulus-response relationship ("bottom-up"). According to this notion a stimulus determines unequivocally a response.

life is characterized by spontaneous activity. This aspect of the subjective is illustrated in Figure 3 in the following way: At first a stimulus has to be defined, i.e., $S = f(H)$; stimulus selection occurs on the basis of an expectation or a hypothesis, and only after a selection has been made can it be said that a reaction is dependent on the stimulus: $R = f(S)$. This concept of perceptual organization is called "top-down." The arrow that goes in both directions on the S-side of Figure 3 is meant to demonstrate this particular idea.

   After these preliminary remarks on some basic features of perception, I now explore the taxonomy of the subjective in some detail. Four classes of elementary psychological functions are discriminated—those of perception, of stimulus processing, of stimulus evaluation, and of response. Let us examine the first, the perceptual domain.

   Since more than 100 years, it has been known that particular lesions in the brain result in specific functional losses. A patient who has suffered a local injury in the occipital lobe may exhibit a circumscribed blindness in his visual field, e.g., a homonymous hemianopsia (Teuber, Battersby, & Bender, 1960). Another patient with an injury to a different occipital site may show that he no

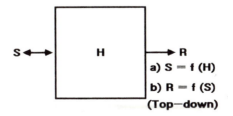

FIGURE 3   Scheme of the modern concept of the stimulus-response relationship. The hypothesis (H) about an event defines the stimulus. Only after such a definition it can be said that the response is a function of the stimulus. The arrow going in both directions is meant to indicate this "top-down" concept.

longer perceives colors (Pöppel et al., 1978). A third patient may no longer be able to recognize faces; he suffers from a so-called prosopagnosia (Meadows, 1974). Although extremely rare, such cases are very instructive.

On the basis of numerous studies on perceptual functions, one can argue that functions are locally represented. This observation allows a more general law on elementary psychological functions to be deduced: The fact that psychological functions are lost with interindividual constancy after circumscribed lesions of the brain provides proof of the existence of these functions, i.e., psychological functions can be defined as those that, in principle, can be lost after circumscribed injuries of the brain.

Using a term from technology, we may refer to those structures (or neuronal algorithms) that implement specific functions as modules. Of the different sensory systems in Fig. 4, only three such systems or modalities are shown: Sv refers to stimuli in the visual system, Sa to those in the auditory system, and St to those in the tactile system. Each sensory system is characterized by a number of modules; in this example, only three such modules are shown for each modality. The different modules may be viewed as the structural or algorithmic correlates of particular perceptual qualities. Such qualities in the visual domain are, for example color, movement, or, perhaps, faces. For taste, these qualities are sweet, sour, salty, or bitter. In case a module is lost, this particular quality is no longer available; for instance, if the module mv2 is missing the patient might be color-blind.

The next functional domain is that of stimulus processing. Here memory and learning functions are summarized. For this domain it can also be argued that the integrity of local neuronal structures is essential for the availability of specific psychological functions. A well-known illustration is provided by the case of H. M., a patient who suffered a selective memory loss following bilateral surgical ablation of the hippocampus. Since the operation, the patient has suffered from a particular loss of memory, i.e., he is no longer capable of storing information in his referential mnemonic system (Scoville & Milner, 1957). His short-term

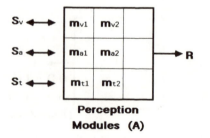

Perception
Modules (A)

FIGURE 4 Scheme of the modular representation of the perceptual systems. Each square is meant to indicate a neuronal structure or a neuronal algorithm representing an elementary psychological function.

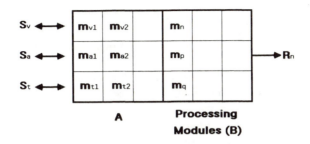

FIGURE 5   Scheme of the modular representation of the perceptual, and processing systems.

memory is apparently quite normal, and he does not seem to have any problems remembering events prior to the operation. Thus, those functions are still available that are necessary to use information from his long-term memory. Only one particular aspect of his memory has been lost—the capacity to store new information.

In conclusion, the functions of stimulus processing also appear to be represented in a modular way in the brain, as is indicated by numerous neuropsychological observations. This idea is visualized in Figure 5. Different learning strategies and different aspects of memory are selectively represented, either in a structural or in a functional (algorithmic) module.

Apart from functions of stimulus acquisition and stimulus processing, the subjective is characterized by functions of stimulus evaluation. This functional domain refers to the emotions. Each perceptual contact with the world is instantaneously accompanied by an emotional evaluation. In particular, pain and pleasure are such basic, essential dimensions (Pöppel, 1982, 1985). For this functional region, it also seems true that different evaluative functions are represented in a modular fashion (Figure 6). The local diencephalic or limbic representation of different emotions has been proven by neuro-ethological and neurological observations (e.g., Ploog, 1980). Lately the integrity of the right

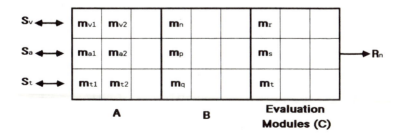

FIGURE 6   Scheme of the modular representation of the perceptual, the processing, and the evaluative systems.

hemisphere has been stressed for the availability of negative emotions, like sorrow (Sackeim et al., 1982). A convincing example has been provided by Olds' experiments (1977), which have resulted in a new paradigm for studying learning. Through electrical stimulation in the hypothalamus, an area could be localized that apparently leads to a positive evaluation of the present situation. If, in the paradigm of operant conditioning, a rat accidentally pushes a lever leading to an electrical stimulation of the so-called pleasure center in the hypothalamus, the animal will form an association between lever and positive emotion and will activate the lever continuously. Analogous stimulations in homologous regions of the human brain have lead to verbal utterances of pleasure.

In Figures 4–6 the different functional areas have been indicated graphically with the same size. This does not imply that these areas are anatomically of equal size. Furthermore, it should not be concluded that every functional region comprises the same number of modules. At present, nothing can be said about the number of such modules, although the number is certainly limited. As the number of modules is not yet known, an open taxonomy with its basic structure is described here.

The final functional domain comprises the functions of motor response (Figure 7). The dogma of the localization of functions historically started with this domain. The French neurologist Broca (1865) was probably the first to stress that spoken language is dependent on the integrity of a circumscribed region in the frontal lobe of the left hemisphere. If this area is destroyed, for instance by a stroke or a trauma, a particular form of aphasia is observed that is named after Broca. On the basis of many other observations—like from work on apraxia or on oculomotor control it can be concluded that this functional region of motor response is also constructed in a modular fashion.

However, sensory input alone is not sufficient to trigger mental functions. For the brain to function or for the subjective to be available, it is necessary for a certain level of activation to exist (Figure 8). The energetic support of the brain is schematically shown here so that only one reservoir supports the different functional regions. However, it is also possible that different regions working in

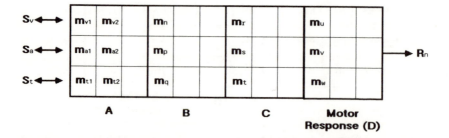

FIGURE 7   Scheme of the modular representation of the perceptual, the processing, the evaluative, the response systems.

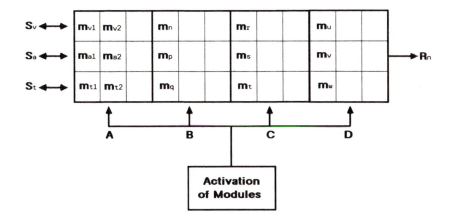

FIGURE 8 Scheme indicating the activation of the various modular systems.

parallel provide the neuronal energy for the different functional regions of the brain. A disturbance in activation can result, in the extreme case, in a coma—in less severe cases, a reduction of vigilance is observed (von Cramon, 1979).

It is now claimed that each intentional act is characterized by the activity of modules in all functional domains. For example: We may see a beautiful face toward which we orient ourselves. We evaluate this stimulus according to its novelty or, as some people say, according to its pertinence or impertinence. We may evaluate this face with respect to its aesthetic value. Without a memory, each situation would be completely new to us. This certainly is not the case; mnemonic information is included in this perceptual act as we compare this face to others or as we refer this face to our mental image of "faciness." As we react to the stimulus, modules from the functional domains of response are in action. Thus, this act is based on the participation of modules from different functional domains. Furthermore, a certain level of activation of the modules has to exist.

In the graphic system used here, the mental state of seeing a beautiful face is characterized by the accentuation of certain modules (Figure 9). The activity of specific modules leads to a new problem of organization of brain states. The hypothesis that different subjective functions are represented in different areas or with different algorithms leads to the question of how the activity of these different regions is temporally coordinated. The problem of such a temporal organization in the brain has been treated by Lashley (1951). The following question arises here: How can one subjective experience in which *different* modules are active be created by the appropriate local activities? What is the underlying mechanism that guarantees that the evaluation of an event is actually related to a perceptual event and not to another one which comes later or earlier?

As a solution of this intracerebral time problem that arises because of the modular representation of functions, the following suggestion is made: Tempor-

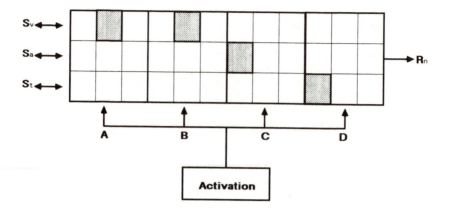

FIGURE 9   Scheme indicating a particular mental state in which the higher neuronal activity of specific modules is shown (grey).

al coordination of psychological functions is provided by neuronal coordination mechanisms, which are expressed as oscillatory processes in neuronal populations. On the basis of such neuronal oscillations, the brain can provide itself with independent temporal states. It can be argued that, within a period of neuronal oscillation, all physically nonsimultaneous events are considered as simultaneous. There are a number of psychophysical observations indicating that, in fact, such high frequency oscillatory processes do exist.

Oscillatory processes can be seen in experiments on choice-reaction time (Madler & Pöppel, 1987; Pöppel, 1968, 1970, 1978, 1985; Pöppel et al., 1978). If a subject or patient has to react to stimuli from the visual or auditory modality in a choice-reaction paradigm, quite often multimodal histograms of the reactions are observed. In Figure 10, one such histogram is shown for a subject who participated in a choice-reaction time experiment where visual or auditory stimuli had to be discriminated before the reaction. Here only the reactions to the auditory stimuli are shown. If the stimulus were continuously processed in the brain, one would expect a uni-modal distribution of choice-reaction time. The multimodality of the histogram, which was observed under stationary conditions, is a clear indication of an oscillitory process that underlies stimulus processing. In a technical sense, one can refer here to relaxation oscillations that are stimulus dependent. In Figure 11, this idea of an oscillatory process is shown graphically (Pöppel, 1970). A stimulus triggers a neuronal oscillation, and the reactions are triggered at particular phases of this oscillation, which results in multimodalities in the reaction time histogram.

The author believes that the neuronal oscillation of a frequency of 30–40 hertz is the formal structure with which events in the environment are identified and temporally ordered. This oscillation is also the formal structure that relates processes in different modules to each other (Pöppel, 1985). With such a

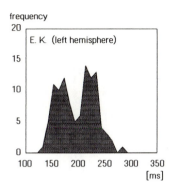

FIGURE 10   Histogram of acoustic choice-reaction of a subject that had to discriminate between optic and acoustic stimuli before the proper response was made. (Only the acoustic response times are shown). Please note the bimodal distribution of the response times.

neuronal oscillation, the brain has a clock (Figure 12) that provides the synchronization of activity in the different modules. However, it should be stressed that, at present, nothing is known about the structural implementation of this neuronal clock. There are two possible ways to reason about the implementation of this brain clock. One is that such a clock is implemented at one particular locus in the brain (like the Formatio reticularis); this structure would digest information from all different sensory organs and then secondarily trigger the different thalamo-cortical regions via fast-conducting pathways. The other idea is that each sensory system has its own neuronal oscillation on the basis of a thalamo-cortical feedback system. In this last case, an additional synchronization mechanism between the different domains would be necessary.

In order to complete the taxonomy of the subjective, some observations from chronobiology must be added. It has been shown that mental or physiological functions can vary considerably (Aschoff, 1981), depending on the time of day. In Figure 13, this fact has been considered, i.e., the activation of the modules underlies a long-term circadian modulation. Different circadian oscillators may be responsible for the circadian modulation of mental and physiological functions. Besides a circadian modulation, infra- or ultradian modulations may also exist, and even a circannual modulation of activation may be possible for the human.

Finally, a further phenomenon of temporal organization has to be considered—namely the phenomenon of temporal integration (Pöppel, 1985). It has already been demonstrated by Wundt (1911) that events which follow each other are integrated up to a certain temporal limit into a perceptual unit. This border of integration has approximately 3 s, as has been indicated by a number of observations (Figure 14). It has been suggested previously (Pöppel, 1985) that a sub-

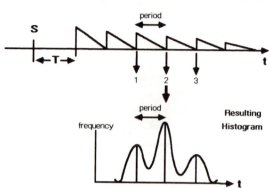

FIGURE 11 Model of a neuronal relaxation oscillator explaining multi-modal response histograms like in Fig. 10. After a constant transduction time (T) a central periodic process is triggered. The period of this central neuronal oscillation is probably close to 30 ms. Motor responses are only triggered at certain phases of this oscillation. This phase dependency of the response leads to the multi-modal distributions in response histograms. The multi-modality therefore is an expression of a temporal information processing that is quantal in nature.

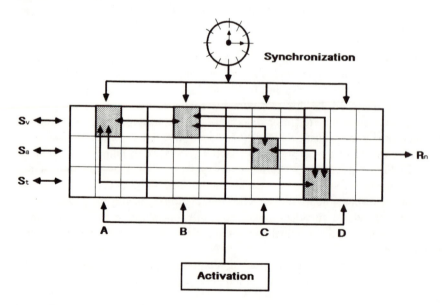

FIGURE 12 Scheme indicating the temporal synchronization of the modules by a central clock.

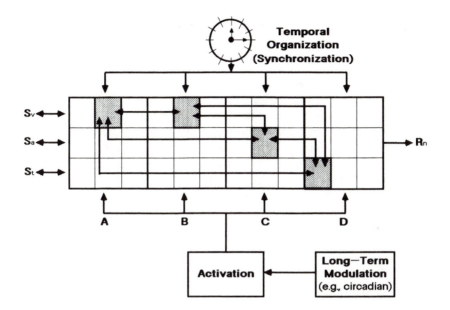

FIGURE 13   Scheme indicating the dependence of the modular system on long-term influences like the circadian rhythms.

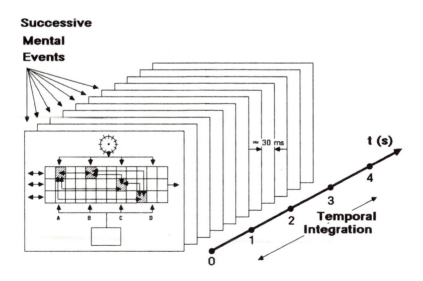

FIGURE 14   Scheme indicating the temporal integration of successive mental events into a unit of not more than a few seconds.

jective representation of this 3-sec-integration interval could be considered as the subjective present, the "now," or as the content of consciousness at a given moment.

This "now," which is conceived here, may at first seem like a mental island within the stream of time. Temporal islands, however, are not typical for the subjective reality of healthy people. The subjective stream of time is characterized by the fact that the islands of "now" are connected which each other. On the basis of this connection of different temporal islands, we obtain the impression of flowing time. The connection of different windows of presence is possible on the basis of the content within consciousness. What we have now and what we have next in consciousness is always dependent on what is represented. Each subsequent content of consciousness is determined by the preceding one. On the basis of this semantic connection of contents in consciousness, we do not realize that each act or each separate content of consciousness is limited to only a few seconds. For our subjective reality, it is important *what* we are aware of and not *how*. Because of this, we do not realize the temporal structure of consciousness, which is the formal background for the content of consciousness. The temporal structure of consciousness itself is not a content of consciousness.

The open taxonomy of the subjective discussed here is biologically oriented. Biological systems can be disturbed. There are four areas within which problems can arise and which can be used to test this taxonomic system. This taxonomy allows the construction of pathological phenomena that can be tested experimentally afterwards: (1) Local modules can be lost. (2) Disturbances may be found in the area of activation and its long-term modulations. (3) Disturbances may be found in the temporal short-term organization and synchronization. (4) Problems may arise in the area of temporal integration and the semantic connection of integrated intervals.

The local loss of a module results in a functional loss. Functions that are based on neuronal modules or discrete neuronal algorithms are then no longer available. Without the integrity of these structures, the psychological repertoire lacks certain essential elements. The modules carry the "whatness" of mental life.

Disturbances or lesions can also be observed in the area of activation. Severe disturbances result in a coma or a reduced state of vigilance. Disturbances in the activation system may even result in depression. In a depression, reasoning may be slowed down, the patient is characterized by sleepiness, reduced ability to concentrate, physical lethargy, and general psychomotor inhibition. All these symptoms can be associated with a disturbance in the area of activation. During depression, typical diurnal changes can also be observed, characterized by severe depression in the morning and an improvement in the afternoon. Some psychiatrists believe that a disturbance in the circadian organization is actually causally related to depression, and certain manic phenomena can be interpreted as an increase in activation due to a poorly controlled circadian oscillator.

Disturbances in the area of temporal organization should theoretically result in completely different pathological phenomena. Certain schizophrenic symptoms could be discussed on the basis of the taxonomy presented here. Is it conceivable that the disturbance of temporal organization may actually lead to schizophrenia? It has been argued that the 30–40 hertz oscillator is essential for event identification. A disturbance in the temporal connection of different modules could conceivably result in defective event identification so that physically defined stimuli no longer can be given an identity. Personal identity might be endangered if the temporal connection between the perception, processing, and evaluation of stimuli is temporally disconnected.

Temporal integration and possible disturbances in this area may lead to different pathological phenomena. This is particularly true for thought disorder. The psychiatrist Bleuler (1969) described such disturbances characteristic of schizophrenic patients in the following way: It appears that the normal connection that is essential to keep the thoughts together is no longer available and that other thoughts may suddenly appear. It is suggested here that a disturbance of the semantic connection of successive integrative units may lead to the discontinuity of mental life, which results in this particular form of schizophrenia.

The taxonomy presented here can only be applied if it can be tested. I believe that such a test is possible through neuropsychological and psychiatric phenomena. A potential test is an advantage of this taxonomy. It provides a conceptual basis for the description of the subjective on the basis of evolutionary reasoning. On the other hand, the taxonomy allows an integrated view of neurological and psychiatric phenomena.

ACKNOWLEDGMENTS

The work reported here was supported by grants from the Deutsche Forschungsgemeinschaft. The author would like to thank Irmgard Mainz, Gabi de Langen and Dr. Barbara Herzberger for their help.

REFERENCES

Aschoff, J. (Ed). (1981). Biological rhythms. *Handbook of Behavioral neurobiology.* New York: Plenum Press.

Bleuler, M. (1969). *Lehrbuch der Psychiatrie* (11th edition). Berlin, Heidelberg, New York: Springer.

Broca, P. (1965). Sur le siège de la faculté du langage articulé. *Bull. Soc. Anthropol., 6,* 337–393.

Cramon, D. von (1979). *Quantitative Bestimmung des Verhaltensdefizits bei Störungen des skalaren Bewußtseins.* Stuttgart: Georg Thieme Verlag.

Darwin, C. (1962). *The origin of species.* New York: Macmillan.

Descartes, R. (1955). *Die Prinzipien der Philosophie*. Hamburg: Felix Meiner. (Originally published 1644).

Lashley, K. (1951). The problem of serial order in behavior. In L. A. Jeffress (Ed.), *Cerebral mechanisms in behavior* (pp. 112–136). New York: Wiley.

Madler, C., & Pöppel, E. (1987). Auditory evoked potentials indicate the loss of neuronal oscillations during general anaesthesia. *Naturwissenschaften, 74*, 42–43.

Meadows J. C. (1974). The anatomical basis of prosopagnosia. *J. Neurol. Neurosurg. Psychiat., 37*, 489–501.

Olds, J. (1977). *Drives and reinforcements*. New York: Raven Press.

Ploog, D. (1980). Emotionen als Produkte des limbischen Systems. *Med. Psychol., 6*, 7–19.

Pöppel, E. (1968). Oszillatorische Komponenten in Reaktionszeiten. *Naturwissenschaften, 55*, 449–450.

Pöppel, E. (1970). Excitability cycles in central intermittency. *Psychol. Forsch., 34*, 1–9.

Pöppel, E. (1978). Time perception. In R. Held, H. W. Leibowitz, & H.-L. Teuber (Eds.), *Handbook of sensory physiology, Vol. VIII, Perception* (pp. 713–729). NY: Springer Verlag.

Pöppel, E. (1982). Lust und Schmerz. *Grundlagen menschlichen Erlebens und Verhaltens*. Berlin: Severin & Siedler.

Pöppel, E. (1985). Grenzen des Bewußtseins. Über Wirklichkeit und Welterfahrung. dva, Stuttgart. English edition (1988) *Mindworks. Time and conscious experience*. Orlando, FL: Academic Press.

Pöppel, E., Brinkmann, R., von Cramon, D., Singer, W. (1978) Association and dissociation of visual functions in a case of bilateral occipital lobe infarction. Archiv für Psychiatrie und Nervenkrankheiten 225:1–21

Popper, K. (1982). In R. Q. Elvee (Ed). The place of mind in nature. *Mind in nature* (pp. 31–59). San Francisco: Harper and Row.

Sackeim, H. A., Greenberg, M. S., Weiman A. L., Gur, R. C., Hungerbuhler, J. P., & Geschwind, N. (1982). Hemispheric asymmetry in the expression of positive and negative emotions. *Archives of Neurology, 39*, 210–218.

Scoville, W. B., Milner, B. (1957). Loss of recent memory after bilateral hippocampal lesion. *J. Neuro. Neurosurg. Psych. 20*, 11–21.

Searle, J. R. (1983). *Intentionality. An essay in the philosophy of mind*. Cambridge, England: Cambridge University Press.

Teuber, H.-L., Battersby, W. S., & Bender, M. B. (1960). *Visual field defects after penetrating missile wounds of the brain*. Cambridge, MA: Harvard University Press.

Wundt, W. (1911). *Einführung in die Psychologie*. Leipzig: R. Voigtländer.

12

Essay on Perception

Jason W. Brown, M. D.

What is the world? How are we to conceive it? The problem is posed in our everyday experience. Presently, there is before me a wide river, trees, and a great bridge that tapers into the distance. The scene has depth, movement, light and color. The clean smell of the water, the warmth of the sun, are part of my perception; there are sounds and voices around me. I am aware of a multitude of other things in the background, my discomfort on the bench where I am sitting, the pen in my hand, the image I am calling up. I am aware also that the perception is given to me all at once in its entirety. I have no sense that it is constructed out of elements. It seems whole and invulnerable. I shift my attention and the world remains fixed. It will be there again when I look away. It presents itself before me and I ingest it with my organs of sense. My body is an object which exists for the perception of others. And on the rim of this perception is an awareness of self. This self-awareness is bound up with an inner commentary. My concept of self as experienced is replete with this commentary which seems to be the equivalent of mind in the context of this perception. But unlike mind, the perception is not experienced as in the mind or even through the mind but as something outside mind in a space that would be vacant if deprived of the objects with which it is so abundantly filled.

This seems a fair account of an everyday experience of such force and immediacy as to encumber any theory of mind which runs counter to its appeal. Yet every day we are reminded of the fragility of the world. We are dizzy and the world spins around us. We struggle to maintain our balance even as the world disintegrates. Object constancies and perceptual illusions remind us that we are *thinking* objects not just seeing them. In the evening the object gives way to a dream imagery that may be more vivid than waking perception. We question the reality of dream only on waking as we regain the world of objects. Now the perception is stable and outside us. But how fixed and stable is this object? Even as we gaze at it we are aware that it is never perceived in the same way. It is noticed differently, it changes with our feelings and interest; the object itself changes in our perception. We ignore this instability to the degree to which the reconstruction is successful. Yet the fragility of the object helps us to recognize its basis in the mind, it helps us to recognize the continuum which exists from the image of the dream to the object in perception in the enlarging representation of a cognized world.

PRELIMINARIES TO A THEORY OF OBJECT FORMATION

Let us being by asking, in what way is perception built up? Is it constructed like a building out of the units of experience? Are the edges, colors, and contours of objects the formative material of which objects are composed?

The conventional approach to perception assumes that an object is the result of a chain of events leading over stations in a sensory pathway. Features of the object are extracted by cells in the visual cortex and reconstructed to patterns which are then relayed to other cortical zones for spatial mapping, recognition and association to prior experience. On this basis, we patch together an object representation. This theory of perception is grounded on parameters of an object itself, its shape, movement, brightness, depth or color, and correlations with cell discharge at various points in the visual pathway. On this account, attributes or isolates of an object are elements in its mental reconstruction while other aspects of an object experience—affect, imagery, awareness, and recognition—are added on as secondary effects after registration.

Pathological Objects

The symptoms of pathology are the data for a different theory of perception.[1] The symptoms of a perceptual disorder are not piecemeal dissolutions of normal objects but a shift to objects of another type. Objects do not degrade into constituents but to more preliminary objects; or the symptoms of a disrupted perception intrude into a completed object as earlier phases in its formation. The pathological fragment is the nucleus of a preobject . . . a formative stage in the object representation. At times this change is brief and restricted to a small part of the visual field, for example a migrainous blindspot or scotoma, a distortion or an hallucination which appears as a part of an otherwise normal object. However, the pathological segment can persist and replace the perception entirely. Here the preobject character of the symptom is apparent; it more clearly constitutes an incompletely developed object embedded in the object field.

Perceptual deficits and hallucinations may occur together in the same modality. Morel (1936a, 1936b) thought that hallucination involved the functions which were lost in a perceptual disorder and that hallucination and perceptual disorders were different ways of looking at the same perception. Following

[1]This paper builds on previous accounts of imagery and patterns of object breakdown which should also be consulted. The pertinent articles are found in Brown (1983a, 1985, 1988).

Morel, one might say that a deficit points to a disrupted stage in percept formation which is embedded in a fully developed object, while an hallucination is the representation deposited at that stage when it becomes a (truncated) endpoint in percept formation.

The inner bond between hallucination and perceptual deficit is illustrated by cases of agnosia. In such cases, an individual may misidentify objects on the basis of their conceptual relationships. Thus, a *fork* might be called a "plate." This is not a language or naming disorder but a disturbance in perception, a disruption of *object meaning*. In dream, the substitution of an object is also determined by its meaning, though affective and symbolic elements predominate. Unlike deficient perceptions, an object substitution in dream is really seen. Of course, the target of a dream perception is an inference from the dynamics of the dreamwork. Were a waking patient to see the objects of his misidentification (seeing a plate instead of a fork)—and there is no evidence that he does—he would be hallucinating like a dreamer. It seems that what is characteristic of the dream perception is the very thing that is lacking in agnosia. However, the form of agnosia that involves object meaning is related to neural substrates—limbic and temporal lobe mechanisms—which are probably also implicated in dream hallucination. Specifically, conceptual errors in agnosia and substitutions in dream hallucination are both linked to similar (?identical) brain areas.

The mechanisms of the dreamwork, substitution, condensation and fusion reflect an *incomplete selection* of the object representation out of its background field. An hallucination is an alternative (pre)object conceptually related to the target. The relationship between the target and the hallucination is determined by the degree to which the hallucinatory preobject develops. In sleep, the lack of external stimulation facilitates autonomous image formation and cognitive withdrawal and leaves an incomplete object—an hallucination—as an endpoint in percept formation.

Disorders of object meaning constitute only one type of visual agnosia. Impaired discrimination of object form is another type. Errors of object form and meaning may occur in the same patient. The change in performance moment to moment reflects the depth of processing for each object formation. When morphological or form-based errors occur we are more likely to think the patient sees the misnamed object. For example, when a *button* is called a "coin" we have no difficulty supposing that the perception is rather more "coin-like" and we explain this deviation on a visuosensory basis. This is not so clearly the case for conceptual errors when object meaning is involved. The symptom is different because it involves a different level in the object. Disorders of object meaning and disorders of object form correspond to the difference between hallucination and illusion which also differ as to momentary depth.

Moreover, as hallucination and disturbed object meaning are related to similar brain areas, disorders in the analysis or specification of object form and distortions or illusional phenomena in imagery are also linked to similar or identical brain areas. However, object meaning and hallucination are linked to *older* brain areas, object form and illusional phenomena are linked to areas of evolutionary *recency*.

Object Formation and Evolutionary Growth

The relation to evolutionary structure is important because it corresponds with direction of processing. That is, given that disorders of object meaning are related to brain structures more archaic than those mediating processing stages underlying form analysis, the implication is that meaning is encoded prior to form in object perception. Specifically, areas supporting analytic perception are entrained subsequent to the activation of semantic or conceptual stages. However, the patient with a disruption of object meaning still appears to see the target object, not the one resulting from the conceptual derailment. In other words, the disruption of early stages in percept formation may not impact on the completion of subsequent stages. How can this be explained?

On the microgenetic theory, sensory information arriving distal to the disrupted segment constrains the process of object formation to model the external object. What survives in an adequate object is the trace of an incompletely traversed conceptual phase. This trace, the incomplete selection of the object, is the symptom of the disorder.

Put differently, errors in object recognition are the substitutive element of an hallucinatory image displayed in a veridical perception. In other words, misrecognition in agnosia is the price the object must pay in order to avoid the fate of an hallucination. Implicit is the idea that object formation proceeds unidirectionally *from* a stage of conceptual analysis *toward* a stage of form analysis and not, as commonly supposed, in the reverse direction.

These remarks establish a core and highly controversial feature of the microgenetic theory of perception, that a conceptual or symbolic stage in the processing of an object representation *precedes* a stage of form analysis. The implications of this theory are profound for it entails that the meaning of an object is extracted prior to its form, that we understand and recognize objects before they are consciously perceived and that, in a very real sense, an object is remembered into perception, recollected like a dream into the world of external objects.

The Meaning of Associated Symptoms

The symptoms of a perceptual disorder are usually accompanied by other manifestations of preliminary cognition. There may be changes in behavior, affect, language, emotion and awareness. These changes are inferred to be intrinsic to the perceptual disorder because they fluctuate moment to moment according to the symptom type. In other words, the affective content or error awareness associated with a perceptual disorder does not depend on the disorder itself but on the particular symptom at a given moment. On these grounds, many nonperceptual symptoms can be construed to be level-specific alterations that reflect stages in the elaboration of a behavior coextensive with that of the disrupted object.

To take an example, objects have an affective content. We may adore an object or the object can be terrifying. We can be amused by hallucinations or frightened by them. The affect may be located in the viewer or in the object representation. An individual may be frightened by a banal hallucination or the hallucination itself may be frightening. Intense affect is a feature of early cognition. In contrast, partial, derived or exteriorized affects characterize fully unfolded objects. Strong affective content in a behavior is a sign that the object is incompletely exteriorized. Unlike the final object, which seems to exist for its own sake as an object in the world, the preobject is fixed in the mind of the perceiver as a content that has not yet attained the status of an independent object. For this reason the object experience is imbued with subjective content from the perceiver. Emotion is a bridge to external objects; it is a sign that the object is not as independent as it seems but that it flows out from the perceiver as an extension of his affective life.

Summary

From such observations we can recover the hidden infrastructure of the perception as it is displayed in pathology, an infrastructure not simply bypassed on the way to the final object but one that accounts for the greater though unexpressed part of its content. Stages given up in the process of object formation persist in the final object as manifestations of early cognition. The feeling of familiarity with the object, the memory or recognition of that or similar objects, its location in a system of concepts and affective tonality, are residues of preliminary phases in object formation. The space of the object and its relation to other objects, depth, distance and constancies, are also achieved in the course of a development in which one level is derived into the next, building a context around that object, in other words building up mind within the object, in sum, elaborating the perceiver for whose pleasure the object seems to exist.

Imagery

The nature of mental imagery is a critical problem in perception for it addresses the interface between private and public experience. Apart from feelings, events experienced as mental can be interpreted as images of one type or another so that a theory of perception which incorporates a theory of images is also a theory on the boundaries of mind in the world.

In the microgeny of perception, images and objects are points on a continuum. An image unfolds over the same neural substrate as a perception. An image is an object that is attenuated, while an object is an image that has undergone a further development. One can say that an image is an object in the mind, while an object is built up on a phase of image development. Conversely, an object is a late stage in the microgeny of images. The progression from image to object enlarges mind to embrace the world of perception. This means that a memory or thought image is not simply a revived and transformed perception but a stage on the way to an external object. When we remember an experience we do not uncover a secondary association but recapture an earlier phase in the original object.

Similarly, dream and hallucination are not fictitious reveries constructed on the remnants of an object experience but signposts on the way to an object that actualize prematurely. The often bizarre content of these images does not indicate a reworking of the perception along independent lines, but the application of subsurface rules which differ from those at a subsequent stage. A dream of events from the preceding day does not entail the transmission of a perception to an image or memory store for later retrieval; in dream, an object recedes into the formative cognition out of which it first emerged.

In psychosis the memory image can be the start of an hallucination and result in an almost real perception, or a fully intrapersonal hallucination can result from an object that begins to degrade. Hallucination can proceed outward to the world, or inward to the mind. We all know the frightening reality of many dreams just as the psychotic knows the frightening unreality of many object experiences. Such observations confirm that objects are retrieved out of long-term memory into short-term memory and perceptual awareness, that the recognition and identification of the object occur early on in perceptual processing so that objects are known before they are consciously seen, and that far from objects existing for mind to scrutinize, mind and mental imagery are elaborated in the course of perceptual growth.

MICROGENY OF OBJECTS

On the microgenetic theory of perception, a representation unfolds from image to object within the phyletic core of the brain, not pieced together from peripheral input. The object begins in upper brainstem as a unified act/percept in a two-dimensional map of the body surface. There is a parallel hierarchy of sensory (physical) and perceptual (mental) levels at successive points corresponding to growth planes in the evolution of the forebrain. The sensory levels act to *constrain* the perceptual development but do not enter directly into the object construction, while the perceptual levels—wholly cognitive and represen-tational—are the contents which undergo transformation (see below). There is no constructive process in which perceptions are build up on the raw material of sensation; rather, objects are *sculpted* in the mind as sensation restricts the degrees of freedom in cognitive processing. An object representation emerges through the inhibition of alternative pathways.

The application of sensory constraint at successive levels to an emerging mental representation leads to a model of an external object that captures successive levels in the representation of physical space. The withdrawal or interruption of sensation (levels of constraint) at one or more levels in percept formation results in a suspension of this modeling effect on the unfolding perceptual configuration. This leads to an attenuated object formation and an object representation that develops along autonomous lines to mental imagery or hallucination. The different types of hallucination and imagery can be viewed as incompletely developed objects which model the world up to a certain point.

The outcome of the microgenetic sequence is an abstract multitiered con-struct unfolding in the brain over evolutionary and maturational stages. Within this construct are successive planes in space formation, in memory and in personality organization. These planes provide a perceptual and cognitive foundation for the development of every object representation. The object grows out of this infrastructure. It does not come to the organism but is a product, an output, very much like an action or a behavior. Moreover, the position in the world to which the object unfolds is like a point on an extended body surface, a point that is not sensed by the body or brought into relation with it but one that extends mind's reach as it expands the body into a world without limits.

Sensation and Perception

On this account, sensation is part of the physical world around the viewer, extrinsic to mind and something to be inferred from the perceptions it generates. Sensations do not become perceptions through an increase in their complexity nor is the perception a distal phase in a chain of sensory processes. Perceptions are not elaborated or built up from sensations but are distinct from sensations from their inception.

Perceptions develop through intrinsic mechanisms; i.e., mechanisms through which mind also develops. In fact, mind and perception are almost synonymous. The configurational series that constitutes the perception elaborates a representation that is mental and autonomous in that it does not utilize external sensory material. Sensation is applied at each level or processing stage in the perceptual series. There is a hierarchy of sensory input that corresponds with the structure of the perceptual representation. Specifically, sensation shapes the developing object representation but does not enter directly into its construction.

The representation is modulated at successive points (moments in the object microgeny), the final object being determined by input that is not part of the developing representation (Figure 1).

Presumably, the perception lays down a track—a configurational series—that is the trace of its development. This track has an influence on subsequent experiences in which a similar configuration is encountered. The original track is activated to the degree to which a novel configuration approaches the (latent) configuration of the preceding experience. Since a perception involves the selection of an object, not its piecemeal construction, and since every object has to be selected from a great many other potential object representations, the recognition, feeling of familiarity, experiential and affective content of the final perception are activated early in the forming object to the extent to which similar prior configurations are approximated. In this way sensory experience enters perception as learning.

A corollary to this theory is that there are no *raw feels* or primitive sensations. The perception of pain does not involve a sensory prime but a percept that is archaic or rudimentary in comparison with other objects. The quality of pain may differ from other perceptual experiences—the pain may not be located in a well-defined body part, it is not object-like, it is subjective and in-trapersonal—but the processing underlying the pain is experienced, or elaborates a representation, that is basically like any other perceptual object. As long as an object experience (pain, touch) is in awareness it is by definition a perception, embedded in mind with other cognitive contents.

STAGES IN PERCEPTUAL MICROGENESIS

Roots of Perception

The perception begins in the upper brainstem reticular core, or tegmentum, as a two-dimensional map of ambient space in which targets are identified on the basis of relative motion, size, and perhaps simple shape and pattern detection. The spatial coordinates of the map are linked to actions of the body. The map is an action schema, a program for body movement on targets which serve as triggers for action. This core is modulated or constrained by sensory input through the wider tectal region, an interface for the transformation of sensory primitives into the spatial map and its action program. Although tectal cells appear to show hemifield organization, the tegmental map is presumed to represent a unitary space.

At this stage, however, space has not exteriorized and there is no external object. The space of the target is part of a private space organized about the body midline. A stimulus is fixed through an orientation of eyes, head and neck toward the locus of the target and seized through a movement of the eyes, or another body part such as the tongue or a limb. There is a tight bond between perception and action. The perception of a stimulus is linked to, one could even say manifested by, an orientation toward the stimulus and this orientation is implemented through older axial and proximal motor systems.

Cases with injury or disease of the brainstem confirm the role of this system in early perception. There may be impaired ballistic (rapid, proximal) reaching of an arm, and neglect or inattention (failure to orient) to one side of space. With bilateral damage, there is complete failure of orientation to stimuli, giving rise to a state of "akinetic mutism," a type of catatonia. This condition is similar to a coma with the eyes open. With large lesions of upper brainstem an individual is comatose, or in a state of persistent sleep.

In normal perception, this level appears as, or represents, a state of dreamless sleep. That is, dreamless sleep reflects the autonomous (sensory-free) operation of this system as a ceiling on cognitive unfolding. The coma that results from extensive damage to upper brainstem displays the contribution of this system to normal perception. Specifically, the cognition of dreamless sleep, coma, and the "eyes open" coma of the akinetic mute, represent a base level in the microgeny of percepts, a level that elaborates a state of perceptual vigilence preparatory to a ballistic movement or an optic grasp, organized about axial and proximal motility in an archaic, unextended, two-dimensional, intrapersonal, preobject space (see Figure 1).

The World of Dream

The two-dimensional cognitive map represented at the level of upper brainstem is derived through mechanisms in the limbic and temporal lobe to a viewer-centered, volumetric space of dream and hallucination. A spatial map of targets for action develops to a preliminary object representation. At the same

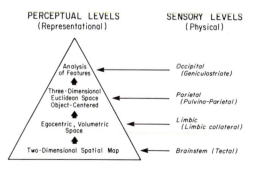

FIGURE 1 Levels of mental representation constrained at successive levels by sensation to model an external object.

time, the object representation—at this stage an image or hallucination—enlarges and fills mental space with content, creating an intrapersonal object in opposition to a viewer that is equally intrapersonal, an observer as much a part of the image development as the image itself.

The limbic preobject is an image in a transitional space which is not wholly intrapersonal but rather a fluid extension of mind into the body surround. The opposition that is set up between image and viewer—which are contents in the same mental surface—is part of the feeling that the image is not wholly intrapersonal. The image is separate from the Self though it has not yet achieved the space of an independent object. The space of dream and hallucination has an object quality; an hallucination may be accepted as real but it is not object-like in its realness. The fact that dreamers and psychotics believe in the reality of their hallucinations should make one pause over the reality of waking percepts but it is not a sign that hallucinatory objects mimic real ones. Hallucination is labile and changing and confluent with a space that has a tangible, viscous quality, not yet the empty medium in which independent objects, fixed and solid, are so reliably situated.

The distortions of dream imagery reveal aspects of the process of object selection. The object-to-be-perceived is derived through systems of symbolic, experiential and affective transformation toward increasing definition and spatial resolution. The emerging perceptual configuration differs from that of the preceding stage in that the bond with motility is less pronounced, responses are less automatic, the target is unreal and its meaning, its affective and conceptual relationships more important in determining the nature of the content that is represented. There is some direct sensory input to this stage by way of collaterals from the optic radiations, but relative freedom from sensory modeling may be necessary for the object to develop autonomously through a stage of personal experience and conceptual knowledge. Specifically, the relaxation of sensory constraints at this transition permits the tectal-derived spatial image to traverse—to be selected through—a stage of symbolic relations and dreamwork mechanisms preliminary to the resolution of the image as a fixed object in the world.

Pathology in this region disrupts the image as it traverses a memory organized about experiential and conceptual relations. Damage to lateral and inferior temporal cortex in monkey gives an impairment in the selection of a visual target from an array of objects. The condition has been interpreted as midway between a memory and a perceptual disorder; retrieval and discrimination are intact. On the microgenetic account, one could say that the lesion disrupts (displays) a stage where the target configuration is emerging within a system of meaning-relations with other potential object representations. In humans with comparable injuries involving the mesial temporo-occipital area, there may be difficulty recognizing common objects, faces or familiar routes. These are forms of visual agnosia (see above) where the problem concerns a conceptual derailment in object selection. Object form and detail are perceived adequately—the object can be described and drawn—but there is a change in the meaning of the object or its relation to prior experience so that the individual can no longer name or categorize the object or describe its function.

Pathology of limbic and temporal lobe regions can produce hallucination. Stimulation of limbic regions produces an hallucination that is more like a dream, while stimulation of temporal neocortex appears to produce an hallucination that is more like a perception. The greater the microgenetic depth of stimulation or evocation of the image, the greater the symbolic and/or conceptual distortion, the more subjective and story-like the experience, and the stronger its affective content. There may be a similarity between normal hypnagogic and "autosymbolic" images (introductory dream images) on falling asleep at night and some cases of hallucination due to temporal lobe damage. The derailment, fusion and condensation that characterize dreamwork mechanisms capture changes in the object representation as it traverses this level.

However, hallucinations are often isolated events without the historical character of dream. In this sense, they are like dream fragments. As with dream, hallucination can range from fantastic images to almost veridical objects. The quality of the hallucination reflects its momentary depth. Thus, cases with temporal lobe lesion may show banal hallucination during the day and bizarre distortion toward evening. Or, the hallucination may first appear at the close of day. These observations suggest that with sleep approaching, imagery recedes to a form characteristic of early cognition, or conversely, that a twilight cognitive regression recaptures an hallucinatory phase in object formation.

According to this account, the spatial map and action program, and the stage of dreamless sleep laid down in upper brainstem as the beginnings of the object representation, are derived through limbic-temporal systems to a stage of affective, experiential and conceptual relations. Aided by a lessening of sensory constraints on object microgeny, an image is transformed along more autonomous paths toward a veridical object. Pathology displays this segment as an hallucinatory endpoint, or the conceptual derailment is buried as an agnosia within an object that is spatially completed at subsequent levels. In deficiency states such as agnosia, object meaning is incomplete, or derailed, though the correct object is achieved, while dream hallucination and dream-like hallucinations in waking mentation reflect the persistent or brief actualization of this level as an endpoint in percept formation (see Figure 2).

Object Relations and Mental States

The hallucination and its volumetric space are selected through the preceding stage and develop to a real external (veridical) object in a three-dimensional Euclidean space. This transition is accomplished through mechanisms in parietal cortex. The object exteriorization occurs from a fluid, subjective space to a space of limb exploration. This is a *manipulation* or grasping space that is not fully

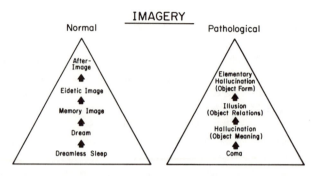

FIGURE 2 Levels of mental representation with a diminution or suspension of sensory input at successive levels.

independent but one that is centered on the action perimeter, the space of the arm's reach. Through this stage there is a consolidation of the forming spatial, temporal and figural qualities of the object as object and surround conform to the constraints of the external world.

Damage to the parietal cortex reveals normal operations underlying object and space representation. In imagery, the change is centered in a perception that is more like an object than a private image. One can say that the image achieves the status of an object so that alterations in real objects (illusions) predominate. Hallucinations may occur but more commonly there are distortions and de-formations of object size, shape, distance or motion (metamorphopsia). The shift from the hallucination of the preceding stage to illusional change in real objects reflects the microgenetic progression toward the final object representation.

Deficiency states tend to mirror changes in pathological imagery. Deficits occur in an external space with impairments of object relations and an alteration in the relation between a viewer and the objects around him. There are disorders of figure-ground perception, depth and relative distance estimation, impaired reaching and grasping of objects, drawing and manipulation. There are a number of disorders related to unilateral and bilateral parietal lobe damage, including such conditions as constructional disability, impaired simultaneous judgments—simultanagnosia—and the Balint syndrome, impaired visuomotor reaching or optic apraxia, spatial inattention, inability to dress oneself—dressing apraxia—and related conditions. These disorders have in common the fact that they are centered in an interactive space between object and viewer, bound up with limb movement on objects in the action perimeter. This occurs because the preobject has exteriorized to an object-centered space that is extrapersonal but not yet fully independent of the viewer.

Many of the spatial impairments associated with parietal lesion are referred to as part of the "right hemisphere syndrome", indicating a preferential link to right-sided damage. The right hemisphere bias appears to be restricted to deficiency states, for hallucination and other forms of abnormal imagery do not show strong laterality effects. The problem of the asymmetric effect of lesions on spatial and other performances, the assimilation of this phenomenon to the microgenetic model and its implication of "parallel" rather than "vertical" processing, are discussed elsewhere (Brown, 1983b, 1988).

Normal image phenomena referable to this stage are characterized by adequate representational targets, similarity to real percepts and a reduced affective content. Memory and eidetic images fall into this category. The memory image is like a dream image which has "come up" to the threshold of awareness, midway between private experience and its perceptual target. If a memory image of a recent event becomes so clear and picturable that it is actually "seen" as if it were still present it is referred to as an eidetic image. Eidetic images usually follow rapidly on object perceptions, but the eidetic image can also occur after a delay. There is a gradual change from eidetic to memory imagery (and to dream) in the forgetting of a perception. This is because hallucination, memory and eidetic imagery lie on a continuum leading to the object perception. Dream hallucination may surface to a memory image. Amnestics describe their memory disorder as like the fading of a dream on awakening. In the same way one can say that an eidetic image is a memory image that has surfaced to an almost real perception.

As the image unfolds through these phases, from dream to memory image to eidetic image and real object, there is a loss of affective strength, of creativity and inventiveness in the image and a progressive reduction in the extent to which the image brings forth new content. These are markers of the subjective origins of the object that are given up in the realization of a fixed and stable world. There is also a change from an image that comes spontaneously and unbidden (dream) to one that occurs to some extent volitionally (memory image), to one that is entrained by an external object (eidetic image), to one that is a fully independent real object. The feeling of spontaneity, purposefulness or independence that is attached to different types of images is generated as a manifestation of a single process of object representation at various moments in its completion. These feelings complement those of automaticity, purposefulness and volition that accompany the action microgeny. Both actions and objects lead out into and elaborate the external world. The active nature of action, the feeling that one is an agent that acts, develops within the action itself, just as the feeling of passivity to images and the feeling of the independence of objects develop within the process of object formation.

A World of Real Objects

In the final segment of the microgenetic process, sensory modeling of the emerging object representation results in the individuation of featural detail and the full exteriorization and *detachment* of an ostensibly real object in an independent, extrapersonal space. This transition is accomplished through mechanisms in primary visual cortex and the circumstriate zone. Specifically, on the microgenetic account, this region is not the initial point of registration for a perception but a sensory-perceptual transform which provides the final modeling to a mental image that has all but completed its perceptual development. The spatial image which has exteriorized into a space of limb activity is analyzed to an independent object in a space that seems public and physical. The articulation of the object into external space coincides with the individuation of features in the object. Relations between objects, between object and space, and between object and perceiver recede into the background of a fully unfolded perception in which object, viewer and space are independent elements.

Thus, within the space of the external environment, submerged in the final percept, there is a concealed space of object relations and limb exploration generated by mechanisms in parietal cortex, a space in which a change in object or perceiver, or the actions of the perceiver on an object, visibly alters the entire perception. This level of space relations, like the preceding stage of recognition and conceptual meaning, persists in the background of the completed percept and provides a context and an underpinning out of which the analysis of object features is derived.

Damage to circumstriate cortex gives disorders of form perception affecting objects, faces and letters. A disturbance of reading (alexia) and object identification (form agnosia) occurs with involvement at this point. The various forms of this disturbance, whether the impairment affects colors, written material or objects, depends on the particular point in the process where the pathology has its maximum impact, and/or the stage of restitution or decay. These disorders are not the result of a piecemeal disarray of independent mechanisms; they are not deletions or fragments but successive moments in a single unfolding process.

Damage to the primary visual cortex results in scotomata or blind spots in the visual field; in severe cases with bilateral damage, cortical blindness. Such patients are not really blind since it is possible to demonstrate perceptions at a more preliminary level. Vision in hemianopic fields was first demonstrated by Bard in 1905, and confirmed by Bender and Krieger in 1951. There is perception of movement, shape, size, some form, and perhaps color. The degree of perception in patients without a striate cortex may be considerable. Semantic priming has even been reported in blind fields.[2]

Hallucinations are common at the onset of a scotoma or in cortical blindness. These hallucinations represent endogenous percepts which become the endpoint in an attenuated object development. Patients are often unaware of cortical scotomata or blindness. This indicates that the scotoma is not an empty spot in the object field but a failure to realize a microgenetic endpoint and thus to elaborate a consciousness of the unrealized portion. The significance of

[2]See Holender (1986).

hallucination and residual vision is that they are truncated object developments which survive destruction of the surface of the perception.

Patients with scotoma may show completion of patterns across gaps in the visual field. There is a celebrated story about the neuropsychologist Hans-Lukas Teuber, who used to recall how Karl Lashley one day "beheaded" him in a migraine scotoma leaving unaffected the geometric pattern on the wall. Such observations along with the experimental studies support the idea of subsurface perceptual gestalts. Parenthetically, the fact that there is completion *in the mind* across "holes" in the brain, though explicable in terms of microgenetic or gestalt theory, could provide an argument for dualism.

Pathological images include elementary hallucinations—lights, flames, geometric patterns—and illusory persistence or multiplication of objects. These phenomena are related to after-images—the residues of a bright object when one looks away—and represent equivalents in imagery of pathological deficiency states. One could say that the image is the mental content within the scotoma, a content ordinarily not accessed into the consciousness of a fully completed object. The after-image and related phenomena differ from eidetic images and hallucinations in that they do not replace but are *superimposed* on object perceptions. They also undergo a change in size in relation to projection distance; i.e., the after-image does not show constancy effects. In other words, the after-image takes on certain of the attributes of physical objects. This is because the after-image arises through primary visual cortex and is extrinsic to—one could say, at the surface of—the developing object perception.

Summary of Perceptual Microgenesis

To sum up, object and space are formed in a rapid unfolding over a series of microstructural transitions. This multitiered process proceeds over a set of autonomous cognitive transformations constrained at successive levels by sensory input to model an external object. There is a transition from an archaic two-dimensional map of somatic space elaborating dreamless sleep and the spatial underpinnings of the object, to the egocentric or volumetric space of dream and hallucination. The object is selected through fields of meaning relations to a three-dimensional Euclidean space. The preobject or image has a holistic or relational quality in the interactive space of limb exploration. From this stage the perception is transformed to an articulated object in a fully independent and extrapersonal "physical" space. At the same time the Self *detaches* from the forming object so that Self and object, which are both laid down by the same process, become distinct and separate representations.

Early stages in this process lay down relations between object and body movement, the link to experience and memory, affective content, relations with Self and other objects, and the situational context within which the object appears. These stages persist abstractly in the final object as a background of knowledge and feeling. At the same time the object proceeds from a representation bound up with action about the body axis to one that is linked to the proximal and distal musculature. In other words, the articulation of an object into external space is accompanied by a parallel microgenesis of action as the act unfolds into discrete and asymmetric digital movements on external objects.

This process is retraced in normal imagery, in the transition from dreamless sleep to dream hallucination, through memory imagery to eidetic images and finally to the after-image. The sequence leads:

• from an image that comes involuntarily (dream); through one that is purposeful or volitional (memory image); to an independent object that seems to interact with the perceiver.

• from a dream image that is filled—or the perceiver is filled—with intense affect; to a memory image that is accompanied by a mild or subtle affective tonality; to an eidetic image devoid of affective content; to an external object where feelings in the object have to be inferred.

• from perceptual or symbolic distortion linked to past experience and distant memory; through a stage of spatial and conceptual resolution; toward increasing referential stability as a memory and then eidetic image; and finally to an independent object.

• from the unconsciousness of deep sleep; through the archaic consciousness of dream; to the introspective consciousness of the memory image; to an awareness distributed over a world of objects that mind itself has created.

In the course of this process, affect and meaning are drawn out from their position in mind to infiltrate surrounding objects. To imbue an object with meaning and emotion is to recede for a moment to a preobject phase. When we do this we withdraw from externality to a stage of imagery that prefigures the object, and we recapture the affect and meaning that were part of the preliminary object development. From a microgenetic point of view, this state is midway between dream and object perception, beyond the vagueness of a memory image that is struggling to the surface and prior to the clear perusal of an object field. Introspection is not a higher state but a regression from the world of objects to an antecedent phase of mental imagery.

SELF KNOWLEDGE AND OBJECT AWARENESS

Objects and Mental Representations

The view that the worlds of inner and outer perception lie on a continuum within the same mental state entails that the knowledge of external objects and self-knowledge are the same kind of knowledge and share common underlying properties. An object is represented as an image in private space or as a "real" object in public space, it develops with, and is qualitatively changed into, different mental spaces, but the same process of object and space representation is involved.

A mental representation—a *conscious* content in the mind, such as an idea or an image—is an object that is truncated in its development. Conversely, an external object—an utterance, an action or a "real" perception—is a mental representation that undergoes further processing. A mental representation, a thought, is a phase in percept formation. Put differently, thoughts make up the infrastructure of objects. The series of states from dream to introspection to percepts retraces the microgeny of objects. From this it follows that observations on inner states, and verbal reports of those observations, are subject to the same limitations as observations directed to external objects. Specifically, both introspection and exteroception (perception) suffer from the same deficiency, namely an inability to access the physical object within the representation and an uncertainty as to the accuracy with which this physical object is represented.

On this view, a representation is the content of a mental state, the nature of which is determined by the surface to which the processing sequence develops. In theory, the process that elaborates a mental state can terminate—or with pathology be attentuated or "sliced"—at any of a possibly infinite number of points on a continuum. The spatiotemporal configuration collapsed over the duration required to generate a representation comprises the content of the mental state. A representation requires time to develop, and the duration of that development has to be incorporated in a definition of a mental state. The state has a temporal context. The content of that state, the representation, is the sum of the potential configurations traversed in the processing while the degree or extent of processing—the endpoint of the processing sequence—determines the level to which the representational content is realized.

Dream and Waking Reality

On this view, there is no clear boundary between inner and outer events, rather a succession of spatial planes leading outward from an intrapsychic core. Of course, in everyday life the distinction of inner and outer is sharply drawn. We peer out of our mental cells and ruminate on a world around us. Objects and ideas could not be more different. Yet in pathological cases, perceptions can actualize at the transition between image and object and the individual does not know whether he is dreaming or awake. This can persist as a more or less permanent condition. Images can appear to invade and replace perceptions or objects can withdraw to image-like states. What is actually happening is that the object, or a part of the object field, has receded to the image that anticipates it, resulting in illusion, hallucination or, more specifically, some level in a pre-perception.

Surely, many of us at one time or another have had a momentary glimpse of this feeling; a perception that is like a remembered dream or an uncertainty as to whether an experience is a dream or a recollection. For many the whole of life is a dream that is experienced. The record of one's life *(Lebensfilm)* unfolds at the moment of death as a dream that has been lived. Shakespeare's remark that life is a dream surrounded by a sleep captures this feeling. What is the difference between a vague memory image of a real experience that is incompletely revived and the memory image of a dream? The microgenetic position is that there is no difference. We are usually able to distinguish the two because objects developing through sensory constraints can be revived with greater resolution into waking consciousness. Except for dreams that are like vivid hallucinations and break through into conscious awareness, most dreams are submerged and "trapped" in subsurface cognition. A dim memory image that recedes to deeper levels in mentation is like a dream that has come up to the threshold of awareness.

The apprehension of this similarity—one could say continuity—between dream and memory images helps us to understand the anguish of the brain-injured patient, for example the patient of Luria (1972), unable to distinguish dream from wakefulness, fixed at a point in object representation that for others is but a fleeting insight. In such a state, objects are invested by thoughts and feel as if they are still part of the perceiver's mind.

Dreams appear distinct from conscious mental states which form a separate domain of knowledge. Conscious mentation is more real to us than dream even though it may be less vivid. There is a different mode of thought during dream and introspection. In spite of these differences, conscious mentation is built on a foundation of dream cognition. Unlike objects, dreams and ideas are positioned in the mind. We find plausible a transition from dream image to idea or mental representation, but not a transition from mental representation to object. The world is more real to us than thought which seems to be a secondary acquisition. Dreams and ideas seem to be deposited by sensory experience, not there before experience and giving rise to it. After all, how can the world we apprehend in perception be an extension of mind if the world was there before mind developed?

Of course, the transformation of ideas to objects has to be quantal—there has to be an emergent step underlying the transition from inner to outer space—or there would be no world at all. The deception of a mind that interacts with real objects is total and unshakable. But the exteriorization of acts and objects is a graded process that can be followed along in its course. An idea is not projected or thrust into the world but develops with the world in stages and only gradually becomes independent of the mind where it originated. We have to understand that the deception of a real world has to be a strong one—there is survival value in the strength of this deception—for otherwise we could not manage in the world—there would be no world to manage in—nor could we consciously interact with minds and objects other than our own.

The implication is that awareness, or consciousness of other objects is part of the consciousness of our own mental states; one cannot exist without the other. The question of the evolutionary selection value of consciousness is, then, bound up with the selection value of an awareness of other objects, not just a state of attentiveness to objects and actions, but an awareness that entails an independent Self that is extrinsic to and looking on those external objects. On this view, introspection is another form of object awareness, the objects being the inner objects (images) or ideas that anticipate external objects rather than the objects themselves.

Other Objects and Other Minds

There are other similarities between introspection and the awareness of external objects. Introspection has for its object the content of a mental state, not the physical (brain) state for which that content is a type of correlate. This is also true for exteroception or the perception of objects. We see an object as a whole, we hear its sound and see its color, not the physical processes responsible for these phenomena. These have to be inferred through analysis or experimentation. The physical process(es) underlying mental representations can be investigated in the same manner if appropriate methods are employed. This follows because the physical correlate of an object perception is of the same kind as the neural correlate of a mental representation. There is continuous flow from the physical world to the neurophysiological underpinnings of mind. A theory on the nature of external objects and the brain states which correspond to object perceptions is also a theory of brain states underlying ideas and the sensory elaboration of ideas to model external objects. In fact, one can go even further and say that there is a still deeper theory on the common basis of mind and world.

The basis in mind for the objects of perception and the ideas of introspection, and the argument that ideas and objects lie on a continuum, entails the solipsist conclusion that one knows only one's own mental content. If the world embracing a mind is continuous with, and another manifestation of, the representational content of that mind, then the incapacity to break through a world of mental representation is matched by the incapacity to perceive a world beyond that of our object representations. Introspection has for its data only mental content, whether internal or external.

But even one's mental content is largely inaccessible to introspection; there is no way to be sure that we are not deluded by the content of our mental states. We may perceive dream images or waking hallucinations as real. The dream or hallucination obtains across different modalities—it is seen, touched, heard— and its apparent reality is confirmed by the collusion of the various perceptual channels. In pathological cases, there are many instances of dissociation—or rather, incongruity—between awareness and behavior. For example, there may be lack of awareness for a defective utterance, for a paralysis of a limb or even for blindness! An individual may insist his aphasic speech is accurate, that he can move his paralyzed arm or that, in spite of failed performances, he can see objects clearly. The implication of these observations is that deviant mental representations entail or generate deviant states of the self and alterations in awareness of mental content, and that what is true in pathology is also true in normal individuals.

Apart from the unreliability of (normal or pathological) introspection, and the fact that the momentary content determines what the self of that moment is, there is the added problem that we enjoy but limited knowledge of our own mental states. We are aware, and incompletely at that, of only the surface of a mental or object representation, of only that fraction of the mental representation that entails awareness. We know only what we are aware that we know, only that part of the representation presented in awareness. What doesn't enter into awareness—and that is the major part of the representational content, including all of that potential content given up in the realization of the final representation—is excluded from the scrutiny of the introspecting state.

But this is only the beginning! There are still greater problems for introspection to resolve. Among these is the fact that the self of the introspective state—the self that is supposedly doing the introspecting—is regenerated each moment by the representational content. The self is a product, not an agent. This means that the content that is surveyed in introspection is not there waiting to be reviewed by an onlooking self, but is thrust into and generates the awareness by which it is accompanied. In other words, mental states introspect themselves and elaborate a self as a part of the available content. Introspection applies to a representation which includes a self concept.

On these grounds, solipsism—though a logical outcome of microgenetic theory—is disingenuous, for we know as little of our mental states as of the world beyond observation. What proof that mental representations are accurate or complete or correspond to experience and memories of lived events? What proof that objects are real or hallucinatory or correspond to objects in the physical world? The corollary to solipsism, that one cannot access any event beyond one's mental representation of it appears the more primary datum.

Introspection

As mentioned, pathological studies indicate that the awareness of a mental representation is bound up with the representation itself, as a part of that representation, and not the expression of a "mind's eye" gazing on mental content. There is a change in the awareness for a given content—a perception, an utterance—when there is damage to the content in question or to the cognitive domain of that content. The change in awareness or introspection is specific to error type and perceptual modality.

For example, an aphasic patient who makes both phonological and semantic errors will tend to be aware of the phonological ones but not the semantic ones. Similarly, a patient with "blindness" due to damage to the visual cortex may be unaware that he is blind, but very much aware of a limb paralysis. The lack of awareness or denial for blindness occurs because the patient is no longer able to generate a memory of, i.e., re-perceive, the (attenuated) world of visual object representations. Awareness is structured, it is elaborated in relation to domain-specific mental representations and is not a general or unitary faculty that floats above or surveys any mental content that surfaces.

Another way of saying this is that a representation incorporates its own awareness, the awareness is *in* the representation. Contents are not derived or accessed into consciousness but elaborate conscious states consistent with their level of derivation. This means that there is no self that introspects mental content; rather the representational content (usually, a language representation) displays itself in the nature of the introspection which it elaborates. Introspection is not a state or component in addition to the state or component that is the object of the introspection. Introspection is a particular state that arises as a coincidence of linguistic and perceptual representations at a given moment. Actually, on the microgenetic view introspection is a kind of withdrawal from the perception of objects to the mental images which anticipate them. The self and other mental contents are deposited by the object development before the object exteriorizes.

Specifically, there are two oppositions set up in the course of object development: (1) an opposition between viewer and external objects; (2) an opposition between viewer and internal representations. On the microgenetic view, these are comparable states, the latter anticipating the former. Both phenomena are a result of the outward development of objects. In the course of this development, a sphere of inner mental (verbal, perceptual) imagery precedes the derivation of the external object. As the object draws outward and becomes independent of mind, mind—that is, the internal or subjective phase of the object development—persists as a type of subjective object in opposition to the objects of the external world. This is the basis for exteroception, the belief in independent objects that impinge on a mind distinct from those objects. Introspection is simply attenuated exteroception, mind gazing on preliminary object representations.

This leads to the apparently paradoxical conclusion that the introspective state is a precursor to a state of object awareness, even though object awareness would appear to be the more primitive function. There is a difference, however, between an awareness or attentiveness to objects and an awareness in which a self surveys an object field that is external and independent of the viewer. Thus, Piaget's description of an awareness of objects and an awareness of activity as early stages in the ontogeny of self-awareness does not obtain when a conscious self scrutinizes objects. An awareness of objects in which the observer is not yet an agent distinct from the objects being viewed is prior to the emergence of a self that is independent of mental contents and external objects.

On this view, introspection is an expression of a perceptual or language behavior, a state of an organism that needs to be explained, not a method of psychological investigation. There are problems in the characterization of the self or self-concept that is supposedly doing the introspecting; there are problems with the observer's access to his own mental content and there are problems with the reliability of verbal report. These problems do not arise through the inability of others to verify mental states and their verbal description, or through the potential for bias, deception or dissimulation on the part of the subject. There is a deeper problem inherent in the nature of introspection that defines the limits of self-knowledge and the knowledge of other objects that has to do with the way in which representations emerge and the nature of intrapsychic content. A fuller understanding of the process through which representations develop is likely to erode the commonsense belief in the existence of a self that scans mental content and vitiate theories of mind built up on metalinguistic data.

The Self as Mental Representation

The feeling of apartness and interaction of a self with objects and other mental contents is a central feature of our conscious life and cannot be simply disregarded. A theory of mind has to account for these phenomena. It also has to account for the structure of mind and how that structure develops. But it need not attribute causal efficacy to contents generated into the introspective state. These contents, like leaves on a tree, are outgrowths of the effective (agentive) or formative structure of mind, part of the crust of new form pouring out from below and not components in mind's creative engine. On this view, introspection is not a shaping activity but a shadow of mental content as it rapidly decays to the past, always a step behind the dynamic of mind and, ultimately, less informative, less genuine, than intuitions developing naturally as the direct manifestations of subsurface processes.

The central point is that the self is also a representation, a self-representation, that is part of the representational content. The self-representation is not confined to one perceptual mode but spans the modalities at a given moment in perception. Contents elaborated in each of the modalities contribute to part of the self-representation. In pathological cases, damage to the perceptual modalities chips away at the self-concept. The self is derived from multiple perceptual contents.

How are the various elements of the self-concept integrated across the different modalities? Given that mental contents are like objects in subjective space, the opposition or contrast between self and mental representation is not found across contents in different perceptual modalities. The content of a tactile, an auditory or visual representation seems part of the same object, unlike the self which seems to observe its own representations. In other words, the opposition is between a self and other mental objects, not among those other mental objects. Moreover, how does a construct such as the self-concept stand in opposition to other mental representations if the self-concept is composed of elements that develop within those representations? The self is generated by, and decomposes in relation to, the representational content of the perceptual modalities but the self has to be more than a composite representation.

One way out of this bind is to think of the self as a type of background configuration which embraces contents in each modality. The process that generates the self-concept, along with other representational content, traverses and revives formative levels in the personality which are not part of the surface content of the separate modalities. That is, the self-concept is laid down in early, formative stages in perceptual microgenesis as a unitary preobject, and it is out of this unitary representation that the contents of the separate modalities differentiate. To return to the metaphor of a tree, one can think of the self as deposited early in the upward growth of structure as it articulates into ever finer arborizations. The fact that the modalities show surface differentiation but are unitary at their base accounts for the unity of a self-representation in which all the modalities have a share. The unity of the self, therefore, is not accomplished secondarily through an interaction or integration across the modalities, but is a unity that underlies the modalities and distributes itself into them.

REFERENCES

Bard, L. (1905). De la persistance des sensations lumineuses dans le champ aveugle des hemianopsiques. *Semaine Medicale, 25,* 253–255.

Bender, M., & Krieger, H. (1951). Visual functions in perimentrically blind fields. *Archives of Neurology and Psychiatry, 65,* 72–99.

Brown, J. W. (1983a). The microstructure of perception: Physiology and patterns of breakdown. *Cognition and Brain Theory, 6,* 145–184.

Brown, J. W. (1983b). Rethinking the right hemisphere. In E. Perecman (Ed.), *Cognitive processing in the right hemisphere.* New York: Academic Press.

Brown, J. W. (1985). Imagery and the microstructure of perception. *Journal of Neurolinguistics, 1,* 89–141.

Brown, J. W. (1988). *The life of the mind.* Hillsdale, NJ: Lawrence Erlbaum Associates.

Holender, D. (1986). Semantic activation without conscious identification. *Behavioral and Brain Sciences, 9,* 1–66.

Luria, A. R. (1972). *The man with a shattered world.* New York: Basic Books.

Morel, F. (1936a). Des bruits d'oreille, des bourdonnements, des hallucinations auditives élémentaires, communes et verbales. *Encephale, 31,* 81–95.

Morel, F. (1936b). De L'application de l'audiométrie en neuropsychiatrie. *Revue de Oto-Neuro-Ophthalmologie, 14,* 161.

Author Index

Subject Index

A

Achromatopsia, 41, 42, 49–52, 62, 63
Acuity, 43–49
Affect, 237, 243
After-image (*see also* Palinopsia), 174, 175, 246, 247
Agnosia, 35, 59–75, 235, 242, 243
  color, 63
  environmental (see topographic)
  facial, 71, 72, 74, 83, 90, 91
  form, 246
  integrative, 89
  object, 68–69, 98, 235, 242
  shape, 83
  topographic, 67, 68, 74, 79, 90–92, 99
Agraphia
  alexia and, 105
Akinetic mutism, 241
Allesthesia
  visual, 70, 177–179
Alexia (*see also* Agraphia), 64, 207, 246
Amblyopia, 42–43
Amnesia (*see also* Memory, Routes), 192, 245
Anatomy, 3–26
Anomia, 64, 209
  color, 63, 210
Anosognosia (*see also* Neglect), 157, 158
Aphasia, 63
  Broca's, 224
  color, 210
Ataxia (*see* Visuomotor ataxia)
Attention (see Neglect)
Auditory-visual synesthesia, 180
Autotopoagnosia (*see also* Neglect), 130

B

Baldwin-Effect (*see also* Evolution), 219
Balint Syndrome, 72, 73, 84, 85, 111
Blindness
  cerebral, 40, 41
  cortical 3, 8, 41, 61, 187, 188, 246, 252
  psychic (*see also* Agnosia), 35
Blindsight (*see also* Scotoma), 246
Broca's aphasia (*see* Aphasia, Broca's)

C

Circadian rhythm, 227, 229, 230
Color (*see* Perception, color)

disorders (*see* Achromatopsia; Agnosia, color)
  naming (*see* Anomia, color)
Coma, 224, 230, 241
Constructional disturbance, 65, 66, 74
Contralateral neglect (*see* Neglect)
Cortical blindness (*see* Blindness, cortical)

D

Dark adaption, 45–49
Defective exploration hypothesis (*see* Neglect, theories)
Denial (*see* Anosognosia, Introspection, Neglect)
Depth perception, 86–89, 98, 105
Depression, 230
Diplopia
  monocular, 175–177
Dream, 233, 235, 238, 241–243, 249, 250
Dressing disturbance, 66, 74
Dual coding theory (*see* Imagery)
Dyschiria, 157, 158

E

Eidetic image (*see* Imagery, eidetic)
Electrical stimulation of brain, 4, 11, 12, 173, 179, 224
Electroencephalography, 189
Emotion, 223, 224, 237
End-stopping, 17
Environment
  coding, 88, 89
  recognition, 68, 90–92, 99
Event-related potential, 189, 190, 198
Evolution, 219
  brain, 131, 235, 236, 238
Exteroception (*see* Perception)

F

Facial agnosia (*see* Agnosia, facial)
Facial matching, 71, 72, 74
Feature-by-feature identification, 90–92
Foveal splitting, 37

G

Geographical disorders (*see* Agnosia, topographical)
Grasping, 86, 106, 244